SEXUALITY AND BEING IN THE POSTSTRUCTURALIST UNIVERSE OF CLARICE LISPECTOR

SEXUALITY AND BEING IN THE POSTSTRUCTURALIST UNIVERSE OF CLARICE LISPECTOR

The Différance of Desire

EARL E. FITZ

UNIVERSITY OF TEXAS PRESS

Austin

TEXAS PAN AMERICAN SERIES
Copyright © 2001 by the University of Texas Press
All rights reserved
Printed in the United States of America
First edition, 2001

Requests for permission to reproduce material from this work should be sent to
Permissions, University of Texas Press, P.O. Box 7819, Austin, TX 78713-7819.

∞ The paper used in this book meets the minimum requirements of ANSI/NISO
Z39.48-1992 (R1997) (Permanence of Paper).

LIBRARY OF CONGRESS CATALOGING-IN-PUBLICATION DATA

Fitz, Earl E.
    Sexuality and being in the poststructuralist universe of Clarice Lispector : the
différance of desire / by Earl E. Fitz — 1st ed.
        p.   cm. — (Texas Pan American series)
    Includes bibliographical references and index.
    ISBN 0-292-72528-0 (alk. paper) — ISBN 0-292-72529-9 (pbk. : alk. paper)
        1. Lispector, Clarice—Criticism and interpretation.   2. Desire in
literature.   3. Sex in literature.   4. Poststructuralism.   I. Title.   II. Series.
PQ9697.L585 Z663   2001
869.3'42—dc21   00-062846

To Juli

CONTENTS

ACKNOWLEDGMENTS

A grateful acknowledgment is made to the University of Minnesota Press for permission to quote from *The Stream of Life*, translated by Elizabeth Lowe and Earl Fitz (1989); and *The Passion according to G. H.*, translated by Ronald W. Sousa (1988). I also would like to acknowledge Carcanet Press for permission to quote from *Near to the Wild Heart*, translated and with an afterword by Giovanni Pontiero (New York: New Directions, 1990).

INTRODUCTION

This book makes three arguments: first, that the style and structuring of Clarice Lispector's novels, stories, and *crônicas* (chronicles) exemplify the issues addressed by poststructural theory; second, that her essentially poststructural *"textes"* also show, chiefly by means of their singular characters, the human face of poststructuralism—the implications this mode of thought has for the public and private identities of real men and women, particularly women; and third, that her narratives are driven by a sense of unfulfilled desire in which her characters develop more as conflicted and fragmented poststructural sites than as stable presences, and that, in a context heavily freighted with both psychosexual and sociopolitical significance, they embody the *désir de l'Autre* (the desire of the Other) that Lacan speaks of in *Écrits*.

While I will seek to demonstrate that a poststructural ethos permeates Lispector's sense of language and of writing, I will thus also argue that it is her expression of human sexuality, in all its conflicted, destabilizing, and boundary-effacing variety, that grounds the powerfully intellectual dimension of her work in human existence's most visceral and urgent drives. In short, desire—presented by Lispector as being inseparable from language—emerges as the ultimate marker of poststructuralism's vital relevance to the lives led by ordinary people. Lispector's depiction of the sexual impulse can therefore be read as the most telling expression of poststructuralism's profoundly human basis, its centrality to the human experience.

Dealing relentlessly with the play of language in the construction of our varied identities, Lispector's narratives illustrate how the basically ontological and epistemological problems posed by poststructural thought appear when they are developed in the context of the human experience by a gifted creative writer rather than by abstract theoreticians. Lispector thus "humanizes" the at times abstruse and, for some, alienating issues broached by poststructural thinkers and shows just how profoundly they pertain to the human condition.

As the extensive criticism of her work shows, Lispector's narratives invite many different approaches, prominent among which are the existential, the phenomenological, the mystical, and the feminist,[1] to cite only a few of the recognized possibilities. And while it does not necessarily cancel any of these out, my argument here will be that only poststructuralism offers a sufficiently comprehensive and language-conscious critical perspective from which to evaluate and interpret the totality of her writing,[2] the basic philosophical and aesthetic principles that inform it as well as its sociopolitical implications and its pertinence to post-Freudian theories of psychoanalysis. In saying this, I must stress that my book does not defend poststructuralist thought per se, although personally I believe that its intellectual significance is beyond dispute. My working premise is that, whether one agrees with it or not, poststructuralism asks important and challenging questions about the relationship of language to human existence, about the nature of human consciousness, and about the political implications that derive from our desire for truth, certainty, and clarity of meaning in an unstable, ambiguous world. This is precisely the turf, thematically and structurally speaking, that Lispector so assiduously cultivated, from the beginning of her literary career in 1944 to her posthumously published final work in 1978, and encompassing her "fiction" as well as her "nonfiction" (a distinction that Lispector, like the later poststructuralists, rejected as meaningless).

In situating Lispector in the context of poststructuralism, I do not claim that she was in any way influenced by the European leaders of poststructural thought (although, given her circle of literary and artistic friends, she would have undoubtedly known about this movement in the early to mid-1970s). My point is rather different: that because for most of her career Lispector was writing what I believe were essentially poststructural texts before poststructuralism as such even existed, we can, now that the basic tenets of poststructuralism are well established, see how revealingly they apply to her work and how well they explain it. Her brilliant debut novel, *Near to the Wild Heart*, appeared in 1944, an entire generation before the recognized advent of poststructuralism, which is usually associated with the publication of Roland Barthes's *S/Z* in 1970, seven years before the Brazilian writer's death. Lispector was, in effect, a poststructuralist without portfolio, a highly original writer and thinker whose lyrical actualizations of what is fundamentally poststructural thought provide, as I will argue in the pages that follow, an effective and complete intellectual context in which to evaluate her work.

But what is poststructuralism? For Jacques Derrida, the French philosopher whose work is fundamental to it, poststructuralism is, at bottom, an interrogation of both language (one that, following the perspective afforded by Saussurean linguistics, privileges the signifier over the signified) and structuralism, its inescapable but paradox-ridden progenitor.[3] More written about than clearly defined, poststructuralism has been understood in a variety of ways but always "[a]s a term loosely applied to an array of critical and intellectual movements, including deconstruction and radical forms of psychoanalytic, feminist, and revisionist Marxist thinking, which are deemed to lie 'beyond' structuralism" (Holman and Harmon 371). Richard Harland, representing a large group of critics who rightly regard deconstruction and poststructuralism as not being synonymous (with the former being one particular actualization of the latter), has suggested that there are three main divisions of poststructuralist thought: the *Tel Quel* group, consisting of Jacques Derrida, Julia Kristeva, and the post-1970 Roland Barthes; a second group consisting of Gilles Deleuze, Félix Guattari, and the later Michel Foucault; and finally, standing alone in a more distinctly sociopolitical context, Jean Baudrillard (Harland 2). As if to further demonstrate the degree of difficulty that exists in defining this term, however, Alex Callinicos divides poststructuralism into two main trends, one consistent with what Richard Rorty has rather antagonistically termed "textualism" *(Consequences of Pragmatism: Essays, 1972–1980:* 139–40) and the other illustrating what Callinicos (borrowing a term from Edward Said and a concept, "power-knowledge," from Foucault) calls "worldly post-structuralism," a way of thinking about language and discourse that maintains its connection to a variety of Realpolitik sociopolitical conditions. Also attempting to establish some parameters for the term poststructuralism is Robert Young, who, in *Untying the Text: A Post-Structuralist Reader* (1981), writes:

> Post-structuralism, then, involves a shift from meaning to staging, or from the signified to the signifier. It may be seen from this how the premises of post-structuralism disallow any denominative, unified, or "proper" definition of itself. Broadly, however, it involves a critique of metaphysics (of the concepts of causality, of identity, of the subject, and of truth), of the theory of the sign, and the acknowledgement and incorporation of psychoanalytic modes of thought. In brief, it may be said that post-structuralism fractures the serene unity of the stable sign and the unified subject. In this respect, the "theoretical" reference points of post-structuralism can be best mapped via the work

of Foucault, Lacan and Derrida, who in different ways have pushed structuralism to its limits. (8)

Arriving at a similar position is Terry Eagleton, who, in "Post-Structuralism," argues:

> If structuralism divided the sign from the referent . . . 'post-structuralism' . . . goes a step further: it divides the signifier from the signified. . . . The implication of all this is that language is a much less stable affair than the classical structuralists had considered. Instead of being a well-defined, clearly demarcated structure containing symmetrical units of signifiers and signifieds, it now begins to look much more like a sprawling limitless web where there is a constant interchange and circulation of elements, where none of the elements is absolutely definable and where everything is caught up and traced through by everything else. (*Literary Theory*, 128–29)

Taking us down a slightly different road, however, is Philip Lewis, who, in "The Post-Structuralist Condition,"[4] prefers the term "critical structuralism" to "poststructuralism," situating "deconstruction" within the context of this "critical structuralism." It is worth noting that Derrida himself has, in *Positions*, taken issue not only with Saussure's concept of the unified sign but with the implications this concept has had on structuralism. Saussure's theory—and, by extension, all structuralist thought—Derrida writes, "leaves open the possibility of thinking a *con cept signified in and of itself*, a concept simply present for thought, independent of a relationship to language, that is of a relationship to a system of signifiers" (*Positions* 19). This condition, which Derrida finds untenable, is one that, in her own fashion, Lispector explores as well.

Indeed, what Toril Moi says of Derrida and his theory of language could easily be taken as a description of Lispector's work as well: "According to the French philosopher Jacques Derrida, language is structured as an endless deferral of meaning, and any search for an essential, absolutely stable meaning must therefore be considered metaphysical. There is no final statement, no fundamental unit, no transcendental signified that is meaningful in itself and thus escapes the ceaseless interplay of deferral and difference" (Moi, *Sexual/Textual Politics*, 9).

Also seeking to elucidate the broad-based and far-reaching implications, both literary and sociopolitical, of poststructural thought is Josué Harari, whose anthology, *Textual Strategies: Perspectives in Post-Structuralist Criticism* (1979), offers a variety of essays that demonstrate another of poststructuralism's main tenets—that since all language is tropelogical and figurative,[5] the language in which we conduct our analysis is necessarily the same as the language being analyzed; that there is, effectively speaking, no valid distinction between "literary" and "non-literary" language, a point the *escritura* (writing) of Clarice Lispector makes manifestly clear.

Another critic who focuses on the interrogation of structuralism that poststructuralism generates is Donald Keesey, who, in "Poststructural Criticism: Language as Context,"[6] has given us an essay that allows us to see the many points of contact between the basic principles of poststructural thought and the narratives of Clarice Lispector. Additionally, we have Mark Poster, whose *Critical Theory and Poststructuralism: In Search of a Context* (1989) argues that poststructuralism's greatest contribution to critical thinking has been its rigorous critique of language as a communicative medium, a concern I also believe to be fundamental to Lispector's oeuvre. Mention should also be made of Robert Con Davis and Ronald Schleifer's *Criticism and Culture* (1991), which, in making reference to poststructuralism's analysis of structuralism, contends that "post-structuralism—taking its impetus, as it often does, in Nietzche's critique of the will to truth (in philosophy) and the impersonality and universality of Kantian aesthetic ideology (in literature)—attempts to transform ways of knowing and the conception of truth" (159). As I shall argue in the chapters that follow, these issues are also implicit in the intensely poetic and philosophical narratives of Clarice Lispector.

In electing to apply a poststructural perspective to Lispector's texts, then, I have opted for what Vincent B. Leitch terms "the more inclusive domain of poststructuralism" over the narrower interpretive mode known as deconstruction, which, though certainly pertinent to Lispector's work,[7] tends not to incorporate "the historical, sociological, and political researches of Foucault and the psychoanalytical formulations of Lacan" (Leitch 290), the latter being an especially important dimension of Lispector's poststructural universe and one that I will examine in more detail in Chapter 6.

After reviewing the work of these and other commentators on poststructuralism, it becomes clear that this particular system of thought resists anything like an easy or clear definition. Nevertheless, running through virtually everyone's discussion of poststructuralism are the following five points, all of which, as I shall demonstrate in the course of my study, are fundamental to Lispector's work:

- There is an acute awareness of and emphasis on the play of language, on language understood as process, as an irresistibly productive semiotic system (what Barthes calls the "scriptible" text);
- It is clear that theoreticians of poststructuralism also tend to focus on what we might term the semantic play that characterizes Lispector's work, the slippage that occurs between and among the signifiers and the signifieds (an issue represented in Derrida's famous neologism, "diffé-rance"; cf. *Positions* 8–10, 14, et al.) and that calls into question the as-sumption that a text can ever possess a single, stable meaning or that such a meaning could ever derive from it;
- There is the importance that is attached to the acts of writing (best un-derstood in Lispector's case as *écriture*, a term Ann Banfield links to the use of "style indirecte libre," or free indirect discourse, a narrative mode extensively cultivated by Lispector)[8] and reading, activities that, by virtue of their ability to unlock and mix the various levels of meaning that a text can generate for us, are demonstrative not only of poststructural theory but of its connection to reader-response theory;
- And as we see in nearly all of Lispector's texts, there is a refusal to make distinctions between "literary" and "nonliterary" language use, between genres, and between language and metalanguage;
- There is the widespread if not unanimous emphasis placed by poststruc-tural critics on language and its relationship to psychoanalysis (Lacan and Julia Kristeva), to the sociopolitical context (Jameson, Lyotard, Spivak, Cixous, Belsey, and Baudrillard), and to the formation of a splintered and conflicted subject (Lacan's linguistically informed unconscious and Kris-teva's "subject-in-process"), an unstable "site" (as in *The Passion according to G. H.*, *The Stream of Life*, or *A Breath of Life: Pulsations*) marked by innumerable forms of conflict and desire, including not only the sexual (in all its myriad manifestations) but the psychological and the ideological as well.

In an attempt to remain true to the basic thrust of poststructural theory, however, I do not offer my argument as the be-all and end-all of criticism on Clarice Lispector, for to do so would be to establish pre-cisely the kind of rigid master discourse that poststructuralist thought disavows. Rather, I employ the poststructural optic as a critical tool, as a way of reading Lispector's deeply complex texts, yet also as a way I feel is particularly germane to her often self-conscious and at least par-tially autobiographical writing and that can account for its most salient characteristics. Thus, my application of poststructuralism to Lispector's work should be understood as being descriptive (rather than prescriptive) in nature, though I do believe it can offer us a surprisingly complete accounting of how and why her texts are as they are.

Although much has been written about Clarice Lispector, her work remains, in an overall sense, largely an enigma to us. This is so, I believe, because of the elusive and ambiguous nature of her *escritura*, the great bulk of which struggles, directly and indirectly, with the twin problems of meaning and communication in human existence. Given the complexity of these issues, Lispector's reader is forced to confront her narratives from a number of interrelated critical and philosophical perspectives, among which the issue of language, in its peculiar relationship to both knowing (epistemology) and being (ontology), emerges as the decisive factor. For Lispector, both literature and philosophy, the two main intellectual grounds of her work, "end in 'language,' which for Lispector is the medium within which such designations as 'literature' and 'philosophy' are made, as well as the medium in and through which alone anything nonlinguistic can be reached" (Sousa, "Once within a Room," viii). Moreover, as Jacques Derrida argues in "The Double Session," "[t]he critical desire—which is also the philosophical desire—can only, as such, attempt to regain . . . lost mastery" (*Dissemination* 230). As we shall see, this urge drives, in a variety of ways, nearly all of Lispector's narratives (Harari 29).

To read Lispector's *escritura/écriture*, then, is to experience language's most basic conflict, to seek but never find, as Derrida conceptualizes it, an elusive "transcendent reading" (*Of Grammatology* 160) that, paralleling both the motivations of Lispector's characters and those of her reader, will eventually yield a more comprehensive and satisfying understanding of her works. Or, again paradoxically, the "truth" we encounter in Lispector's world suggests, à la Derrida ("Structure, Sign, and Play in the Discourse of the Human Sciences," *Modern Criticism and Theory*, ed. David Lodge), that there is no stable center that can be viewed from the outside of its structure, no truth that does not depend for its "truthfulness" on some other structure, center, or truth. To recognize this crucial parallel between Derridean theory and Lispector's sense of writing goes a long way toward revealing the nature of the distinctive ambiguity, or "undecidability," that marks her narratives.[9] In short, Lispector's "*textes*" dramatically demonstrate that, as Derrida puts it,

> there was no center, that the center could not be thought in the form
> of a present-being, that the center had no natural site, that it was not

a fixed locus but a function, a sort of nonlocus in which an infinite number of sign-substitutes came into play. (*Writing and Difference* 280)

As we see so powerfully developed in *The Passion according to G. H.* (1964) or *The Apple in the Dark* (1961), the "transcendent" truth that G. H., Martim, and a host of other Lispectorian characters are in quest of reveals itself to be a function not merely of language but of language's elusiveness, its irradicable "free play." Her intensely textualized world is thus one in which, through her characters, language interrogates being, which is to say, it interrogates itself.

To desire this state of perfect communication and satisfaction but never to attain it, Lispector implies, is what being "near to the wild heart" of life is really like, and it dramatizes both the intensely human dimension of her writing and its poststructural ethos. As when we are in love (another of Lispector's most basic motifs), we are constantly seduced and tortured by language, by doubts about the sincerity of the other, about reliability and meaning, by what the very language that we use to express our love, our sense of being and identity, leads us to hope for and desire, by the seductive but maddening skein of signifiers and signifieds that this language dangles eternally before us.

As Lispector herself explains the nature of this paradoxical condition, "What cannot be expressed only comes to me through the breakdown of language. Only when the structure breaks down do I succeed in achieving what the structure failed to achieve" (*Near to the Wild Heart* 192). Strongly suggesting a close affinity between Lispector and at least some of her characters, G. H., one of her most enigmatic creations, expresses an almost identical sentiment about language and its relationship to both writing and being:

> Reality is raw material, language the way I seek it—and how I don't find it. But it is from seeking and not finding that what I have not known is born, and I instantly recognize it. Language is my human endeavor. I have fatefully to go seeking and fatefully I return with empty hands. But—I return with the unsayable. The unsayable can be given me only through the failure of my language. Only when the construct falters do I reach what it could not accomplish. (*Passion* 170)

"To write," Derrida argues, as if in reference to G. H. and a host of other Lispectorian characters, "is to have the passion of the origin" (*Writing and Difference* 295). Thus it is that, like so many of Lispector's characters, G. H. comes to sense, if not fully realize, that everything she "sees" or even conceives of is inescapably from her perspective within the "prison house of language," a perspective from which she can never escape. Not even Macabéa, the pathetic protagonist of Lispector's most overtly political narrative, *The Hour of the Star* (1977), can get beyond the web of words that ensnares not only her and her (dim) perceptions of her predicament but those (much more acute, if no more successful) of her similarly language-entrapped male narrator, Rodrigo S. M.

This constantly self-interrogating play of language is, I believe, the source of Lispector's reputation as a "difficult" and hermetic writer, and it stands as one of the most distinctive aspects of her creative vision. The nature of her work, therefore, is such that regardless of the critical lens we use to examine it, other plausible readings will inevitably arise. Instead of functioning as stable semantic structures, with discernible centers that determine single, recognizable meanings, Lispector's texts reveal themselves to be a constantly evolving network of signs, the free play of signifieds and signifiers.

In generating such an acutely language-conscious world, Lispector thus explores what J. Hillis Miller understands as the "situation" of humankind as "something encountered in our relations to other people, especially relations involving love, betrayal, and the ultimate betrayal by the other of our love for him or her, the death of the other" (Miller 22). In Lispector's language-inscribed world, our quest to understand inevitably exists just one word, one meaning, one interpretation away. Brilliantly captured in the semiotic complexities of her "apple" (*The Apple in the Dark*), the biblical symbol of perfect decoding that lies forever just out of our reach, our struggle to understand inevitably takes place "in the dark," just beyond our capacity to grasp what we desire to grasp and always one sign away.

This is the poststructural dilemma, it is Martim's dilemma, and it is our dilemma. And like Martim, in some ways (his confused passivity, for example) exemplary of a certain type of Lispectorian character (and in contrast to a creation like Joana, who may be considered as exemplary of another, more aggressive class of Lispectorian characters), in the end we may have no other recourse except to abandon our quests to "know" or possess this perfect, Logos-like state of being and return, meekly, to the false security of our conventional wisdoms, structures, and codes of conduct and signification, to the "paralyzing security" (*Passion* 12) of the "third leg" that G. H. senses she has lost as she begins her descent into the inescapable and destabilizing play of language. What is unique about Lispector's work in this respect is that, through characters as diverse as

Ana, Joana, Martim, and the all but genderless "voice" in *The Stream of Life*, it leads the reader not only to confront the terrifying arbitrariness of human existence but to understand the full extent to which we must deal with the changing conventions of others even as we seek, moment to epiphany-like moment, to create our own identities and "meanings"; we see, in other words, how powerfully the semantically productive self-referentiality of language serves as the most revealing paradigm for Lispector's fictive world.

Portrayed in human, if, perhaps, less than noble terms, G. H.'s near, partial, or pseudo transformation, defined by the destabilizing flow of language, exemplifies our human quest for Logos, an idealized state of perfect harmony and communication that, as Lacan views it, is nothing more than a figment of our verbally constituted imagination. Seen to be merely a linguistic artifice, a construct of our desire, this Logos never-theless exhibits a powerful hold on our human consciousness (which, as Lacan has argued, is itself a verbal construct) and leads us inexorably in quest of a perfection that we can never attain. Our pursuit of Logos must end, as it does for so many Lispectorian characters, in exhaustion, frus-tration, and anxiety, qualities that stem from language's inherent elusive-ness. For Lispector, these qualities characterize the human condition, which her texts reveal overwhelmingly to be a matter of our human quest—through language—for a stable and ambiguity-free knowledge that will forever elude us. Indeed, the very concept we have of this quest (the signified) is itself a maze of words, one born, paradoxically, of our all too human desire that such a perfect state of being exist, God-like, for us. It is this self-consciously conflictive attitude about the relation-ship between language, being, and meaning that animates Lispector's singular style, and that lies, restively, behind her sense of her own work as constituting a "humble quest"[10] for something that lies forever be-yond it.

Both encoding and conveying this quest, the self-conscious act of writing is fundamental to Lispector's texts, and it marks one of her work's most vital links to poststructural thought, which, as Sharon Crowley ob-serves, views writing as "a manifestation of desire," "a reach for author-ity." As is evident in Lispector's narratives, "Invention begins in the encounter with one's own text" (Crowley 98). The common denomina-tor of all these pressures and tensions, however, and both effecting and affecting all the others, is language, the taproot of Lispector's conscious-ness, as a writer and as a human being, and, as in Lacanian psychoanaly-sis, an endlessly generative semiotic system bound up in the process of self-mutation, of undercutting its own consolidating structurations and meanings. What happens in texts like "The Burned Sinner and the Harmonious Angels," "The Egg and the Chicken," "Two Stories My Way," *The Besieged City*, or *A Breath of Life*, therefore, is that Lispector plumbs the depths of a mysterious and protean desire, one constantly disruptive of the structures that would encase and restrict it, and featuring the primacy of the signifier (language) over the signified in a semantically fecund correspondence that Lacan famously describes as the "incessant sliding of the signified under the signifier" (*Écrits: A Selection* 154).

In Lispector's world, from *Near to the Wild Heart* (1944) onward, concepts of identity thus begin to emerge in her texts not as issues to be wrestled with and then resolved but as irreconcilable paradoxes, self-inquisitorial discourses that are as insoluble for the author and characters as they are for the reader. And, as a text like *The Stream of Life* illustrates, these systems relentlessly double back on themselves, undercutting not only their own apparent unity but also the reader's ability to rein them in with the sense of closure expected of a simpler narrative or of a single interpretive stance. The result, with its stylistic manifestation being that singularly acute, narrated "from within" (Nunes 1977 and Lindstrom 1982) self-consciousness that characterizes Lispector's best work, is that, again paradoxically, the more Lispector's characters struggle with the self-referential fluidity of language, the more they find themselves enmeshed in it. Of all Lispector's linguistically self-conscious characters, however, only Joana, from Lispector's first novel, and Lóri, from *An Apprenticeship, or The Book of Delights* (1969), give the reader any real reason to feel that one day they might escape the imprisoning effect that language—read *phallogocentric* discourse—has had on their development as human beings. Yet even their cases are ultimately rendered moot because of the conflicting desires they realize are defining them. This predicament is especially prominent in terms of Lispector's women characters, who are depicted as seeking a personally satisfying sense of psychological, political, and sexual identity within androcentric social structures. This same struggle, which is still being waged, albeit (I believe) in a more openly poststructural fashion, both in Lispector's last published text, *The Hour of the Star* (1977), and in her posthumously published dramatic novel, *A Breath of Life* (1978), typifies her work more completely than perhaps any other single theme.

Although the macrostructures of Lispector's texts (*The Apple in the Dark*, for example, but even the structurally more radical "Fifth Story" and "Two Stories My Way") often suggest the neat order and unified coherence of structuralism, the real anarchy of even these texts, the true drama of their language (to reframe the argument of Benedito Nunes), takes place not merely in the context of language but actually in language, as a direct function of its semantic vicissitudes. As with poetry, a close reading of these and other Lispectorian texts reveals an endless "dissemination" of meaning that cannot be pinned down or delimited (*Positions* 86–87), a dispersal of meaning, moreover, in which the reader must take an active part. In reading Lispector, we are made aware that the most fundamental force in her world is the semantic elusiveness of language itself, the system or structure that, always in play, generates ever more plausible meanings or interpretational strategies. Against high structuralism's belief in stabilized, and therefore explainable, orders, forms, and meanings, Lispector's texts, constantly probing the undecidability of language, challenge the notion that any such stability can be achieved through language, and especially through writing and reading, the two focal points of her work. Lispector's world thus actualizes the world of poststructuralist thought, showing us what it looks like not when written as literary theory but as a provocative amalgam of fiction, poetry, and philosophy and as it pertains to the human condition, to the everyday lives of men, women, and children. As if written to exemplify poststructuralist theory, texts like *The Stream of Life*, "The Egg and the Chicken," and "Two Stories My Way" flaunt their free play, their relentless "différance," and their endless deferrals of meaning and closure.

From Joana and Martim to the voices in *The Stream of Life* and *A Breath of Life*, and from the frustrated old woman of "In Search of Dignity" to the contemplative (and possibly autobiographical) narrator of "That's Where I'm Going," Lispector's characters anthropomorphize poststructuralism, dramatizing its human face while simultaneously reminding us that "human culture is a system of sign systems, and that the source and pattern for these systems is language" (Keesey 343). As with G. H., Martim, or Ana (of "Love"), Lispector's men and women often choose to live out their lives by rejecting as too powerful and too radically transforming those epiphanic moments when our seemingly well-controlled language use suddenly and unexpectedly turns back on itself and on us and we lose control of it and of our sense of identity in general. Yet even in these cases her texts drive home the realization that to a great extent our worlds, our social, political, philosophical, and sexual constructs, are, finally, just that—constructs—self-referential verbal artifices that change meaning and significance in accordance with changing circumstances. As readers, we follow Lispector as her narratives wrestle, sometimes (as in *Soulstorm*) wryly and subversively (Vieira), with the implications of this worldview, which, as exemplified in the characters who inhabit her stories, novels, and "chronicles," amounts to nothing less than a deeply humanistic critique of language's poststructural relationship to reality, identity and being, for, with every "sopro de vida" or "breath of life" that we humans take, we cannot escape "living language," however frustrating this condition may be.

Very close, I believe, to Derrida's concept of "différance," this constantly self-destabilizing semantic tension is the basic building block of Lispector's narratives and it explains why, in her themes, structures, and characterizations, her work paradoxically exudes both a sense of "unity" and "control" and a sense of plurisignation and fragmentation, the loss of control and of unity. Or, to cast this tension in a slightly different context, Lispector's fictions show us how language, that most definitively human of our traits, structures our awareness of our existence at the same instant or moment (these also being key Lispectorian motifs) that it "deconstructs" it. The result of this type of structuring and "destructuring," as we see replayed time and time again in Lispector's work, is a recognition of our deep human need to order things, to go in quest of a state of perfect communication (Logos, or Lispector's "state of grace") even as we fail to attain it. As Lacan might say, however, because such a desire is itself an evolving verbal construct deriving from the same conscious and unconscious language structures that engender our quest (which, similarly, is also a function of our language system), it will forever elude us, as it eludes Lispector's characters, among whom very few emerge from their quest believing they have a chance to succeed, to become something new. But because Lispector writes literature and not philosophy per se, her narratives are able to humanize the seemingly sterile and alien poststructural condition by making the reader feel the confusion, anger, fear, and frustration that arise from it and that, at its deepest level (the "primitivism," the quest for the *matéria prima* of life that permeates Lispector's work), define our condition as human beings, as the self-conscious language animal. Possessed of one of the most unique voices in all of twentieth-century literature, Clarice Lispector is a writer who deserves a much greater audience than she has so far received.

Prior to the work of the Swiss linguist Ferdinand de Saussure (1857–1913), the widely accepted view was that language had a virtually tangible relationship to reality, that words connected directly to objects and ideas in the universe. When it occurred, the problem of ambiguity was believed to be merely a function of careless language use—the wrong word used in the wrong place at the wrong time. Clarity in meaning was held to be fully attainable through careful reading and writing. However, after Saussure's revolutionary theory (that language is a self-referential system of arbitrarily and conventionally related signs with no necessary relation to anything outside the language system itself), all these beliefs in the stability of language and in its relationship to reality were seriously challenged. As Robert Scholes describes it, Saussure, "amplified by Roland Barthes and others, has taught us to recognize an unbridgeable gap between words and things, signs and referents. . . . Signs do not refer to things, they signify concepts, and concepts are aspects of thought, not of reality" (*Semiotics and Interpretation* 24). The entire concept of meaning, perhaps the most crucial of all language issues, was thus called into question by Saussurean linguistics.

While social scientists have generally disregarded Saussure's challenge, literary scholars (and, to a degree, historians like Hayden White) have taken his theory quite seriously, so much so that one can, indeed, say that the nature of meaning—in language and therefore in literature—has emerged as the defining issue of literary criticism in the post-Saussure era. Such seminal movements as semiotics, psychoanalysis, structuralism, and poststructuralism[1] rest directly on it, as do the closely related issues of reader-response theory, feminism, Marxism, phenomenology, and critical questions involving gender, race, authorial intention, the role of the reader, and power. All these concerns, as Barbara Johnson has shown ("Writing," *Critical Terms for Literary Study*, 39–49), can be seen as reflections of our ongoing attempt to understand the relationship between language, writing, and meaning, the issue that, restively, has been at the heart of literary theory for most of the twentieth century.

Few fiction writers, however, have probed the length and breadth of this problem as relentlessly or as imaginatively as the Brazilian author Clarice Lispector (1920–77). Esteemed in Brazil, France, and elsewhere "as an important contemporary philosopher dealing with the relationships between language and human (especially female) subjecthood" (Sousa, "Once within a Room," vii), Lispector is a writer whose work relentlessly probes the semantic and referential play of language use—and the implication this play has for the ways we live out our lives. Relating the issues of language and meaning to problems of individual human identities and to the larger social, political, and economic issues that surround them, Lispector spent a lifetime writing texts that struggled with such issues as: How does one achieve an authentic and satisfying sense of being? On what does one's identity depend? Where does the "real" meaning of language reside? How can one know? What does it mean to "know" something? Is there any one "real," "true," and "stable" meaning? If so, why can't we all know and agree about it? On the other hand, if meaning is unstable and mutable, how can we ever hope to communicate with each other? Or even with ourselves? And, finally, could the seemingly insurmountable differences that divide us be mitigated if we could achieve a new level of awareness about language and its unique ability to determine our identities and to shape the ways we view the world about us? Returning us to the ancient epistemological fount of philosophy and poetry, Lispector's generically hybrid texts can, collectively, be taken as a grand and endlessly self-reflective discourse on language and being, with the problem of meaning (and therefore of identity, both individual and cultural) functioning as their thematic and structural ground.

In many ways, one can say that the great quest that motivates so much of what Lispector wrote was a desire to bridge what she seems to have intuited as the unbridgeable gap that separated the signifier from its signified,[2] the word from its referent, a kaleidoscopic self from an uncertain and unknowable other. This desire to root human existence in language[3] is what drives one of Lispector's most underappreciated characters (and perhaps one of her many alter egos), Ângela Pralini, to declare, in *A Breath of Life*, "I like words. . . . I want to write words so clasped together, one in another, that there are no spaces between them and between me" (my translation). That this desire, pandemic to her narratives, was never realized—except in her eventual realization that behind one word lies yet another word,[4] that "writing consumes writing" ("escrever consome escrever"; *Um sopro de vida* 77)—only confirms her status as a writer driven by a deeply poststructural outlook, one that, however, also demonstrates its relevance to a wide range of human experiences and conditions. Stressing two main points—that while the great majority of Lispector's texts can be said to struggle intrinsically with the issues involved in *écriture*, many of them also interrogate these same issues in more overt, extrinsic ways—I will show in this chapter how Lispector's work demonstrates Derrida's famous assertion that "language bears within itself the necessity of its own critique" ("Structure, Sign, and Play," 114–15).

Notoriously difficult to define (as we have seen),[5] poststructuralism involves not a rejection but a rethinking of structuralism's basic principles, especially those relating to what, before Saussure and Derrida, had been considered the supposed stability of the linguistic sign and, consequently, of meaning. By challenging the idea (implicit in Saussure's linguistics) that the signifier (the word) and the signified (the concept or thing to which it refers) were perfectly and symmetrically unified, the poststructural reaction (which is often said to have begun in the United States with Jacques Derrida's 1966 Johns Hopkins address, "Structure, Sign, and Play in the Discourse of the Human Sciences")[6] called for a new consideration of the ways that language generated, or, as Derrida would have it, "disseminated," meaning. If the structuralists had argued for the inescapable separation of the word from its referent, the poststructuralists saw an additional and equally inescapable division: between the two components of the sign itself, between the signifier and the signified. The startling result of this line of thought was that language suddenly revealed itself to be a much more unstable and fluid system of signification than even the structuralists, with their belief in neatly balanced structures and oppositions, had envisioned. As a direct consequence of its critique of structuralist thought, poststructural theory generates a new way of thinking about meaning, one which, as a function of language's inherent mutability and semantic arbitrariness, now becomes a matter of production, of sociopolitical and cultural "staging," as it ebbs and flows throughout the interlocking but endlessly productive chains of signifiers (words) that constitute any given language system. Because, as Derrida has argued, a complete or perfect meaning cannot, in such an unstable condition, ever be fully present in any one sign,[7] the concept of meaning itself becomes problematic. Meaning, paradoxically, is both there ("present") and not there ("absent") in a given text, which is, of course, composed of many words, or signs (each one of which is semantically polyvalent). Meaning, therefore, becomes a matter of how each reader connects and reconnects each word/sign with the others that surround and sustain it, making it a problem, finally, of interpretation rather than of the "discovery" of the "single," "perfect" solution (which, in the poststructural view, cannot exist). To read (or write) as a poststructuralist, then, is to "read" and "write" the endless free-play process of psycholinguistic and cultural signification, an experience that constitutes not only the basic stylistic ground of Clarice Lispector's work but its overall thematic orientation as well. More precisely, I will try to show that the problem of signification, which, in its connection to the creation of one's protean identity, functions as the most mesmerizing and compelling thematic aspect of the Brazilian writer's texts, is most thoroughly appreciated in Lispector's world when considered in terms of a particularly feminist brand of poststructuralism, one that, expanding from its psychological underpinnings, projects our language-based individual identities into the context of the larger social, political, and economic structures that so powerfully influence our lives.

This means that, in addition to undertaking "a critique of metaphysics (of the concept of causality, of identity, of the subject, and of truth), of the theory of the sign, and the acknowledgment and incorporation of psychoanalytic modes of thought" (Young, "Post-Structuralism: An Introduction," *Untying the Text*, 8), Lispector's texts also explore "the relation between language, subjectivity, social organization and power" (Weedon 12), particularly (though not exclusively) as these relate to the possibilities available to women existing in patriarchal social structures. "For poststructuralist theory,"—as we see in texts like *Near to the Wild Heart*, "The Burned Sinner and the Harmonious Angels,"[8] "The Message," "Plaza Mauá," "*The Passion according to G. H.*," and *The Stream of Life*—"the common factor in the analysis of social organization, social meanings, power, and the individual consciousness is *language*" (Weedon 21). For Clarice Lispector's texts, as for poststructural theory in general, "[l]anguage is the place where actual and possible forms of social organization and their likely social and political consequences are defined and contested" (21). Although late Lispector works like *The Hour of the Star* and "Beauty and the Beast, or The Wound Too Great" possess a fairly obvious political dimension (the problems associated with poverty, malnutrition, and ignorance), all her narratives project language as "the place where our sense of ourselves, our subjectivity is *constructed*" (21). For Lispector, subjectivity, which is sometimes mistakenly taken as a solipsism that is thought to limit the importance of her work, becomes not only "a site of disunity and conflict" but an onto-logical force ". . . central to the process of political change" (21). This most distinctive quality of Lispector's work—that in presenting lan-guage as the ever-changing locus of both subjectivity and sociopolitical organization it structures itself by moving back and forth, thematically speaking, simultaneously upholding and undermining the same posi-tions—is, as I shall demonstrate, what makes it the epitome of poststruc-tural writing.

As becomes quickly apparent to the attentive reader, Lispector's texts, in their semantic and structural plasticity, present meaning less as a function of external, objective, or verifiable referents than of language's irremediably productive nature. This explains why her work seems so opaque, so tangled, and so open to interpretations that are not merely diverse but often in conflict. From Joana (of *Near to the Wild Heart*) to the male "author" and female protagonists in *The Hour of the Star* and *A Breath of Life*, Lispector's language-defined subjects are anxiously aware that not even they can imbue their identities with the kind of perfect stability and meaning that we, adrift in an ever-changing and uncertain world, desire. The nature of language—which, in Lispector's world, constantly thrusts itself forward as a self-referential system of signs en-gaged in an endless process of signification and resignification—simply does not permit it, except, of course, as a self-eliding illusion, the ill-understood quest for which drives many of Lispector's most compelling characters, including Joana, Martim (*The Apple in the Dark*), G. H. (*The Passion according to G. H.*), the voice of *The Stream of Life*, and Rodrigo S. M. (*The Hour of the Star*).

Yet as a careful reading of her complete works also makes clear there is more to Lispector's poststructuralism than a "mere" critique of the inter-action between language, meaning, and human existence. Humanizing these deeply philosophical issues, Lispector's seductively self-conscious and lyrical narratives expand the interplay of language and being on the subjective, even autobiographical,[9] level into a metaphorically empow-ered speculation concerning the nature of identity and of both socio-political and textual power structures. It is Lispector's unique talent, however, not just to show how these structures inhibit personal freedom (as many writers have done) but, by means of various and endlessly com-peting discourses within and among the texts themselves (the constantly evolving positions of the reader, the characters, and the voices involved), to draw the reader into an actual experiencing (through her or his interpretation of the characters' interpretations) of the ever evolving ways language shapes and gives meaning to the world. As works like *Near to the Wild Heart*, *The Passion according to G. H.*, and *The Stream of Life* demonstrate, it is a mistake to regard poststructuralism as an ineluctably nihilistic, antihumanistic, and apolitical mode of thought. To the contrary, the basis of the intense sentience experienced by Lispector's most powerful characters (G. H., for example, or Joana) is language's engulfing of us, the realization that although as human beings we claim to possess language, if we are "lucky" enough (like G. H. or the voice in *The Stream of Life*) or are sufficiently "cursed" (like Ana, of "Love," or Martim), we come to realize how much it possesses us, how irresistibly it shapes and determines our lives. In unexpected and singular fashion, then, Lispector's poststructuralism actually stems from what is perhaps Western civilization's most deeply rooted humanistic tradition—the role language plays in defining our essential humanity, our sense not only of who and what we are but also of who and what we might become.

In contrast, however, to the position of traditional humanists, who hold that it is we who control language (and not vice versa), that language has "correct" references external to itself, and that the world will either be explained well or poorly (depending on our ability to match the right word with the right referent), Lispector's poststructural humanism posits an anxious and acutely language-conscious existence in which "[t]he signifier floats away from the signified, 'jouissance' dissolves meaning, the semiotic disrupts the symbolic, 'différance' inserts a gap between signifier and signified, and power disorganizes established knowledge" (Selden 102). Whether dealing with issues of theme, characterization, or style, these gaps or fissures (what Derrida calls "moments of aporia") in the development of Lispector's texts are a distinctive feature of her work. They represent the mysterious interstices between things and thoughts, between words and their referents, which eventually reveal themselves to be other words whose meanings are themselves in a state of constant flux, a state of affairs that sums up the essential nature of Lispector's most definitive characters. As G. H., for example, writes, making reference to her "secret quest":

> I went into what exists between the number one and the number two, how . . . Between two musical notes there exists another note, between two facts there exists another fact, between two grains of sand . . . there exists an interval of space, there exists a sensing between sensing—in the interstices of primordial matter there is the mysterious,

fiery line that is the world's breathing, and the world's continual
breathing is what we hear and call silence. (*Passion* 90)

Summing up this profoundly verbal perception of human existence is
the narrator of "That's Where I'm Going," one of Lispector's most
thoroughly hybrid narratives, who declares, "At the tip of a word is a
word" (*Soulstorm* 146).

Descriptive of poststructuralism's actual operation, these quotes accurately sum up what happens in a typical Lispector novel, story, or
"*crônica.*" Page by page, line by line, and word by word, her narratives
surge and swell within and against themselves; and the narrative structure that, in a more traditional writer, would govern them, refuses here
to coalesce into the production of a single, coherent, and unambiguous
meaning. By constantly calling into question their own quest for truth
or Logos,[10] works like "The Fifth Story," "Two Stories My Way," and
A Breath of Life advance the inescapably unstable nature of signification
as the most definitive quality of human existence. Moreover, Lispector
presents this signification as a fluid process, one antithetical to what we
ordinarily understand as the "discovery" of "meaning," the signifiers of
which, in Lispector's deceptively "simple" words, "lead a chameleon-
like existence, changing their colours with each new context" (Selden 73).

One of the most significant of these "new contexts," and one that at
once both humanizes and politicizes Lispector's poststructuralism, is the
feminism implicit in her work.[11] From *Near to the Wild Heart* to *Family
Ties* and pulsing steadily through such later works as *The Apple in the
Dark, The Stream of Life, An Apprenticeship,* or *The Book of Delights, The
Stations of the Body* and *A Breath of Life,* as well as through her fascinating "*crônicas,*" Lispector's feminist-oriented poststructuralism (Barbosa
1997: 94–95) examines the issue of power not merely in terms of male/
female relations but in terms of how language determines the various—
and often conflicting—identities (intellectual, emotional, professional,
social, and sexual, for example) that come into play as we enter into
our various psychological and cultural relationships, which, themselves
functions of language, are also unstable, uncertain, and unpredictable.
Female characters like G. H., Joana, the "Burned Sinner," and the voice
of *The Stream of Life,* for example, as well as several male characters
(Rodrigo S. M., Martim, or the "author" of *A Breath of Life*) come to life
in Lispector's narratives as acutely conscious states of mind whose painfully self-scrutinized existences inevitably end up reflecting the ways we
respond to the patriarchal structures that dominate our lives. To para-

phrase Chris Weedon on Althusserian Marxism, Lispector's feminist poststructuralism leads us to see language as the unstable but fundamental force that, via the conflicting discourses it endlessly engenders, emerges as the only mechanism we have that can give meaning to the world.

But while the sociopolitical and economic status of women as a class is inherent in nearly all of Lispector's narratives, it is, in a number of cases, their powerful "jouissance," their psychosexual sense of female pleasure that gradually emerges as one of their most potent qualities. With *The Stream of Life* being designated by Hélène Cixous as the "finest practice of her concept of 'l'écriture féminine,'"[12] Lispector's texts most emphatically write the female body. And, as Mara Gálvez-Breton writes,[13] like Luce Irigaray, who argues for a symbiotic relationship between what she sees as a plural, autoerotic, and finally, subversive female sexuality and language, Lispector's female characters (as early as Joana, in 1944) confront and then satisfy their desires through their discoveries of their own bodies. At times, this is accomplished, as in *Near to the Wild Heart*, and (more overtly) in "Footsteps," by the act of masturbation and by the attainment of a new and psychologically empowering kind of language, one that is intensely poetic and that, as Cristina Ferreira Pinto suggests (Pinto 1990), defies the strictures of patriarchal discourse. While this would seem to be an accurate description of Joana's self-liberating experience in Lispector's first novel (written when the author was in her early twenties), it applies, in varying degrees, to her later works as well, particularly *The Stream of Life*, a text sometimes described as "orgasmic" in nature, and *A Breath of Life*. For Lispector, then, as for a number of French feminist theoreticians, there is a close, even integral connection between female desire and pleasure ("jouissance") and the metaphoric, imagistic language and the transgressive, nonlinear, open-ended structurations that inscribe the puissance that marks her best work. The connection between the philosophical orientation of Lispector's texts and the power of her antiphallogocentric voices (male, female, androgynous, and what we might call, as with Martim and Vitória, gender "inverting," or effacing)[14] thus leads us to read her work as an indictment of the warping power wielded by androcentric society, a power that, as works like "The Message," *The Apple in the Dark*, and *The Hour of the Star* imply, distorts the development of both women and men.

A crucial aspect of this tendency is the extent to which Lispector emphasizes the act of writing in her work. Cixous, in fact, elaborates on this point in her foreword to *The Stream of Life* (the English translation), where she observes that "if there is a subject of this text, or an object, it is on the question of writing. *The Stream of Life* is about writing, as a verbal activity. I write you. . . . The vital theme of this text is writing, all the questions of writing. Everything is organized around the mystery of writing" (*Stream of Life* xv). Omnipresent in her work, this same concern with "writing" and its relation to being also appears in *A Breath of Life*, the posthumously published work in which a male "author" declares, "It's curious, the sensation of writing. Upon writing, I think neither about the reader nor about me: at this moment I am . . . the words actually said" (my translation). By linking the ontologically self-affirming acts of writing (and reading) to the "writing degree zero"[15] creation, or "birthing," of one's manifold identities, Lispector transforms the issues of "being female," being a woman (merging the issues of biology and gender in a phallocentric world), being a man, and, simply, "being," and gives them prime psychological and political importance in her work.

Yet even the early novels, *Near to the Wild Heart* (1944), *The Chandelier* (1946), and *The Besieged City* (1948), reflect what we can now see as a similar sense of language and being. These texts, like the later ones, "disseminate," or spin out a "web-like complexity of signs . . . ," that structure themselves around "the back and forth, present and absent, forward and sideways movement of language in its actual processes" (Eagleton 132). A prototypical case is that of Joana, whose fragmented development as a character is cast in precisely this "back and forth, present and absent, and forward and sideways movement," as her very different roles in the tangled love triangles—involving first she, Otávio, and Lídia, and then "the man" and his "woman," or "wife"—make especially clear.[16]

The same is essentially true for Virgínia, the protagonist of *The Chandelier*, a novel often read in conjunction with *Near to the Wild Heart*.[17] Like Joana, her predecessor, Virgínia's struggle to gain an authentic identity reveals itself to be essentially a psycholinguistic problem; the real conflict thus is over whose system of signification, theirs or someone else's, will generate an authentic and satisfying identity for these two young women. As Ronald W. Sousa observes, referring to Virgínia's situation in *The Chandelier*, "Ultimately problematized in this set of relationships is woman's place in the socio-symbolic order; it is an issue that freights meditation on language throughout Lispector's work, moving it from the categorical and anchoring it in the analogical and the socio-symbolic" ("*O lustre,*" in *Clarice Lispector: A Bio-Bibliography*, 88).

In terms of its importance to her later work, this language-sensitive process of self-discovery and self-empowerment can be said to be a paradigm of Lispector's entire career, which can itself be taken as the literary embodiment of poststructuralism's human side as well as a questioning of structuralism's scientific pretensions.

Although *The Chandelier* is often read as another version of *Near to the Wild Heart*, there are several important differences. First, for however much Virgínia and Joana employ language in the formulation, or construction, of their identities, Virgínia's experiencing of this process seems less spontaneous than does Joana's. Yet it is largely as a result of this more studied linking of human consciousness and outer reality that *The Chandelier* makes more explicit the paradoxical problem so fundamental to Lispector's fictive universe: that language can be dealt with only through language. The degree to which this phenomenological orientation is emphasized in *The Chandelier* causes it to lapse occasionally into a kind of tediousness that is not found in the fresher, more dynamic *Near to the Wild Heart*, published two years earlier. In comparing the two novels on this point, it seems as if Lispector were trying, in *The Chandelier*, to see how far she could take the role of language in the psychocultural development of a main character.

And, indeed, Virgínia's development as a protagonist constitutes another major distinction between the two novels. Although, like Joana, Virgínia grows as a character largely in terms of the different relationships she has with various people, what is unique to her case is her particular relationship to the men in her life. Beginning in adolescence, with her brother, Daniel, but continuing on into her adulthood, with her lover, Vicente, Virgínia's quest for an identity is more bound up with men's opinions and expectations of her than was the case with Joana, whose relationships with men function more as mechanisms by which she could effect her own emancipation from the confines of orthodox gendering.

Interestingly, however, Virgínia's relationships with women (chiefly her mother and her older sister) are, as in the case of Joana (with the mysterious "mulher da voz"; with Lídia, her husband's pregnant mistress; and with the female lover of the nameless "homem" that Joana seduces), more complex and volatile than her relationships with men. Eventually, however, Virgínia, like Joana (though to a lesser degree), comes to achieve a measure, at least, of independence from the expectations that the men in her life place on her. It is in this context that *The Chandelier* makes its point about the predetermined roles women are expected to assume in an androcentric social structure, but it does so, in vintage Lispectorian style, by emphasizing language both as a weblike trap and as the anarchically liberating force that, once we come to understand its only arbitrary connection to external reality and its unique ability to determine what that reality means for us, can make us different people, freer and less susceptible to the constricting pressures of convention and conformity.

The struggle to resist these latter pressures constitutes the tension of Virgínia's story more than it does Joana's, and, indeed, Joana ultimately achieves a kind of apprehensive and vaguely staged liberation at the end of her novel while Virgínia's ends in her death, the victim (like Macabéa, of *The Hour of the Star*) of a hit-and-run driver. It is important to remember, however, that although Virgínia is perhaps overall less successful than Joana in breaking free of the gender demands that society has imposed on her, she, too, possesses a rich and vital "inner world," one that is intensely language based and that makes the reader feel how profoundly discourse not only shapes but informs our world, our personal sense of reality and being. Joana's development as an adult character, in fact, is characterized most of all by precisely this type of lyrically self-conscious and self-creative use of language, one effect of which, however, is to drive her ever deeper into the "silence" of her own "inner world" and to render her more and more incapable of functioning in the more fixed, rigid, and conventional world of other people— the world, that is, of ordinary society. It is in this spirit that Sousa discusses *The Chandelier* as a "perverse Bildungsroman," one in which Virgínia comes to discover, late in the novel, that her life has been a series of debilitating conflicts between "an interior self-construction that is all she has to rely on" and "the understanding that such self-construction is necessarily always fragmentary and momentary, susceptible to specific emotions and manias" (Sousa, "*O lustre*," 89). This is why, Professor Sousa explains, late in the novel Virgínia speaks of "a day-to-day 'negotiation' of life rather than of any position that is systematically fixed" (89). The essential fluidity of Virgínia's conception of life, as manifested most crucially of all in the language use that inscribes it, thus expresses what, for so many of Lispector's characters, is a fundamentally poststructural sense of existence, one in which everything is "negotiated," moment to moment, by our living by, through, and in language, where as Lacan has characterized it, the signified forever "slides" beneath the signifier, which floats away, reconnecting with other signifiers. It is this failure to connect the signified with a stabilizing signifier that explains the fragmented and conflicted development of Lispector's characters and that characterizes the self-interrogating style that brings them to life.

When, as in *S/Z* (1970), Barthes advocated a more open and dynamic concept of structure, one that distinguished between "lisible" (readerly) and "scriptible" (writerly) texts, he was attempting to give a theoretical justification for a kind of writing that Lispector had been practicing since 1944. As Barthes outlines it, and as Lispector practiced it, "scriptible" writing is not a thing or an end, but a process, the readerly production of meaning that, being a part of the process itself, can never be regarded as stable, completed, or ultimate; words always lead to more words, a concept Lispector dramatizes in texts like "That's Where I'm Going" and "The Obedient Ones." The five "codes" that Barthes says are shared by the author and reader are instances of "parole" that cannot be grounded in any ultimate language use.[18] Since such texts are thus "coded" only tangentially to some other reality, the problem of representation addressed in "Sarrasine," for example, shows itself to be similar to the way the same problem is treated in many of Lispector's texts. In both cases representation is ultimately replaced by reflexivity, a point underscored by Lispector in her heavy use of reflexive verbs and self-reflective syntactical structures. For Barthes, moreover, realism (as a literary mode) is based on a spurious assumption, namely, that the linguistics sign is somehow inherently linked to the external reality it purports to express. In his view, as in Lispector's, the realist (or "representational") sign is meretricious because it obscures its true status as a linguistic sign by generating the illusion that through it the reader (or listener) can perceive "reality" as it "really" is and that this can occur without the intervention of the sign itself. This position, however appealing, "denies the *productive* character of language" (Eagleton 136), which is perhaps the most distinctive characteristic of Lispector's narratives, a point she alludes to in "The 'True' Novel," a *crônica* dated 22 August 1970, where she decries the traditional realistic novel for much the same reason that Barthes does—because it is boring. If for Barthes, realism is the literary ideology of the prestructuralist age, then perhaps we should say that Clarice Lispector offers us the ideology of poststructuralism, an ideology, as we shall see, by no means devoid of sociopolitical significance.

In Lispector's fictive world, then, it is precisely the "productive character of language," its semantic fertility, that emerges as the basic subject matter of her texts, the mysterious *matéria prima* that G. H., seeking ultimate truths (or "transcendental signifiers"), eventually comes to find as the eternally elusive essence of human existence. Lispector's post-1961 work, where the language of such texts as *The Apple in the Dark*, *The Passion according to G. H.*, *The Stream of Life*, and *A Breath of Life* tends not to present itself as functioning in a mimetically representational fashion, is especially antirealistic in the poststructuralist sense. As these and other of her texts show, for Lispector, language, in all its arbitrariness, mutability, and autogenously productive power, was simultaneously the object of her narratives and the unstable, unreliable, and elusive medium of their expression. For Lispector's characters, there is no getting outside of language; the world is indeed text and, to paraphrase Heidegger (a philosopher who, along with Husserl and Wittgenstein, has special importance for Lispector's work),[19] the limits of one's world truly are the limits of one's language.

This casting of language itself as the primary focus, as the élan vital of existence (and therefore of identity), reaches its zenith in *The Stream of Life*, a text that, as we have seen, is essentially about writing, understood, again, as *écriture*. Thus, for Clarice Lispector (as for the later Barthes), language—and not some external reality—was simultaneously both the subject and object of her work, which, after *The Apple in the Dark* (1961), can easily be read as exemplifying Barthes's theory about those texts in which there is no single, definitive meaning and which are structured around semantically inexhaustible webs of signifiers, signified, codes, and constantly realigning fragments of codes. Yet while this basically poststructuralist orientation predominates in her later works, it is also powerfully present (though less overtly so) in Lispector's first novel, *Near to the Wild Heart*, which suggests that although she would undertake different variations on it, Lispector's basic sense of language, which I believe is essentially poststructural in nature, was fully operational as early as 1944.[20]

Fundamental to poststructural thought, "différance," Jacques Derrida's neologism for the imprecision and unreliability of language—its endless differing, deferring, and deferral—forms both the structural and the thematic basis of Clarice Lispector's fictional constructs. In texts from *Near to the Wild Heart* (1944), *The Chandelier* (1946), and *The Passion according to G. H.* (1964) to *A Breath of Life* (1978), the destabilizing force of "différance" permeates her work. According to Derrida (*Of Grammatology*, 1976), all language use—and not just that of "literature" (where it is more obvious)—involves the decentering play of "diffé-rance," and this helps explain why certain of Lispector's ostensibly "fic-tional" texts (like *The Passion according to G. H.*, *The Stream of Life*, or *The Hour of the Star*) often seem like "nonfiction" while many of her ostensibly "nonfiction" pieces, like "Forgiving God" (*Discovering the World*, 19 September 1970), seem "fictional," or literary. Lispector's early recognition of the free play inherent in language (its "différance," its "dissemination") has dissolved for her the borders between genres.

Speaking as a professor of philosophy, Derrida conceived of "diffé-rance" as a counterbalance or antidote to what he viewed as Western culture's basic "logocentrism," that is, its (for him) overweening and ultimately unjustifiable faith in a perfect, absolute, and self-evident Logos, in the Word (of God, law, or "man"—never woman), in truth, meaning, and reason. Arguing that, since Plato, Western thought has "privileged" Logos (and all the hierarchies of power that derive from it) by placing it at the center of all discourse,[21] Derrida, in what has been a radical challenge to the intellectual foundations of Western culture and civilization, thus views "logocentrism" as the error of mistaking what is arbitrary, mutable, and differential for what we wish to understand as "necessary," "proper," "natural," and immutable. Jonathan Culler, interpreting Derrida on this key point, defines "logocentrism" as "the orientation of philosophy toward an order of meaning—thought, truth, reason, logic, the Word—conceived as existing in itself, as foundation."[22] Greatly indebted to Saussure's linguistics (especially to the Swiss linguist's revolutionary assertion that in language there are only differences without positive terms) and to the philosophies of Nietzsche, Heidegger, and Husserl, Derrida's concept of "logocentrism" thus contextualizes such decisive concepts as "logic," "truth," and "meaning" as functions not of stable and verifiable realities but of the free play of signifiers and signifieds, the ever fluid relationship between arbitrarily and differentially linked linguistic signs.

By challenging the privileged "centering" of Logos in Western civilization, Derrida has led us, in what constitutes a powerful critique of structuralist thought, to reconsider not only who and what we are but also what we believe in and on what basis we believe it, an issue that Martim embodies in *The Apple in the Dark*, that Rodrigo S. M. (possibly Clarice Lispector) wrestles with in *The Hour of the Star*, and that several characters attempt to decipher in *A Breath of Life*.[23] Surveying the evolution of Western thought and social organization, Derrida, in the tradition of Descartes, Nietzsche, and Husserl, interrogates (as Lispector's narratives also do) our accepted modes of receiving, processing, and generating knowledge. Further, he asks that we speculate whether, on the basis of our heightened appreciation of language, we have not been seeing a gradual but widespread shift away from a "logocentric metaphysic of presence" and toward a recognition that human existence is more capricious and arbitrary than logical and fixed, that human existence (like Saussure's linguistic sign) is the spontaneous interplay of differences without positive terms, this latter point accounting for the unique kind of ambiguity that permeates Lispector's language-conscious texts.

In terms of philosophy, then, it is apparent that such concerns as these speak to traditional problems of epistemology and ontology. Yet because Derrida's thought also directly addresses such issues as "truth" and "meaning," it relates in an immediate and integral fashion to literature, which, like philosophy, occurs by, through, and in language. The difference, as Plato demonstrated in *The Republic* and elsewhere, is one of language use (often defined merely as an issue of style) and authorial intention. Derrida, however, like Lispector, asserts that there is a deeper, more fundamental problem at work here—the self-referential and semantically unstable nature of language itself. Upholding Saussure's view that a language is a closed sign system (his "langue") composed of arbitrarily connected signifiers and signifieds that do not possess absolute or substantive references beyond themselves and that enjoy no positive terms external to the language system itself, Derrida argues (in a way analogous to Carnap, Wittgenstein, and the other Logical Positivists) that language itself—and not its style or the intention of its author—is the real issue here, the inescapable variable in the generation, transmission, and reception of both "truth" and "meaning," this, too, being a fundamental characteristic of Lispector's writing.

Taken in their entirety, the decentering, self-questioning voices and narratives produced between 1944 and 1978 by Clarice Lispector give us a body of literary work that expresses the peculiar ethos of our time. Like all truly outstanding writers, Lispector possessed a highly unique voice, one that, in her case, captured the poststructural sense of language—and of silence—that serves so tellingly to describe our late-twentieth-century condition, our hopeful but anxiety-ridden malaise. At its poetic and philosophical heart, the "savage heart" of Lispector's method was the speaking (or, more apropos of her case, writing) subject (usually feminine) struggling self-consciously with language, with its endless semantic productivity and its mercurial relationship to identity. Her many voices labor to discover or create meaning in an intertextual world of words, a fluid, constantly self-transforming system of signs that produces neither a single, perfect meaning nor a stable, externally defined existence. When we read a text like *Near to the Wild Heart*, *The Passion according to G. H.*, *The Stream of Life*, or *The Hour of the Star*, we find ourselves participating in a paean to human existence as defined by language, a poststructural poem that, by showing us how words ceaselessly make and remake us, finally transcends being as stasis and becomes being as process.

Struggling with the essential poststructural conundrum, the female voice of *The Stream of Life* (1973),[24] for example, declares early on that, "I'm aware that everything I know I cannot say, I know only by painting or pronouncing syllables blind of meaning" (*SL* 5). This realization leads the narrative voice to confront the paradoxical "secret harmony of disharmony" (*SL* 6), which, in turn, elicits a readerly response that, recalling Derrida's reservations about the alleged primacy of spoken language, stresses writing as language's most continuously fluid and potent form of expression:

> I don't want what is already made but what is tortuously in the making. My unbalanced words are the luxury of my silence. I write in acrobatic, aerial pirouettes. (*SL* 6)

Cast as a positive, fecund force, this silence emerges not as the failure of language to communicate but as the embodiment of Cixous's "écriture féminine," a kind of writing that, as Verena Andermatt Conley explains, "leads to an undoing of the hierarchies and oppositions that determine the limits of most conscious life. By virtue of its poetry that comes from the rapport of the body to the social world, *écriture féminine* disrupts social practices in the ways it both discerns and literally rewrites them. . . . 'écriture féminine' . . . effectively redeems [the human subject] through the ways it offers anyone, male or female, a *living* relation with language and experience" (Cixous, *Reading with C. L.*, vii–viii). Utilizing language as would a poststructural theoretician, then, the metafictional voice of *The Stream of Life* then writes her voice, stressing once again the transformative interplay of language and being:

> To interpret and shape myself I need new signs and new articulations in forms which are found both on this side of my human history and on the other. (*SL* 15)

This process of linguistic self-realization then continues to intensify and expand, as we see in the following line: "I transfigure reality, and then another reality, dreamy and somnambulant, creates me in turn" (*SL* 15). Metaphorically expanding the argument that language does not reflect reality so much as it creates—and constantly transforms—it, *The Stream of Life* reaches its zenith when its narrator, finally embracing the verbal nature of being, writes: "I'm in a trance. I penetrate the surrounding air. What fever: I can't stop living. I'm this dense jungle of words that wrap themselves thickly around what I feel and think and experience and that transform all that I am into something from me" (*SL* 54–55). For Cixous a text that explores the connection between pleasure and writing (*SL* xi, xv–xvi), *The Stream of Life* luxuriates in the poststructural "slippage" of writing, its ceaseless play of signifiers and its endlessly self-referential coding and decoding. As its female voice expresses this language-as-body-based condition:

> I'm waiting for the next sentence. . . . I can stand it because I ate my own placenta. . . .
> My eyes are closed. I'm pure unconsciousness. They've already cut the umbilical cord: I'm loose in the universe. I don't think but I feel the *it*. With eyes closed I search blindly for the breast: I want thick milk. . . . A pulsating I is taking shape. (*SL* 26, 27–28)

This self-consciously formative "I" then continues, alluding, Derrida-like, to the birthing "play" of both "structures" and "signs," a basic feature of the human condition and one with which we must all contend:

> It suddenly occurred to me that it's not necessary to have order to live. There's no pattern to follow and there's not even pattern itself: I am born. (28)

Projecting existence as a function of the self-generating play of language, and thereby underscoring its inescapable mutability, the "I" of *The Stream of Life* then begins to question the concept of gender in her new, language-determined and archetypal conception of being:

> I'm still not ready to speak of "him" or "her." I point to "that." "*That*" is universal law. Birth and death. Birth. Death. Birth and . . . like the world breathing.
> I'm pure '*it*' that was rhythmically pulsating. (*SL* 28)[25]

By presenting (via language) human existence as an eternal process of birth, death, and rebirth, and by emphasizing the primacy of the neuter or gender-free demonstrative pronoun (cast as the "universal law"), the voice of *The Stream of Life* explores a sense of being that simultaneously recognizes our human desire for order and structure as well as our terrifying realization that language, with its self-referential instability and imprecision, is the only thing that stands between us and utter chaos, utter nothingness.

When the voice/text of *The Stream of Life* tells us, then, "You who read me, help me to be born" (*SL* 27) she-it is telling us that we all, readers as well as writers and narrators, are born and exist in the context of language, and to come (again through language) to a realization of this condition is to be born into the "marvelous scandal" of poststructural existence, the experiencing of which constitutes the warp and woof of Lispector's world:

I'm the heart of the shadows.

. . .

Now the shadows are dissipating.

. . .

Marvelous scandal . . . I am born.

(27)

As we can see, no small part of Lispector's power as a writer lies in her ability both to dramatize our quest for perfect knowledge and understanding (Logos) in her texts and, in virtually the same breath (her "breath of life"), to lead the reader to realize that the fulfillment of this quest is an illusion, a chimerical desire that, though unattainable, will forever spur us on, restively luring us (in an actualization of "différance") to seek after that which will forever elude us, Logos itself. Her characters thus project themselves into a multidimensional awareness of their pathos and triumph only to later discover these very levels and kinds of awareness changing and ebbing away, even as they labor to retain and understand them. That this fluctuating, language-based consciousness gradually establishes itself as the most poignant expression of the human condition is the realization that Lispector's texts lead us to over and over again. As her narratives show, for however much we desire clarity, stability, knowledge, and perfect understanding in our lives, we can never attain them, and that because of this we necessarily find ourselves eternally "bewitched," like the voice at the "end" of *The Stream of Life*, by the parlous, symbolic nature of human existence. Like Martim, of *The Apple in the Dark*, we are stumbling fearfully around in the darkness of our anxieties and frustration, or we are forced to recognize, as the self-conscious authorial voices in *The Hour of the Star* and *A Breath of Life* do, that we exist in a never-ending web of words: "I'm a writer who's afraid of the snare of words: the words I speak hide others. . . . Writing is a stone thrown into a deep well" (my translation). But either way, as Lispector's reader finally comes to realize, what really matters is language—speaking, reading, thinking, but above all writing—because to use language and to be aware of doing so is not only to be, but to be in the most complete, most human, and most expressive mode available to us, this being the force that drives Lispector's most definitive texts.

For Lispector, writing was a deeply personal—and deeply passionate—act not only of self-affirmation but of actual self-creation; to write was to exist.[26] This, too, led her texts toward an inward turning, a sometimes comic but often anguished contemplation of being as defined by language itself, of writing (as Barthes suggests in *Writing Degree Zero*) as an "intransitive" act rather than as a commentary on or representation of some event or situation in the real world. Because it seems likely that Lispector was aware of herself as a marginalized author (a middle-class woman of Jewish ancestry in a nominally Catholic culture)[27] in a marginalized nation (Brazil) at the same time she was so preoccupied with the nature and function of language in regard to the human condition, one is led to wonder whether a major conflict in her life was how to reconcile these two poles—the linguistic and the cultural—in her work. One of Lispector's greatest works, however, *The Hour of the Star*, can, as we shall see, easily be read both psychoanalytically and politically, as a compelling attempt to synthesize her views on language, identity, and creativity (Pinto 1987) with her social conscience, specifically the tragic plight of people in Brazil's lower classes.

If Lispector's great Ur-theme is the relationship between language and reality (with art—and especially literary, or verbal, art—functioning as a conflicted middle ground), then her basic technique is to show how language constantly undercuts and dislocates itself. The result, in Lispector's world, is a semantically unstable milieu, one in which men and women are bound up in the ceaseless play of verbal signs that are more iconic and more self-referential than they are mimetic descriptions of material reality. As Alfred MacAdam and Flora Shiminovich put it, Lispector's writing points to "the possibility of a language that resists fixity and binary (male-female) oppositions. Hers is a language in the process of being reinvented" (MacAdam and Shiminovich 259). Thus, as Lispector demonstrates through her characters' struggles to "know" and to "understand,"[28] human existence reveals itself to be a problem of poststructural ontology: How, given these apparent truths about the fluidity and arbitrariness of language (and about its problematic relationship to three-dimensional reality), do we live? How can we know who and what we really are? On what basis can we make the endless decisions that must be made? Where does power lie? How can we know what to do, how to act, what to believe? This, I believe, is the philosophical-cum-sociopolitical context in which Lispector's *escritura*, is best studied, and it illustrates the relevance of poststructural thought to the larger human experience.

Chapter 2

A SEMIOTICS OF BEING:
STYLE, STRUCTURE, AND MEANING
IN A POSTSTRUCTURAL KEY

Although there remains much to be said for regarding Clarice Lispector's texts as examples of what Ralph Freedman has termed lyrical narrative,[1] after some thirty years of studying her work I now feel that we understand it best if we regard it as being fundamentally poetic in nature. Indeed, I believe Lispector should be read as essentially a poet rather than a narrativist,[2] for to do so provides us with both a different set of generic expectations with which to approach her very complex work and a critical orientation that better enables us to appreciate what her texts are doing, to themselves (via their semantically destabilizing self-referentiality) and to their reader's reception of them. There would seem to be, moreover, a special affinity between the dynamics of poetry and poststructural theory, an affinity that, as suggested by Julia Kristeva in *Revolution in Poetic Language* and as exemplified by Lispector in *The Apple in the Dark, The Passion according to G. H.*, or *The Stream of Life*, animates the Brazilian writer's best work. In this chapter, therefore, I will examine, from the perspective afforded us by modern semiotics, how the identifying stylistic features of Lispector's work—its language, syntax, and modes of discourse—bear out her manifestly poststructural conceptualization of life and writing.

In reading these and other of Lispector's texts ("The Fifth Story," for example, or "Where You Were at Night"), the reader is struck again and again by the degree to which her ever language-conscious texts require the reader to deal not with action, as in the world of narrative, but with the transformative power and mystery of poetic language and the relationships between the signs that give it form. In reading her post-1961 works especially (an exception being the relatively stark, austere stories in *The Stations of the Body* [*Soulstorm*]), one feels that Lispector's most expressive style is profoundly poetic, even mythopoeic, and that in its patterning and play of images, its semantic diffuseness, and its distinctive punctuation it achieves the kind of beguiling rhythm patterns and seductive semantic verbal suspension that we associate with good lyric poetry. As in a poem, the words of Lispector's lyrically charged narratives actually play the same role as action does in the more traditional forms of the novel and short story. As Guimãres Rosa once suggested,[3] Lispector's words are "incantatory," richly imbued with polysemous ambiguity and continuously liberated, through her unmistakable syntax, from their standard or "correct" meanings. This preoccupation with language explains why, in her most celebrated work, action and setting are subsumed in wave after wave of language-oriented consciousness, particularly on the part of the reader who comes to realize that the text s/he is reading is constantly reinventing itself. Reading Lispector's densely lyrical fiction, then, is tantamount to reading poetry since in both cases what is involved is a

> search for the unknown, for something that lies at the heart of experience but cannot be pointed out or described without being altered or diminished—something that . . . is not knowledge because it is never revealed. It is mysterious or opaque, and even as it invites the reader, it wards him off. (Strand xv)[4]

Like poetry, Lispector's work "endorses a state of verbal suspension" because, as we see in texts like *The Stream of Life*, "Where You Were at Night," and *A Breath of Life*, it features, "language performing at its most beguiling and seductive while being, at the same time, elusive, seeming to mock one's desire for reduction, for plain and available order" (xv). Reconnecting the ancient epistemological link between philosophy and poetry, Lispector's texts cultivate not only the semantically vague areas that lie not only "between the lines" (which is where she says real knowledge is gained)[5] but also "between the words" in the interstices that constitute the shifting relationships within and among the words themselves. This decidedly poststructural sense of writing is a prime feature not only of Lispector's basic style but of language's inherent mystery and ambiguity, its tendency toward self-referentiality, erasure, destabilization, and contingency. In certain fundamental ways, then, poetry has more in common with poststructural theory than one might ordinarily think. And if a reader were seeking a writer in whose texts there were blended together a poststructural conceptualization of language and a deeply poetic style with a need to create narratives of a decidedly sociopolitical and philosophical nature, she or he would have to be greatly impressed by the work of Clarice Lispector.

As we read, for example, in *The Stream of Life*, a 1973 work that for many of Lispector's readers represents her maximum achievement, "I transmit to you not a message of ideas but rather an instinctive volup-tuousness of what is hidden in nature and that I sense" (*SL* 16). Openly utilizing what, for Lispector, is the linguistically rooted mystery, ambi-guity, and ambivalence of human existence, this same poetically charged and acutely self-conscious voice goes on to declare that the text we are reading—*The Stream of Life*—is not a traditional narrative but "a feast of words" that, as verbal "signos," or signs, "are more gesture than voice" (16). Awash in desire and wanting "raw, bloody life" (17), the text's mercurial voice then declares, paradoxically, that

> from the lack of meaning will be born a meaning, as from me light, ethereal life is inexplicably born. The dense jungle of words wraps itself thickly around what I feel and life, and transforms everything I am into something of my own that remains beyond me.
>
> Nature is all-encompassing: it coils around me and is sexually alive. (17)

With the narrator thus establishing an ontological relationship with her own text that parallels, in distinctly poststructural fashion, the relation-ship each of us has with language (that, inescapably, we are defined si-multaneously as both self and other by a force, language, that constantly "transforms" us all), the reader—gaining ingress into the play of this text by approaching it as a poem rather than a traditional narrative—experiences, dissemination-like, a multiplicity of "births": of words, of meanings, of levels of awareness, of being itself:

> I'm a heart beating in the world.
> You who read me, help me to be born.
> Wait: it's getting dark. Darker.
> And darker.
> . . .
> It continues on.
> . . .
> I was born. (27)

Although this same poetic style and structuring characterizes the great majority of Lispector's texts, it is more prominent in certain ones (*The Foreign Legion, Where You Were at Night, The Stream of Life,* or *A Breath of Life,* for example) than in others (*Family Ties, The Stations of the Body,* "Beauty and the Beast," *The Besieged City, An Apprenticeship,* or *The Book of Delights,* or *The Hour of the Star*). Still other of her works, how-ever, more hybrid in nature, oscillate between the decentering polysemy of poetry and the centering, or stabilizing, lure of orthodox narrative (*Near to the Wild Heart, The Chandelier, The Apple in the Dark, Clandestine Happiness,* and *The Passion according to G. H.*).

When G. H., for example, declares early in her narrative that "[w]ord and form will be the plank on top of which I shall float over billows of silence" (*Passion* 12), she is laying the groundwork for a later developing meditation on the mercurial relationship between words and their referents and between language, meaning, and being. Because for G. H., "[t]ruth doesn't make sense" (11), and because for her, meaning involves "a profound loss of meaning" (27), one in which, paradoxically, "what seems a lack of meaning . . . is what meaning there is" (27), she can also declare, "But what an abyss between the word and what it sought to do" (59). She will later expand and personalize this idea, saying, "My error . . . had to be the part of truth: for only when I err do I get away from what I know and what I understand" (101). Seen more and more as an unstable factor of the fluid relationship between words as well as between words and objects, truth, for G. H., emerges as an elusive entity, one that she will never possess or understand completely.[6] Yet as a poststructural hero, G. H., like Lispector's other characters, is ensnared in a web of words[7] eternally and frustratedly in quest of the one thing (an ultimate beginning; a clear, stable meaning; Logos itself) that will eternally elude her. Enveloped by the semiotic self-referentiality of language and, like the reader, seduced by a style that is at once intensely poetic and philosophical, G. H., like Martim before her, finds herself trapped inside an endlessly elastic "web of spaces" (37) that, exemplifying Derrida's "espacement," or "spacing," derives from the interplay of words whose off-setting meanings are generated by the related but different meanings of other words. Thus, G. H.'s world is a semiotic labyrinth, one in which everything is language and where even the "nude" charcoal sketches—in which, as if illustrating Lacan's "mirror stage" in reverse, G. H. sees herself—are iconic signs that demand interpretation even as they are interpreting, and being interpreted by, other signs. Here, as elsewhere in Lispector's world, the anarchic spirit of a poetically charged "différance" reigns supreme.

As we see in *The Apple in the Dark* and *The Passion according to G. H.,* the primary effect of this oscillation between the discourse of poetry and that of narrative is to lead the reader to feel the dark, mysterious, irrational, and ultimately anarchical pull of poetry, which, like George Steiner, Lispector presents as "maximal language use,"[8] as language given "free rein" to generate its own semiotic field. Embodying the particular kinds of poetic writing that would later be associated, albeit problematically, with Cixous's concept of "writing the body"⁹ and, earlier, with Derrida's poststructural sense of *écriture*,¹⁰ G. H.'s "writing voice"¹¹ confronts us with the intimate yet ephemeral connection between language and being, Lispector's most basic theme:

> I, who before lived on words of charity, or pride—or something. But what an abyss between the word and what it sought to do. (59)

Living out this vital linkage, G. H. then goes on to declare that:

> Every word of ours—in that time that we called empty—every word was as light and empty as a butterfly: the inner word fluttered against the mouth, the words were said but we didn't hear them. (111)

G. H. concludes, finally, with an erotically charged question:

> Or is all this just my still wanting the pleasures of the words for things? or is it my still wanting the orgasm of utmost beauty, of understanding, of the consummate act of love? (135–36)

Emerging from this poetic and philosophical matrix, a distinctive stylistic feature of *The Passion according to G. H.* turns out to be precisely this sense of space that separates and isolates not only words but human beings as well, an issue that is akin to Derrida's twin concepts of "supplément" (which implies both an addition, or supplement, and a substitution) and "différance" (*Of Grammatology* XLIII–LXVII; and *Speech and Phenomena* 141). As G. H. expresses it, in a way that clearly equates "the enigma" of life (its meaning) with language:

> I had found the enigma itself. . . . And I was not even touching the thing. I was just touching the space that goes from me to the vital core . . . I don't know, I don't know. For the thing can never be really touched. The vital core is a finger pointing to it . . . the dark is the dark's vital core, and something's vital core is never reached. (*Passion* 130–31)

And then, as if to demonstrate not only "supplément" and "différance" but "espacement" as well, G. H. concludes:

> But it is I who should keep myself from giving the things a name. A name is an accretion, and it inhibits contact with the thing. The name of the thing is an interval for the thing. The will to accretion is great . . . because bare things are so wearing. (133)

Arguably the most overtly political of her works, and the last of Lispector's novels to be published during her lifetime (appearing in October 1977, some three months before her death on 10 December), *The Hour of the Star* is, for many readers and critics, her masterpiece. A subtle, ironic text that weaves a fairly obvious discourse on the devastating effects of poverty with a very sophisticated discourse on the nature of fiction and its relationship to reality, this eighth novel "represents," for Marta Peixoto, "overlapping systems of oppression and a young woman absolutely crushed by them" at the same time that it functions as, "a meditation on the difficulties of writing about poverty" ("*The Hour of the Star*," in *Clarice Lispector: A Bio-Bibliography*, 39). For Peixoto, *The Hour of the Star* is structured around three interlocking "textual interactions": the first involves "the implicit connection between Lispector and her male narrator, Rodrigo S. M." ("*Hour of the Star*" 40); the second deals with the narrator's very complex relationship with his "creation," the waif, Macabéa; while the third focuses on the interaction between the metafictional narrator, Rodrigo S. M., and the "encoded reader," or narratee,[12] who, often addressed in the plural, would seem to represent Brazil's literate public, especially its middle and upper classes, people who, if they so desired, have the political power to make changes in their country's socioeconomic structures.

While the figures of Rodrigo, the narrator, and Macabéa, the character, often seem to meld into a single portrait of Lispector herself, the text of *The Hour of the Star* also takes up what we have seen is a seminal Lispectorian theme, the relationship of language to reality. What is unique in regard to this theme's pertinence to this novel, however, is that the question is cast in terms usually reserved only for aesthetics: What is the relationship between Lispector's (or Rodrigo's) art and the text's reality? What is the mimetic quality of Rodrigo's self-conscious narration? Can language ever tell the "truth" about anything or anyone, as Rodrigo says he wishes to do for Macabéa, or does language continually alter the truth, constantly transforming it into something that tantalizes us but which we can never possess or know in any immutable way? This concern with verisimilitude and mimesis, the truthful representation of reality, becomes especially apparent in the relationship between Rodrigo and his "invention," Macabéa, where it speaks to the question of how one represents the truth of a character who in so many ways literally embodies Derrida's concept of "différance," "differing" from nearly all normative standards of interpretation and, through her narrator, endlessly deferring any definitive judgment about her. Rodrigo, however, wishes to believe that he can indeed "capture" the sundry social and psychological truths of Macabéa, a creature so without hope or recourse that she virtually has no voice, except insofar as her narrator will give her one. At the same time, however (and in a way that works against the affirmation of traditional mimesis in this text), Rodrigo also suggests that if mimesis is not actually an impossibility, its ability to represent "truthfully" the "reality" of a character like Macabéa is certainly compromised by such seemingly insurmountable differences as class, culture, and gender, which, in this text, "are not smoothed over but played up as points of friction" (Peixoto, "*Hour of the Star*," 40). The ultimate brilliance of *The Hour of the Star*, however, may be that while Rodrigo cannot always transcend these differences, the reader, identifying with the narratee, can, which allows the pathetic Macabéa, "adrift in the great unconquerable city" (*The Hour of the Star* 80), to eventually represent not only women as victims of an oppressive social structure but men as well, both sexes coming to reveal themselves as hapless human beings "engulfed in the brutality of life" (Peixoto, "*Hour of the Star*," 41).

Renowned, then, as one of Lispector's most politically conscious texts, *The Hour of the Star* (1977) also cultivates what is perhaps her most defining theme, the uncertain but nonetheless vital relationship between language and being. Cast here in terms of mimesis, the novel's symbiotic interplay of language and human existence manifests itself through the textually aware divagations of a self-conscious male narrator, one Rodrigo S. M., whose relationship to "his" character, Macabéa, and to the reader allows him to question whether art (and in particular, art that depends on language for its representation) can ever "represent" reality in a "truthful" fashion. Can language ever "represent" reality, or does it create (that is, "re-present") reality, changing its "truths" as it changes our consciousness of it? Implicit in all of Lispector's works, and explicit in many of them, this issue attains its most complete expression in *The Hour of the Star*.

In the second half of the novel especially, images of reality-as-language abound. For example, the narrator writes of "[s]earching for the word in darkness" (70), while, in discussing how, without knowing it, Macabéa will not merely be "changed" by crossing the street (an action that will lead directly to her death), she will be changed "by words" (79), since "the word is divine" (my translation). In Lispector's frame of reference, the "divinity" of the word suggests not only language's transformative power but its inherently metaphysical relation to reality, which, as we have seen in the case of Macabéa's demise, "was . . . changed by words" (my translation).

The words of the narrator, Rodrigo S. M., thus imply that the relationships and attitudes we normally think of as defining human reality are functions of language; either the literal creation of nominalistic reality and our subsequent contemplation of it (as in the case of literature) or in the social science world of "objective facts," where we must still use language to describe, delimit, and above all, determine the "meaning," or implications, of what are otherwise assumed to be nonlinguistically dependent "facts." It is as if, through the self-conscious voice of her narrator, Rodrigo S. M., Clarice Lispector, in her final novel, is suggesting that as long as human beings inhabit this planet, language, the most distinctly human of tools, will humanize everything we touch, invent, or know, including the category of knowledge that we categorize as empirical (which, like Macabéa's "poverty," comes to have meaning for us only when we actualize it in language). Thus it is that the narrator of this final Lispector novel to be published within her lifetime makes a point of addressing not once but twice his (and perhaps his creator's) attitude toward "facts": first, he declares (after laboring, frustratingly, to "tell the truth" about his "creation," Macabéa: "I am becoming interested in facts: facts are solid stones. There is no means of avoiding them" (70)—an image to which he then adds the following transformative metaphor: "Facts are words expressed throughout the world" (70).

The second of the narrator's two references to the place "facts" have in writing (or in literary art) appears almost immediately after the first. After trying to determine exactly "what happened" as Macabéa proceeded to consult Madame Carlota (a clairvoyant whose advice she was seeking), the narrator, expressing considerable dissatisfaction with this particular discursive method, interjects his own story with the following exasperated declaration:

> How tiresome to have to grapple with facts. Everyday matters annihilate and I'm not in the mood for writing this story which is merely a form of catharsis. I see that I am writing here and there about myself. . . . I find it exhausting to have to describe things. (72)

The thrust of the semiotic perspective outlined by these words is not, of course, that the "factual" world does not exist; only that for Rodrigo, the narrator of the novel, as for Clarice Lispector herself, the "factual" world comes to mean something to us, to "signify," as it were, only when human beings "re-present," or "transform," "factual" reality into language. Put another way, objective facts mean something to us only when they are transformed—that is, interpreted—by language, as Macabéa was, literally and figuratively.

Although this same sense that language determines the nature of our identities and existences permeates Lispector's early texts, it received its first systematic presentation in her 1961 novel, *The Apple in the Dark*, a dense, slow-moving text that, in 1967, Gregory Rabassa perceptively regarded as "the high point in the development of Miss Lispector's work, the point toward which she was striving and to which her later novel [*The Passion according to G. H.*] is, in a sense, a footnote." [13] With images of darkness, silence (a function of language), and the wasteland dominating the atmosphere and tone, the text tells us, first, that Martim (one of Lispector's rare male protagonists) "had no words for what was happening," that "he had no words for anything" (*Apple* 23). Later, in a description that embodies Derrida's sense of "dissemination" ("a continual flickering, spilling and defusing of meaning . . . which cannot be easily contained with the categories of the text's structure, or within the categories of a conventional critical approach to it"),[14] we are told that

> what made Martim feel such perfection was the fact that his words had in some way gone beyond what he had wanted to say. And even though he felt deceived by them he preferred what he had said to what he had really wanted to say because of the much more certain way in which things go beyond us. (36)

The epitome of one kind of poststructural protagonist (the pathetic, timorous antihero), Martim, in a telling phrase that captures the spirit of the Nietzschian and poststructural concept of language as a "prisonhouse," is characterized in the following fashion: "At some unidentifiable point, that man had become prisoner of a ring of words" (37).

Martim's dilemma (a dilemma that, like G. H., he does not ever fully comprehend, "prisoner" that he is in "a ring of words"), then, is the quintessential poststructural dilemma: because language can never entirely do what we want it to do (express perfect truth perfectly) or be what we want it to be (a stable, reliable system of signification, a mechanism by which "the Truth" can be both perfectly perceived and expressed), we are forced to live out our lives thrashing about in a sea of uncertainty, doubt, frustration, miscommunication, and isolation.

But while Lispector's texts most certainly do transport the reader into these areas, they do so most poignantly when, as in *The Stream of Life*, *A Breath of Life*, and in sections of nearly all her other works, she privileges her lyrical vision (over her need for narrative), and allows the mystery and incantatory power of poetry to enrich the essentially philosophical basis of her language-conscious ontologies.[15] By developing the philosophical principles of poststructuralism in the context of a poetically rendered sense of anxiety and desire, Lispector has succeeded in humanizing it, transforming it from a deracinated and arcane philosophy to a depiction of the way life is conceived of and lived by people like Joana, Martim, G. H., or the voice of *The Stream of Life*, all of whom are painfully aware of being lost within the eternal play of language and who seek, by means of their quests for what Derrida conceptualizes as the "transcendental signifier,"[16] to resolve this deeply unsettling situation.

One key question that comes out of a poststructural approach to Lispector's work is the following: Does Lispector's alleged mysticism point to or otherwise suggest a kind of alternative sense of language and existence, and if so, does it refute the scientific pretensions of the formalists and structuralists? We know that for Derrida, neither the object of inquiry (language) nor the method of inquiry (again language) is stable enough to warrant the claim of "scientific" analysis. As the French philosopher sees it, any discourse that views itself as "scientific" cannot escape being logocentric and, hence, led astray by its own erroneous assumptions about truth and its supposed verifiability, stability, and transparency. According to Derrida (*Of Grammatology* and *Dissemination*), the language of literary discourse or analysis—like that of literature itself—is inescapably unstable (because it cannot escape from its inherent "différance") and therefore unscientific. The question Lispector's texts lead us to ponder, however, is this: If our language use cannot be scientific and logical (that is, objectively verifiable), then what is it? Mystical? Poetic? Or perhaps poststructural, structured, as we see in texts like *The Passion according to G. H.*, *The Stream of Life*, and *A Breath of Life*, around, on, and through the eternal ebb and flow of semiotically productive chains of signifiers? If our discourses cannot be described as scientific, then what are they like? What is the nature of "truth," or of being, vis-à-vis language? Could it not be poststructural, an eternal quest for something forever elusive and protean, a quest for a perfection and stability that can never be attained? Such a paradoxical concept of truth might well be said to be Lispector's signature theme, the issue she struggled with, as a person and as a writer, throughout her long and active career. If language was the great theme for Barthes, then perhaps it would be accurate to say that for Clarice Lispector the unstable process of linguistic signification, what we might call the ontology of language, was the defining focus.

Consistent with their fundamentally poetic style, Lispector's texts are also more revealingly studied in terms of the poststructural term "structuration" than in the context of more traditional concepts of structure and form. Focusing on the interplay of differences among and within texts, "structuration" accounts for the "diachronic" dimension of a text, its "change" through time, the semantic and aesthetic evolutions it undergoes and that it generates. Coined by Derrida to replace what, for him, was the more rigid term, "structuralism," which focuses on a text's "synchronic" or time-stopped dimension (its function as langue, or system, as opposed to its more mercurial parole, its individual speech acts, its moment-to-moment uniqueness), the term "structuration" finds constant expression in the self-referentiality and semiotic complexity that characterize Lispector's texts. From *Near to the Wild Heart* to *A Breath of Life*, Lispector's narratives tend overwhelmingly to embody Derrida's belief that language must always exhibit a semantic surplus ("supplément"; *Dissemination* 109–10, 156–71; and *Of Grammatology*) over what we futilely wish its "exact," "perfect," or "stable" meaning to be. Thus, as a preeminently poststructural *texte* like *The Stream of Life* illustrates, language is always in the process of signifying both more and less than we think it is. Whether in terms of syntax (stylistically, the key to penetrating Lispector's unique worldview) or in terms of larger units of textual organization, like paragraphs, chapters, plots, or story lines, Lispector's narratives relentlessly undercut themselves, drawing the reader into an endless process of semantic "construction" and "deconstruction." At every level of their structuration, Lispector's fictions both center and decenter themselves. By thus challenging or subverting their own authority, however, they leave the unsuspecting reader (along with their characters) in a frustrating quandary, not knowing what to think or believe. Far from being a sign of a carelessly written piece of work, however, it is precisely this absence of certainty that exemplifies the complexity and instability of the poststructural universe.

While *The Apple in the Dark* is her most protracted example of the destabilizing process of signification, and *The Stream of Life* her most succinct, all of Lispector's texts have this feature in common; to one degree or another, they all deny the reader not only the stable, ostensibly reliable logocentric outlook we are taught to seek and expect but even the veracity or truth (or at least the apparent truth) of their own vision.

"Living language" in the fullest, most ontologically complete sense of the term, Lispector's characters show us how life is lived—problematically and with great uncertainty—when the full extent of its transformative relationship to language is made manifest. While, as we will shortly see, this integral aspect of Lispector's work collides with what many commentators regard as the essential "nihilism" of poststructural analysis,[17] at the level of structuration it constitutes a fascinating aspect of her work, one that I believe marks Clarice Lispector as the poststructural writer par excellence, a writer whose works relentlessly probe the unstable relationship between language and being.

In works as diverse as *Near to the Wild Heart, The Apple in the Dark, The Passion according to G. H., The Stream of Life, A Breath of Life*, "The Fifth Story," "Two Stories My Way," and "A Complicated Case," Lispector creates fictive worlds that resonate self-referentially with the semantic fecundity of words. She imbues her texts with an infinitely rich and anarchic sense of language that critics like Barthes, Derrida, Cixous, and Kristeva have all made much of. Such an approach to writing (one of Lispector's most definitive metaphors and themes) suggests that, as in the works cited above, at any given moment a text's meaning is simultaneously a function of arbitrary and differential interrelationships (ranging from word to word, line to line, text to text, and reader to text—all considered diachronically) and interpretations, the free play of simultaneously expanding and contracting webs of signifiers (words) and their interacting systems of signification and erasure. Approaching her texts from this critical perspective helps explain why rereading her narratives produces not merely different reactions in the reader but radically different reactions, yet none of which ever quite cancel out the others.

Along with "Two Stories My Way," another of Lispector's most structurally unique narratives, "The Fifth Story" has been described as "a disquisition on literary genre" (Maria Angélica Lopes 78). Developing a self-consciously intertextual discourse on how one story is, in a sense, all stories, "The Fifth Story" features five separate but closely related narratives, all of which, like Barthes's "codes," are linked literally together as variations on a single line: "I was complaining about the cockroaches" (*FL* 75). As each "story" grows and expands (the second, third, and fourth stories being distinguished by the progressive psychological development of the gender-free narrative "I"), the reader begins to understand how the "same" story becomes "different" as it recasts itself into other, ever-changing forms. The question of structure, or genre, is thus seen to be subservient to the function of language, which, as always in Lispector's world, is synonymous with being. Put another way, "The Fifth Story" is perhaps best approached as a concise and self-exemplifying commentary on the nature of literary form, a commentary, however, that suggests that genres change because language is constantly going beyond them, that, indeed, genres exist only because (as with the "meanings" of words) we arbitrarily choose to agree that (for a time at least) they exist as valid objects. Just as "the depravity of existence" (77) can "shatter" one's "internal form" (77), so, too, does language determine that genre must be understood as in terms of flux, or evolution, rather than anything fixed or rigid. Lispector also elaborates this point in the *crônica* "Form and Content" (20 December 1969), arguing that form is always a function of content (which, for her, is inevitably a function of language).

While certain of her works (*The Stream of Life*, "The Fifth Story," or "Two Stories My Way," for example) demonstrate this process more obviously than others (such as *Near to the Wild Heart, The Chandelier, The Besieged City, The Hour of the Star*, or "A Complicated Case"), they all develop within it. In "The Fifth Story," as we have seen, Lispector creates a text that is composed of five closely connected narratives. Mirrored in each other, these five stories, the texts of which vary only slightly from each other, lead the reader to conclude that, Borges-like, there exists within them an infinite number of these stories and their "readings," their self-appraising and refractive intertextuality. Each story thus "means something" only in relation to the other stories, as in Saussurean linguistics, where a word "means something" only in relation to other words in the same system. Employing a self-conscious first-person narrator-protagonist who is gender-neutral[18] and a structure that, as in "Two Stories My Way," openly flaunts its "différance," "The Fifth Story" not only presents a poststructural interpretation of "truth" (that it is a variable, a function of the constantly evolving structures that generate and sustain it), it literally embodies it. In this short but endlessly self-referential *texte*, form has become content.

Another of Lispector's short fictions that achieves this same end, and perhaps, from a stylistic perspective, even more effectively, is "A Complicated Case," an intrinsically metafictional work (once again featuring a self-conscious first-person narrator) that also flaunts a distinctly poststructural mode of expression. What differs here is that this narrator is more flagrantly unreliable, admitting openly to his or her inability to comprehend the meaning of the events being narrated. As if describing the tenuous relationship between language and reality, the once again gender-neutral narrative voice declares, "The realism here is invented. . . . I guess at reality" (*Soulstorm* 50). Similar to what occurs in "The Fifth Story," the reader of this spare, oblique narrative comes to feel that the "reality" we all "guess at" is largely determined by the shifting, self-referential, and interlocking verbal structures that our language both manifests and generates. In short, our sense of "reality" is much more a function of language than we would have otherwise thought. Because the reader, too, is, like Martim and this story's narrative voice, trapped inside language and its constant restructuring, the most striking feature of "A Complicated Case" is that its self-questioning text—its structuration—reveals itself to be much more complex, interrelated, and open than even the events depicted; words,[19] the reader comes to realize, signify more to each other (and their various syntactic and structural configurations) than to any reality external to them. Thus, as this enigmatic text makes abundantly clear, there is an inescapable void between the physical world of things, actions, and events and the attempt of language to describe, interpret, and finally (re)create them. Any sense of orthodox "realism" that the reader might wish to find in this text is, of necessity, pure invention, a "fiction" that, recalling both Borges's and Derrida's objections to logocentrism, shies away from the true nature of language's relationship with reality.

A final feature of Lispector's poststructural sense of style and structure has to do with the nature of "the center," a metaphor that, conceptually speaking, refers to a text's most basic ordering principle, that (normally thematic) feature that determines the alignment and relationships of all the other elements. A distinguishing feature of nearly all Lispector's narratives, the absence (or constant shifting) of this ordered and ordering "center" effectively demonstrates the point Derrida has made about the privileged role the "center" obtains in classical structuralist thought. As Derrida explained it, in "Structure, Sign, and Play in the Discourse of the Human Sciences," the

> "center" is ". . . a point of presence, a fixed origin," the purpose of which . . . was not only to orient, balance, and organize the structure . . . but above all to make sure that the organizing principle of the structure would limit what we might call the *play* of the structure. By orienting and organizing the coherence of the system, the center of a structure permits the play of its elements inside the total form. And even today the notion of a structure lacking any center represents the unthinkable itself. (109)

Because it is precisely this "free play" that constitutes the basic ordering force of Lispector's texts, we can see, in the constant semantic decentering at work in narratives like *The Stream of Life*, *A Breath of Life*, "The Fifth Story," "A Complicated Case," "He Soaked Me Up," and "Plaza Mauá" (the latter two utilizing the shifting complexities of human sexuality to effect the decentering), how deeply this fundamental poststructural concept infuses the Brazilian writer's work. Moreover, if we interpret Derrida's discussion concerning the relationship of a "center" to its structure as resting on a discourse on "the structurality of structure" ("Structure, Sign, and Play," Lodge 109), we understand more clearly the relevance his argument has for Lispector's texts when he writes, paradoxically,[20] that "it has always been thought that the center, which is by definition unique, constituted that very thing within a structure which governs the structure, while escaping structurality" (109). Thus, as we see in texts like *The Stream of Life*, "Where You Were at Night," "A Report on a Thing," "That's Where I'm Going" (which presents a distinctly positive poststructural ontology), "Silence," and "Soulstorm," Derrida's 1966 critique of traditional Western epistemology's sense of the "center"[21] comes vividly to life in Lispector's work. Just as Derrida shows this unquestioning faith in the perfection and immutability of the "center" as the seat of all "Truth" and knowledge (Logos) to be unfounded because it cannot overcome the play of "différance" inherent in language, so, too, does Clarice Lispector show us that, in terms of both our private and public lives, this "center," or self, is neither more nor less than language use itself, and language, for Clarice Lispector's characters, does not describe human existence so much as it defines it. Her greatest works, like *The Passion according to G. H.*, *The Stream of Life*, "Family Ties," "The Message," "Plaza Mauá," or *The Hour of the Star*, poignantly play out this most human of dramas, that of our being fated to seek perfect understanding and knowledge[22] by means of a mechanism (language) that is inherently flawed, that cannot do what we want it to do, but from which we cannot escape[23] and without which we would not be what we are.

Lispector's ironic, open-ended, essentially plotless, and thematically ambiguous[24] texts thus demonstrate, in fictional form, not only the "structurality of structure" of which Derrida speaks but why it is that language cannot ever create anything but a "momentary" and spurious "center," a "center" that is not the "center" because it is constantly changing, decentering, and undercutting itself, just as Lispector's texts do; what is "true," "valid," or "appropriate" one moment (or in one section of a narrative like "The Fifth Story") is "untrue," "invalid," or "inappropriate" the next moment (or in the next line). Things change, and, in Lispector's world, they do so in, through, and by means of language—our use of it, our conscious creation of it ("lalande," for example, from *Near to the Wild Heart,* or the "it" from *The Stream of Life*)[25] and our transmission and reception of it, in terms of our own multiple selves as well as those of others. This ceaselessly shifting quality of Lispector's narratives is manifested structurally and thematically in her work by poststructural "free play," a fundamental feature of her texts that sustains itself by means of lyrically resonant patterns of such basic images as the "now instant" or the "moment," silence, and fluidity, all expressed in terms of a great variety of contexts, including physical and textual birth, time, water, death, desire, emotional and intellectual repercussions,[26] and ambivalent feelings, especially involving sexuality, the interplay of love and hate, darkness, words, and the human body (presented in typically but not exclusively female terms).[27]

In summary, other than the general concept of "structuration," the single poststructural feature that most distinguishes the form Lispector's texts take is undoubtedly their denial of the reader's appeal to or expectation of the kind of "either/or" thinking that, as Derrida argues, has long dominated Western epistemological systems. Condemned by a variety of post-Saussurean theorists as not only simplistic but intellectually straitjacketing, such seemingly essential "binary oppositions" as true/false, correct/incorrect, right/wrong, or even male/female are, in Lispector's fluid, open texts, constantly being uncoupled and broken up, realigned and "reinscribed" (to use Derrida's term) in an endless process of signification and resignification. Structurally, then, what we see in works from *Near to the Wild Heart* and "Love" to *The Stream of Life,* "Plaza Mauá," and *A Breath of Life* is how and why these "binary oppositions" (so defining of classical structuralist analysis) constantly undercut and regroup themselves to differing and deferring effect, thus manifesting the fundamental play of "différance" that characterizes Lispector's writing. Achieved chiefly by means of her unorthodox syntax (and the unusual punctuation that accompanies it), Lispector's most identifying structural feature is, finally, her texts' systemic dissolution of these "binary oppositions." By subverting what we can understand as established (phal)logocentric assumptions (and, by syntactically rearranging them, showing how artificial and convention bound they are), Lispector's structurations reflect and embody both our human need for logical order[28] and the anxiety of our confrontation not only with the anarchy of language but, through it, with the relativity of our social, political, and psychological structures.

Through the struggles of characters as diverse as Joana, Martim, "He-she/She-he" (from "Where You Were at Night"), Carla and Cel-sinho (from "Plaza Mauá"), or Macabéa, the texts of Clarice Lispector involve us in life as it is lived with a poststructural consciousness, one in which we use language to question the false sense of order, security, rectitude, and identity that language (Logos) simultaneously seeks to provide. This explains, structurally speaking, why her works only rarely offer the definitive beginnings and middles that conventional plot structures call for, as well as why so few of them ("That's Where I'm Going" and *An Apprenticeship, or The Book of Delights* are the chief exceptions) have conclusive, much less "happy," endings. Whether we resist phallo-gocentrism and the allure of its power, control, and violence[29] (as most but not all of her most memorable characters do, including Joana, G. H., the narrator of *The Stream of Life*, and Carla and Celsinho), or whether we capitulate to its pressures and seductiveness (as, for example, Ana, Martim, and Macabéa do), we cannot escape it, and it is here that the drama of Lispector's texts—the drama of life-as-language—resides.

Extrapolating from the fluid sense of structuration that Lispector's texts evince, one can more easily appreciate the essentially poststructural nature of meaning inherent in her work. While it is easy to read Lis-pector's words (her diction is quite simple), it is very difficult, as in *The Stream of Life*, to feel confident about what they mean. For Lispector, as for Barthes and Derrida,[30] meaning—in language and therefore in lit-erature—is a matter of production, of contrast, relationships, and imagi-nation. The fundamental poststructural concept of *écriture* emerges, for example, almost immediately as the primary contextual ground of *The Stream of Life*'s narrative voice, who, after first declaring, "I'm not play-ing with words" (*SL* 14), then self-consciously writes:

> Writing . . . is the way followed by someone who uses words like bait: a word fishing for what is not a word. When the non-word—the whatever's between the lines—bites the bait, something's been writ-ten. (14)

Then, in a declaration that expresses not only Derrida's concepts of "sous-écriture" and "supplementarity" (*Of Grammatology* XVI–XVII, 19, 44–64, 281–302), this voice says:

> [T]he non-word, in biting the bait, incorporates it. . . . I transfigure reality, and then in turn another reality . . . creates me in turn. . . .

Words . . . I move carefully among them, for they can turn menacing;
. . . With this sentence, I give birth to a scene, as in the flash of a
camera. (*SL* 14–15)

While *The Stream of Life* is the most distilled of all Lispector's texts in
expressing this poststructural sense of how writing itself (*écriture*) is the
most powerful, most complete manifestation of plurisignation that we
have, this same consciousness of meaning as never being fully or perfectly encapsulated in a single verbal sign (that is, a word) or structure
(the sentence, paragraph, or plot, for example) but as being "a kind of
constant flickering of presence and absence together" (Eagleton 128) is
found, to one degree or another, in virtually everything Lispector wrote.
It is, in short, a benchmark of her work.

Also exemplifying this tendency is "That's Where I'm Going," a
little-known narrative from *Where You Were at Night* that is much ad-
mired by Hélène Cixous,[31] and in which Lispector creates a fully developed poststructural consciousness that is strikingly positive and optimistic. An exhilarating affirmation of how one might live not only
happily and successfully but authentically and honestly as well by accepting a personal ontology of "becoming" (change) rather than "being" (stasis), this underappreciated short text shows how potentiality can
be a reality we can successfully embrace. As this text's self-conscious
narrator observes, struggling with the problem of identity as an issue of
how one sign is always linked to another sign, "It is to myself that I'm
going" (146). Then, expanding this idea to include the inevitability of
personal transformation, we are told that, again via language, "I trans-
mute myself" (147), a concept that gains meaning only in terms of other
words and the spaces (Derrida's "espacement" and Lispector's "fishing
between the lines") between them, for, as we have seen, "At the tip of a
word is a word" (146). Cast more and more in a poststructural key, it is
the concept of human experience understood as a confrontation with the
semiotic productivity of language—and not an attempt at semantic closure—that Lispector's tale leads us to contemplate.

A similar (though less optimistic) expression of poststructuralism's
concern with the problem of language and meaning can be found in
"Silence," another of the powerful short narratives that compose the
generically hybrid collection of *Where You Were at Night*. Focusing more
on the repercussions that stem from the struggle to communicate (with
a conflicted self and with an uncertain other), which can be regarded as
one of Lispector's most trademark subjects, "Silence" presents yet an-

other take on poststructural ontology, one that links the semantic in-stability of words with our struggle to understand language as the most essential aspect of the human condition and to use it to break out of the solipsism that, as an aspect of language itself, works to imprison us. Al-though, we are told, "meaning" is there, "in the very heart of a word" (*Soulstorm* 152), it is also, paradoxically, "not there," that is, existing, as in the interplay of Derrida's "presence" and "absence," only in a frag-mented and sporadic fashion and not in the perfect, complete form that we humans seek. Silence, yet another of Lispector's most fundamental motifs,[32] is thus presented here as the "meaning" that, though it reposes "in the very heart of a word," serves only to torment us since we can never possess it completely; its full semantic "presence," as Derrida would assert, is always denied us. Functioning as deeply affecting ex-amples of this basic poststructural conundrum, Lispector's texts all mock our human desire for clarity, closure, order, and stability. They show us, in ways poststructural theory cannot, what it means, in human terms, to realize that the more one comes to understand language, the more shift-ing, arbitrary, and parlous our sense of existence is revealed to be.

Even in a 1961 work like *The Apple in the Dark*, which represents a decisive stylistic, structural, and thematic turning point in terms of Lis-pector's development as a writer, one can feel the compelling power of Lispector's lyrically charged narrative, one in which, as in pure poetry, the reader is led not only to discover a real preference for language use that openly generates multiple meanings (a form of semantic birthing) but also to suspect that in such texts "something beyond 'meaning' is being communicated, something that originated not with the poet but in the first dim light of language, in some period of 'beforeness'" (Strand xv). More than this, it becomes clear that this "something beyond 'meaning'" is essentially the object of the great psycholinguistic quests undertaken in such texts as *The Apple in the Dark*, *The Passion according to G. H.*, *The Stream of Life*, "Where You Were at Night," "Soulstorm," and *A Breath of Life*.[33]

It is interesting to note in this same regard that when Mark Strand remarks that "reading poetry is often a search for the unknown" (xv), he is expressing an attitude about the nature of a particular type of language use that closely resembles a revelation Lispector made about the nature of her own writing in "The 'True' Novel," a *crônica* dated 22 August 1970. Expressing boredom with the mimeticism of "true novels" and "with their web of facts and descriptions" (*DW* 400), she goes on to say, "[W]hat guides me in my writing is always a sense of research and discovery" (400). Echoing Strand's contention that reading poetry involves a search (or, as Lispector would put it in "Humility and Technique," a quest) for what is not known, she declares, "Following my intuition is my method of writing. . . . I continue to follow my intuition without knowing where it will lead me. . . . I enjoy writing as long as I do not know what is going to happen next" (400). Moreover, when Strand observes that, for him, poetry involves a search for something ". . . that lies at the heart of experience but cannot be pointed out or described without being altered" (Strand xv), he could easily be describing what happens in texts like *The Passion according to G. H.*, *The Stream of Life*, or *A Breath of Life*, where Lispector's psychodynamic language is constantly in the process of transforming itself and the realities with which it deals.[34] Strand's belief that poetry, while not "knowledge" in and of itself, is an "avowal of being" (xv) is basically reiterated by Lispector when, finally, she sums up her own feelings about this issue by writing, "Frankly, I do not understand myself. Yet I slowly carry on writing without even knowing where I am heading," adding, "I truly feel that I am heading towards something more human" (*DW* 401).

As the stories of Martim and G. H. show us, however, Lispector's texts inevitably force us to confront the frustration resulting from our search for something (Logos) that, trapped as we are in the self-referentiality and supplementarity of language, we cannot even define, much less control. The more pathetic of the two, Martim's case exemplifies this dilemma and, in so doing, establishes him as one of Lispector's most human protagonists. More continuously "decentering," and resisting interpretational closure or any definitive "master" reading, texts like *The Apple in the Dark*, *The Passion according to G. H.*, *The Stream of Life*, "That's Where I'm Going," "Where You Were at Night," "In Search of Dignity," "A Report on a Thing," "A Manifest of the City," and "Silence" (the latter six titles from *Where You Were at Night*) embody the simultaneously stabilizing and destabilizing nature of language use by utilizing words that, alone and in patterns (Lispector's structurations), undercut the very interpretations that, approached from some other perspective, they seem to sustain.

This distinctive characteristic of Lispector's mature style is appreciated most keenly at the junction of poststructural theory and feminism, a junction that has great importance for our better understanding of her work and the various levels of meaning it has for us. Though often considered more in terms of its stylistic or structural importance to Lispector's work, Cixous's concept of "l'écriture féminine" (perhaps, as

Christiane Makward has suggested,[35] better understood as "writing the body" rather than the more literal—and misleading—"feminine writing") is, I believe, more useful when applied to the Brazilian writer's texts as an epistemological issue, a question of how we claim to "know" things. Thus, as Verena Conley notes, when Cixous first encountered Lispector's "voice" (in bilingual editions or in French translation; *Reading with Clarice Lispector* vii–viii), she discovered not so much a particular style (though this was, of course, an important aspect of the experience) as a truly unique Weltanschauung, a sense of reality, being, and knowledge that "embodied itself" in language: "I embody myself in voluptuous and unintelligible phrases that spiral outward beyond words" (*SL* 14) and that would lead to an undeniable urge "to feed directly from the placenta" (3).

But as Marta Peixoto has suggested, while Cixous has certainly done Lispector a service by calling attention to her work, she may have also done her an even greater disservice by seeming to limit her, by making her appear (to those who have not read her in depth) to be more one-dimensionally nurturing than she really is, and, finally, by depicting a Lispector far less darkly violent, transgressive, and perverse than her texts reveal her to be.[36] Semantically speaking, however, the concept of "l'écriture féminine" does speak to Lispector's powerful and continuous presentation of the female body as one source—though not, thinking of Irigaray's *Speculum of the Other Woman*,[37] the only one—of identity. Challenging what, on one level, could thus be taken as Lispector's advancement of the primacy of the female body and psyche is, however, the continuous degendering and deoppositioning of language (and, through language, of being) that infuses her texts and that makes them so generative of multiple interpretations.

Yet Lispector does not so much privilege the female body per se as employ it as a locus of energy, a point of departure. In a way that recalls Derrida's "deconstructive" strategy, Lispector tends first to reverse the "normal" male/female opposition (in which the male element—the first element—is the privileged one) and then, to resist the formation of a merely reversed hierarchy (that of female/male), to "reinscribe" what is now the second, or "inferior," term (male) back into the newly "superior" term (female). The result, as we shall see in a later chapter, is the creation of what can be thought of as transgendered and transgendering subjects, characters who, by means of the language that they use to inscribe themselves and that is used to describe them, get beyond standard gender-bound identities. By presenting, as in *Near to the Wild Heart, An*

Apprenticeship, or The Book of Delights, "The Message," "Plaza Mauá," and "Where You Were at Night," this crucial Derridean interpretive maneuver as an unending process of psycholinguistic self-creation (variant of the birth motif), Lispector elaborates in poignantly human terms the basic tensions, conflicts, and frustrations of poststructural thought.

Because as a system of thought poststructuralism centers so intensely on the entwined issues of language and being, it possesses a disturbingly intimate dimension, and this, in contrast to the more detached discourses of Barthes and Derrida, is what Clarice Lispector gives us, intimacy and intensity being hallmarks of her work. And while it seems clear that, combining, at times, erotically charged female body imagery[38] with the related problems of human desire ("Footsteps," "Life *au Naturel*" and *A Breath of Life*) and meaning ("A Manifest of the City," "Silence," and "Soulstorm"), Lispector's lyrically rendered *escritura* merges a number of stylistic and semantic issues, its most powerful presence in her work would seem to be the kind of "reversing" and "reinscribing" force it exerts on the "uncoupling" of the many binary oppositions she deals with in her narratives. Prominent among these, however, is the male/female opposition, the subverting of which helps explain why the issues of androgyny, gender, and power have such a pervasive presence in her narratives.

Lispector's abiding concern with the problems of language, writing, and meaning was not limited to her fiction, however. In "Since One Feels Obliged to Write" and "Miraculous Fishing" (both originally from the nonfiction "Fundo de Gaveta" section of *The Foreign Legion* [1964]), for example, Lispector writes about how a writer, like a reader, must work "between the lines" as well as in the "gaps" or "spaces" not only between words but within them as well. Echoing here Derrida's sense of how the "aporia," or indeterminateness of language, affect the production, transmission, and reception of meaning, Lispector's extensive comments on the nature of her own writing also illustrate many of the most definitive aspects of poststructural thought. In "Since One Feels Obliged to Write . . . ," for example, Lispector writes, "Since one feels obliged to write, let it be without obscuring the space between the lines with words" (*Foreign Legion* 114). The ironic and paradoxical dimensions of this statement about writing, in which a comprehension of the fluid interconnectedness between and among words is clearly implied, are later refined and developed in "Miraculous Fishing," one of Lispector's most revealing discussions of how and why she writes as she does. Metaphorically equating the act of writing with that of fishing, with the bait being the word, Lispector observes that the word then fishes for "something that is not a word" (*FL* 119), an image that parallels Saussure's claim that a sign means something only in relation to the other signs in its system. In typically enigmatic Lispectorian fashion, she goes on to say that when the "non-word" "bites" the "bait" (which, of course, is another word), "something has been written" (*FL* 119). She concludes this brief but concise discussion of how she gets things done by observing, in a way that recalls Derrida's "supplément," that "the non-word upon taking the bait, has assimilated it" (*FL* 119). The implication, of course, is that the act of writing, like the act of reading, is, as she says in "Adventure," a never-ending process of cross-fertilization, one in which a single word (a locus of diverse meanings) attracts and is attracted by other words that it incorporates (and that incorporate it), semiotically speaking, in a ceaseless exchange of suggestion and meaning that takes place "between the lines," where the reader, activating his or her own interpretational codes, enters the free play that is the process of signification. When one applies this theory of writing (and reading) to a work like *The Passion according to G. H.*, which was published in 1964, the same year that "Miraculous Fishing" first appeared, it is easy to see what it means, structurally and thematically, to Lispector's sense of herself as a writer, to her narratives, and to her readers. Put another way, *The Passion according to G. H.*, one of the most thoroughly poststructural texts Lispector ever wrote, epitomizes the kind of writing alluded to more theoretically in "Miraculous Fishing," a piece that, along with a few others ("Writing, Humility, Technique," "Um momento de desânimo," "Sôbre escrever," "Form and Content," "Adventure," and "Writing," for example), can be considered her "ars poetica" or "literary testament" (Affonso Romano de Sant'Anna and Elizabeth Lowe, quoted in Lopes, 78).

"Writing," indeed, another important nonfiction selection from *The Foreign Legion* (1964), finds Lispector making an analogy between writing and music and suggesting that within the "frustrating discomfort of disorder" (*FL* 211) with which a writer struggles, it is also true that "order constrains" (211), that words, as functions of systems, constantly impose their own structures. Going on to say that because she felt herself incapable of "dressing up an idea in words" (211), Lispector's manner of writing—in a sense the heart of her style—was that "[w]hat comes to the surface is already expressed in words or simply fails to exist" (211), an attitude that comes very close to embodying Derrida's argument that, because of language's innate self-referentiality, all that is written has, in a sense, already been written.[39]

For Lispector, then, existence is virtually synonymous with language, with our use of words; to write is to live, to be, which explains the powerfully ontological pressure that her narratives generate. Closely related to the idea of writing as a quest for understanding (a quest that, in Lispector's world, leads, time after time, back to language) is the sense that for Lispector (as for Derrida) writing—and not speaking—constitutes the taproot of language use, its most complete and mysterious form of expression. With only one major exception (*An Apprenticeship, or The Book of Delights*, 1969), all of Lispector's narratives privilege writing over speaking. A close examination of Lispector's novels, stories, and *crônicas*, in fact, quickly reveals not only how infrequently spoken dialogue is used but also—and more importantly—how thin, barren, and awkward it is, especially in contrast to the poetic richness and semantic fertility that mark the ebb and flow of her silent, inner language use, which the reader receives and processes as nonspoken language. Thus, Derrida's rejection of "phonocentrism" in favor of written language finds full and eloquent expression in the endlessly self-reflective and silent world of Lispectorian *écriture*.

Between the 1964 "nonfiction" pieces of *The Foreign Legion* and the *crônicas* that she wrote for the *Jornal do Brasil* between 1967 and 1973, Clarice Lispector actually devoted a great deal of time to discussing her own techniques and her development as a writer. In "The Unreality of Realism" (20 January 1968), for example, she alludes to the "nonrealistic" character of her own narratives by challenging the legitimacy of the term, "realism," as it applies "to any form of human expression which [like writing] is conscious and self-controlled" (*DW* 94). Making a similar point in "The Columnist" (22 June 1963), Lispector muses on the differences between how she writes her *crônicas* (where she believes she "chats" with her readers) and how she writes "literature," a form of writing in which, altering her style a bit, she tries "to communicate in depth" with herself and with her reader (*DW* 151). As these discussions show, by questioning the relationship between art and life, Lispector broaches, in theoretical terms, the driving force of so much of her work—the transformation of reality through language.

Punctuation, long regarded as one of the most singular features of her writing, is also discussed by Lispector. In "Note to the Typesetter" (4 February 1968), to cite one exemplary case, she writes, "Punctuation shows how a sentence breathes, and this is how my sentences breathe. And however odd you find my phrasing, all I ask is that you respect it" (*DW* 101); in "To the Rhythm of My Typewriter" (17 April 1971) she reiterates this point, adding that "I myself write as I breathe" (*DW* 447).

Syntax, another distinctive aspect of her writing, also comes under self-critical scrutiny. In "Speaking of Journeys" (12 June 1971), for example, Lispector (responding to Gregory Rabassa's contention that, because of her syntax, her work is more difficult to translate than that of Guimarães Rosa) declares that she is "not aware that there is anything very unusual about my syntax" (*DW* 463), a statement that, ironically enough, would seem to suggest that Lispector was more aware of how her sentences were structured than she chose to let on. It is, indeed, virtually impossible to imagine how Lispector could have cultivated the themes and issues that were her literary signatures without also assiduously and meticulously cultivating a particular kind of syntax, one that would produce in the mind of the reader precisely the semantic ambiguity, ambivalence, and fluidity she dealt with so intensely in her thematics. A discussion of syntax also occurs in "Reply Overdue" (21 February 1970), a fascinating discussion by Lispector of a certain critic's review of her third novel, *The Besieged City* (1949). Stressing that her syntax was never a case of merely showing how a character comes to comprehend and discuss reality, it followed, for Lispector, that syntax "can change reality even while creating it" (*DW* 354). She then adds, "Our way of looking at a man also creates that man. Our way of seeing determines our perception of reality" (355). Lispector concludes this revealing discussion by offering up what we might well regard as her final word on what the critics take to be the relevance of syntax in her narratives:

> I fail to see how these threads, amongst others in the narrative, could have all been lost amidst what you describe as the book's "verbal magic." Ever since I published my first novel, critics have insisted on discussing my unusual phrasing. But believe me, what I was striving for—and have achieved, damn it—is to communicate through those phrases, and not simply to have invented phrases for their own sake. (355)

Later, however, and sounding like a cross between Mallarmé and Barthes, she writes, in "What Pedro Bloch Told Me" (17 November 1973), "Words stifle everything: love, truth, the world" (*DW* 621). Interpreting her own style as "an obstacle which must be overcome," Lispector also makes it clear that she sought to write "without having to rely on my natural style" ("Style," *DW* 190; 12 October 1968).

This pronouncement, however, should be read in the context of her revelations in "Adventure" (4 October 1969) that "I write because of my inability to understand except through the process of writing" (a statement Derrida himself might have made) and in "Humility and Technique" (4 October 1969) that "[t]his way or 'style' (!) has been called several things, but never what it really and exclusively is: a humble quest" (*DW* 308–9). Lispector expands on this same point in "About Writing" (20 December 1969), saying, "As I write, I become conscious of things I knew all the time without being aware that I knew them" (*DW* 331).

Lispector also discussed her style in a number of other *crônicas:* "Form and Content" (20 December 1969), where she contends that content determines form; "The Making of a Novel" (2 May 1970), where she declares herself to be "quite hopeless when it comes to editing," adding that "I am incapable of narrating an idea, and do not know how to 'embellish an idea with words'" and that "the greatest drawback about writing is that one has to use words" (*DW* 371–72); and, as we have seen, "The True Novel" (22 August 1970), where Lispector defends the kind of novel she writes against the traditional realistic novel—which she finds boring—and stresses her own penchant for writing as "Research and Discovery" (*DW* 400) via a syntax that will "convey as faithfully as possible what I am thinking when I write" (400). In this same *crônica* Lispector also identifies "intuition" as her basic method of writing: "Following my intuition is my method of writing. . . . I only enjoy writing as long as I do not know what is going to happen next" (400).

Finally, in "Words from the Typewriter" (29 May 1971), Lispector wrote about her personal sense of being as a function of writing, her quest (as a writer) for silence (which, for Lispector as for Lacan, was tantamount to a Nirvana-like state of perfect communication) and her reader's response to it:

> I feel I have almost achieved my freedom. To the point of no longer needing to write. If I could I would leave my space on this page blank: filled with the greatest silence. And readers, on seeing this blank space, would fill it with their own desires. (*DW* 457)

Whether appearing as "fiction" or as "nonfiction," distinctions that Lispector tended to disregard (Mathie 133), the richly ambiguous and poetic style that Lispector characteristically employs thus merges with her thematic focus on writing a semiotics of being, one that, for the reader as much as for her characters, would embody the poststructural outlook and the form it takes when applied to the human condition. Cultivating fluid, self-referential "structurations" that emphasize the constantly evolving process of meaning, Clarice Lispector presents herself as a writer for whom human existence is defined most essentially as a moment-to-moment negotiation of language, the nearly always frustrating quest to possess what must always elude us—perfect, immutable knowledge.

The pressures of eroticism and desire permeate Lispector's texts. From *Near to the Wild Heart* (1944) to *A Breath of Life* (1977), sexual energy and a quest for pleasure are driving, albeit destabilizing, forces within her work. Though typically muted (and, at times, seemingly repressed), these primal urges are, moreover, never separated from their characters' verbal struggles to (re)create and express themselves. Indeed, recalling Shoshana Felman's argument in "Turning the Screw of Interpretation,"[1] Clarice Lispector not only explores the relations between sexuality and language, she grounds both sexuality and desire in language. The result of this is not what one might expect, however, for while her texts are virtually devoid of explicit sexual description (the sex act itself never gaining a prominent representation anywhere in them), they are infused with a pulsating eroticism that is both vital and acutely gender conscious, merging (as in *The Stream of Life*) the segregating and divisive distinctions of "him" and "her" into a more common "it," or into the dual-gendered character "Ela-ele" (She-he), from "Where You Were at Night." As we shall see, Clarice Lispector's multifaceted subjects, the loci of her texts, tend to develop themselves more in terms of shifting sites of desire than in terms of any determining origin, action, or stable presence. What this means in terms of their development is that for Lispector "desire in language" (to paraphrase Julia Kristeva) emerges as the great force that, lubricating the play of desire between the conscious and unconscious mind, leads her characters to exemplify what Lacan terms the "discours de l'Autre" (the discourse of the Other; *Écrits* 312). For Lacan the object of this "discourse" is the "désir de l'Autre" (the desire of the Other), a realization that we desire only in terms of something else, the other, which, in Lispector's texts, often manifests itself in the various forms of sexuality and sexual expression that infuse her work. To read Lispector's narratives in terms of sexual desire, then, is to discover not only the intimate nexus between language and being that animates them but also the deeply erotic impulse that, transgressing the prohibitions that separate the permissible from the forbidden, constantly dissolves barriers, psychological as well as cultural, within them.

As is evident in such texts as *Near to the Wild Heart*, "Miss Algrave," "The Imitation of the Rose," "The Message," "The Solution," "Clandestine Happiness," "Pig Latin," "Remnants of Carnival," "One Hundred Years of Pardon," "The Waters of the World," "Irresistible Incarnation," "The First Kiss," *The Stations of the Body* (*Soulstorm*), "Where You Were at Night," and "Interrupted Story" (written when its author was fourteen), in Lispector's world sexuality, "[l]ike rhetoric, . . . generated conflicting forces and complex contradictions, revealing a lack of unity and an essential ambiguity."[2] Or, as Felman puts it, even more apropos of Lispector's case, "sexuality *is* rhetoric, since it essentially consists of ambiguity: it is the co-existence of dynamically antagonistic meanings" (Felman, "Turning the Screw of Interpretation," 112). According to Vincent Leitch, and in a way again fully applicable to Lispector's work, "What Felman advocated was a new psychoanalytical criticism derived from Lacan that renounced the old search for meaning and content in favor of inquiry into procedures and methods of reading meaning. For her, as for other deconstructors, meaning was never final, literal, fixed; it remained contradictory, unreadable, rhetorical" (Leitch 293).

As we shall see, however, one can also argue that, taken in its entirety, Lispector's career as a writer also comes close to exemplifying Harold Bloom's "self," the poetic "subject" or "psyche" in whom "[t]he powers of language, simultaneously constituting and deconstituting the self, produced internal cleavages" (296). Though more apparent in certain texts than in others, a strong and, seemingly, sexually charged autobiographical impulse animates Lispector's work.

In either case, however, a close reading of all Lispector's texts shows clearly that for the Brazilian writer sexuality is a powerfully transforming force in human existence. Though the sex act itself is described neither salaciously nor graphically (indeed, it barely exists in her novels and stories except in oblique, metaphoric language), the sexual impulse, presented as being inseparable from the fecundity and seductiveness of language itself, functions as the chief animating force in a number of her greatest works, including the revolutionary *Near to the Wild Heart* (arguably Latin America's first New Novel), the sensual *Stream of Life*, and a number of seductive short fictions, including "In Search of Dignity," "Plaza Mauá," "Soulstorm," "Life *au Naturel*," and "Um dia a menos." For the main characters in these (and other) texts, sexuality not only animates them, it alters them, psychologically and physiologically, leading and allowing them to become (again, through language) something they had not been before.

In the two-page-long "Life *au Naturel*," for example, an unnamed woman's unfulfilled desire leads her to take the initiative with a man and consummate their passion. Presenting her desire as a "fome," a hunger that, though she is not conscious of it, she will move to satisfy, the text's development amounts not only to an intense depiction of sexual desire fulfilled but also to a philosophical commentary on the transitoriness of human existence—and on our need to act on what we feel and know to be our most basic needs.

Yet as powerful as it is, the story's erotic impulse is muted, carefully coded in deeply poetic language. Paralleling the combustion of the logs her male lover places on the fire, the woman's passion finally bursts into flame, metaphorically speaking, as she takes the man's hand in hers:

> She harries the moment, she devours its fire, and the fire sweetly burns, burns, and blazes. So, she who knows that everything will end takes the man's free hand, and taking it in hers sweetly burns, burns, and blazes. (*Soulstorm* 169)

Subtly forwarding the suggestion of female empowerment through a combination of eroticism and decisive action, Lispector also manages here to sound the carpe diem theme as well, a tactic that implies just how vital the sexual impulse is to Lispector's overall sense of the ephemerality of the human condition:

> Ah, and to think that it will end, that in itself it cannot last. No, she isn't referring to the fire, she is thinking of what she feels. What one feels never lasts, what one feels always ends, and can never again return. (*Soulstorm* 168–69)

While such erotically driven metamorphoses can be exhilarating and liberating (as in "The Waters of the World," *An Apprenticeship, or The Book of Delights*, "Miss Algrave," "The First Kiss," and "Life *au Naturel*"), they can also be (or turn) confusing and debilitating ("The Message," *The Apple in the Dark*, "Plaza Mauá," "Where You Were at Night," and "Soulstorm") and even tragic (as in "The Burned Sinner and the Harmonious Angels," "Footsteps," "Um dia a menos," "In Search of Dignity," and *The Hour of the Star*). What Lispector consistently presents, then, is a narrative world in which sexuality, regardless of the form or expression it takes, is a powerful, potentially life-transforming force, one that is ignored or repressed only at great risk to our well-being, a point poignantly made in the conclusion of the very sensual and desire-filled "One Hundred Years of Pardon" from *Clandestine Happiness:*

> [A] thief of roses and pitangas has one hundred years of pardon. The pitangas, for example, are the very ones who ask to be plucked, instead of maturing and dying on the branch, virgins. (my translation)

A more pointed commentary on sexual mores can be found in Lispector's 1948–49 drama, "The Burned Sinner and the Harmonious Angels," a little-known work that though reminiscent, in its symbols and dialogue, of medieval morality plays also speaks to modern relationships involving the issues of sexuality and power in a sociopolitical context.[3] Ostensibly about adultery, "A pecadora e os anjos harmoniosos" mounts an allegorical discourse on the destructive impact that sexual double standards have on social, moral, and political structures. Featuring a female protagonist (the "pecadora," or sinner, of the title) who, ironically, never speaks, the play develops around the issue of female empowerment as manifested in transgressive sexual expression. The drama can thus be understood as a form of early Lispectorian experimentation with the psychological and political ramifications of female power and pleasure. Condemned to death by a male tribunal for having entered into an adulterous affair, the woman only smiles enigmatically, utterly unrepentant for her actions and thereby incurring the vengeful wrath of her male-dominated society. Revealingly described as chattel, as a woman "who belonged to no one" (FL 159), the "sinner" elicits a telling political response in the reader, however, because while her fate is to be burned at the stake, her partner in the "crime," a man, will go unpunished.

Yet true to her constantly destabilizing approach to writing, Lispector deftly shows this same man—outwardly the beneficiary of society's double standard on the issue of adultery—having his own doubts about the morality of what is going to happen and about his part in it: "Alas, I have not been sent to the stake. I share the same sign and destiny, yet my tragedy will never be consumed by fire" (158–59). Although the man, equally guilty of the "crime," does not explicitly mention any remorse that he might be feeling for escaping the punishment to be meted out to the woman, and although his statement is veiled with respect to its precise meaning, it does seem to imply some degree of recognition on his part not only of the tragic injustice that is their society's execution of the female "sinner" but of his own guilt as well. Suggesting, then, as she does elsewhere, that phallocentric social mores, ethical codes, and political structures exert a deleterious influence not only on women but on men as well (though not, as this play makes clear, in similar or equal ways),[4] Lispector succeeds, in "The Burned Sinner and the Harmonious Angels," in grafting a strong political message onto a subtle yet effective depiction of female sexuality and desire.

A very basic conflict in her texts, from *Near to the Wild Heart* and "The Burned Sinner and the Harmonious Angels" to *A Breath of Life*, thus stems from our very basic human need to express our sexuality while living in cultures whose codes of conduct (economic and social as well as sexual and moral) send deeply conflicting messages: We are told to flaunt our sexuality, as we do through our modes of dress, our art and music, and to use it to sell merchandise, but we are forbidden under pain of legal penalty and public censure from actually engaging in or depicting sex, except within a strictly limited set of activities and circumstances, chiefly those occurring within heterosexual marriages involving young or middle-aged men and women. A surprising number of Lispector's texts thus actually deal with such ostensibly "deviant" sexual behaviors as masturbation, transvestism, rape, geriatric sex, and homosexuality, as well as with such "acceptable" issues as sexual repression, neurosis, and androgyny.

In "In Search of Dignity," for example, from the hybrid collection of short narratives *Where You Were at Night* (1974), Lispector presents the fictitious Senhora Jorge B. Xavier, a nearly seventy-year-old woman who lusts, like "a bitch on all fours" (80), after a real Brazilian pop singer, Roberto Carlos. Featuring a destabilizing touch of mordant humor and yet built around ever more intense images of desire and passion, "In Search of Dignity" shows its elderly protagonist progressively moving down "a dark passageway of sensuality" (83), one in which "lechery was her damnation. It was a lowly hunger: she wanted to eat Roberto Carlos' mouth. She wasn't romantic, she was coarse in matters of love" (83). Painfully conscious of her own urgent needs and of society's hypocritical attitudes regarding age and sexual desire, she knew that "[i]n old men, she had certainly seen lascivious stares. But in old women, never" (83). Yet because she knows she was "imprisoned by desire, out of season" (84), Senhora Jorge B. Xavier cannot help but worry about her attractiveness to the object of her desires:

> Her lips, lightly rouged, were they still kissable? Or might it be, perhaps, nauseating to kiss the mouth of an old woman? She examined her lips from close, and without expression. . . .

It was then that Senhora Jorge B. Xavier suddenly bent over the basin as if to vomit up her very guts and interrupted her life with a shattering silence: there must be a way o u t! (84)

By contrasting the droll, perhaps parodic, tone of the rest of the story with the suddenly and dramatically anguished tone of the final paragraph, Lispector effectively reminds the reader that for however much this old woman's lustful pursuit of the youthful pop singer—himself depicted in androgynous terms, as having a "virginal-girlish face" (82)—appears at first glance to be ludicrous and scornful, for her it is an issue of desperate importance, one that will either affirm or deny her very existence.

Yet for all the roles that these various issues play in Lispector's work, what is most singular about her expression of sexuality is the extent to which it comes to fruition through language, the extent to which, though always altering our sense of identity and being, it may, depending on other equally unpredictable factors and circumstances (the "proprieties" of gender, age, race, and class, for example), be either a positive or a negative force in our lives, one leading us toward happiness and fulfillment or toward frustration and a sense of failure or death. Expressive of the complex poststructural worldview, specifically in regard to the poststructural understanding of the term "desire," Lispector's texts deny both easy answers (or even clear questions) and the presence of stable, unambiguous truths. Presenting sexuality, then, as a metaphorically cloaked and profoundly destabilizing force in human affairs, both psychologically and socially, Lispector's texts create an elusive, ultimately unknowable yet erotically charged world in which not only desire but the meaning of desire is fluid, unstable, transgressive, and murky.

But even within such an uncertain universe, certain categories of sexually based tensions can be discerned: heterosexuality, homosexuality, transvestism, androgyny, and masturbation—the latter a force in Lispector's work that dramatically underscores the essential solipsism that torments so many of her characters and that accentuates their primal need to express a unified and coherent self, a goal which, as a function of language, is never totally achieved.

Perhaps more effectively than other forms of sexual expression in Lispector's work, it is the act of masturbation, as in the cases of Joana[5] and Cândida Raposo or as depicted in "Where You Were at Night" and *The Stream of Life*,[6] that, as we shall see, emerges as the ultimate expression of the seductive voluptuousness of language itself, as the one act that most viscerally connects language to being. In the novel version of

The Hour of the Star, for example, Macabéa's unexpected sexuality is presented as standing in stark if ironic contrast to the poverty of her circumstances and surroundings ("she often dreamed about sex . . . but her sex made its demands like a sunflower germinating in a tomb," [*Hour* 33, 70]), while in the film version her sexuality is expressed in the scene where, seemingly, she is masturbating in her sleep. Achieving the same thematic ends as the book version, this scene is both affective and deeply expressive of Macabéa's plight because it implies that her sexuality can only assert itself when she is asleep and perhaps dreaming, that is, when her conscious mind cannot repress her sexual urge, which the film presents as perhaps Macabéa's only satisfying form of self-expression, pathetic though it may be. The film version is thus actually more poignant on this score because the viewer both sees and hears Macabéa in the throes of (self-induced) sexual passion while simultaneously taking in the full extent of the suffocating poverty that envelops her. It is a powerful, revealing scene, and it effectively dramatizes what is a more objectively stated issue in the book.

Comprising the bulk of Lispector's sexually charged material, however, heterosexually oriented narratives have appeared throughout her career. Her first novel (*Near to the Wild Heart*), for example, utilizes a narrative structure in which Joana's development toward self-discovery and realization is paralleled by a similar stylistic progression from suggestive to openly sensual imagery, one that, moreover, throws into stark contrast the poverty of her marriage's sexuality with the lushness and beauty of what may be her autoerotic, or masturbatory, sexuality. Though never explicitly sexual, the scenes that, late in the book, depict Joana preparing to leave her phallogocentrically trapped husband and strike out on her own are dominated by powerful female body imagery (especially involving breasts and wombs) and by an overwhelming, if as yet inchoate, sense of female power and psychosexual pleasure. As if eavesdropping on the mental flow of the psychological and physiological "awakening" of Joana, the reader apprehends, for example, that

> she had been fascinated to discover her own body. The renewal had been hers, she had not given herself rapturously to this man and had remained isolated. . . . She could feel the world gently throbbing in her breast, her body ached as if she were bearing the femininity of all women. (*Heart* 126)

And later the reader discovers in a similar vein that

she [Joana] felt a great desire to melt away until her fibres merged with the beginning of things. To form but one substance, rose-coloured and sweet—breathing gently like a rising and falling womb. . . . What word could convey just then that something had not condensed and lived more freely? (175)

Although in this first novel Joana eventually has both a husband and a (male) lover, whom she dominates, her sex life with these men is not the primary ground of the novel's eroticism; indeed, the sex act itself is more implied than expressed in the depictions that involve them. Rather, as evidenced in the passages cited above, Joana's emergent sexuality, which closely parallels her discovery of self, emanates from the fluid and increasingly free interplay of her own body and mind, all this taking form in a free play of language in which the issues of psychosexual need or desire merge with those of gender and being. In short, Joana takes possession of herself, her identity, only when she possesses herself sexually.

As the text shows, the language that expresses the spirit of Eros that animates Joana is overwhelmingly self-referential; it does not refer in the main to any sexual activity beyond that engendered by Joana herself. Indeed, while the least erotically charged encounter Joana experiences must surely be the one she orchestrates with the pathetic and nameless man she very deliberately and calculatingly picks up, her most sensual experiences are those in which her body, the locus of the text's structurations, and of Joana's sense of self as the primary site of desire and being, seems, in language that is intensely poetic, to arouse and pleasure itself. Although relatively early in Joana's transformation, the reader learns, for example:

At night, between the sheets, the slightest movement or unexpected thought awakened her to herself.

. . . she opened her eyes wide, perceived her own body plunged into reassuring contentment. . . . Joana . . . Joana . . . she softly called to herself. And her body scarcely responded, quietly echoing: Joana. (92)

Later, in a parallel scene that more openly links the climactic play of autoarousal to the play of language, we learn that

release came and Joana trembled at its impulse . . . Because gentle and sweet as daybreak in a forest, inspiration came. . . . she uttered in a whisper words born at that moment . . . new and fragile buds . . . less than words, . . . disconnected syllables, meaningless, lukewarm, that flowed and criss-crossed, fertilized, . . . reborn in a single being only to separate immediately, breathing, breathing . . . (127)

With the essential poststructural fluidity of language and meaning here exhibiting its sensually poetic foundation, the text's narrative voice then moves, shortly before the final page (which suggests less a conclusion than a new beginning), to achieve for Joana a kind of mind-clearing structural and erotic climax, one that, in the manner of Derrida, simultaneously undermines both the notion of the "center" and of the self as a stable, unified presence:

> Joana found it difficult to think clearly—there was something in the garden that dislocated her from the centre. . . . Something was trying to move inside her, responding, and through the dark cavities of her body, waves came surging, . . . she . . . found herself being pulled further and further back in sweet vertigo, by gentle fingers. . . . She examined herself, suddenly alert as if she had advanced too far. . . . The pink waves darkened, the dream fled. (174–75)

In terms, then, of the role sexuality plays in this extraordinary 1944 novel, written when its author was in her early twenties, the reader is left feeling that it is Joana's private, self-induced, and thoroughly relished autoeroticism—and not an eroticism involving either her husband or her lover—that in large part empowers this text with such viscerally decentering force.

Joana, however, is not the only Lispector protagonist to engage in sexual release by means of masturbation. In "Footsteps," a spare, almost minimalist story from *The Stations of the Body*, Lispector presents the reader with Dona Cândida Raposo, an eighty-one-year-old widow who is still "troubled" by the pangs of unfulfilled sexual desire. For Dona Raposo, the text tells us, "the desire for pleasure didn't pass away" (48). This "desire for pleasure," moreover, quickly establishes itself as the defining aspect of life itself. Not only has this one aspect never gone away; it has become a source of suffering and frustration, a living "hell" (48), when, as in the case of this "shameless" old woman (whom no one "wants" anymore), it cannot be sated by any kind of sexual activity that is sanctioned by society. Caught between a realization of her sexual vitality, her sexual needs, and society's refusal to recognize an old person's sexuality as "acceptable,"[7] Dona Raposo thinks first about paying for sex and then, viewing that option as not viable either, elects to take care of her sexual frustration herself. As she puts it, to her gynecologist, "And . . . and what if I take care of it myself?" (49). With the doctor opining that this might help, Dona Raposo proceeds to rely on the solitary act of masturbation to alleviate her suffering: "That night she did what she could and, alone, satisfied herself. Silent fireworks" (49).

The otherwise droll and perhaps parodic (Peixoto, *Passionate Fictions*, 73) quality of this story is suddenly and dramatically transformed into an expression of acute ontological pathos, however, by what the text then tells us: "Afterward she cried. She was ashamed. From then on she used the same method. It was always sad. That's life, Senhora Raposo, that's life. Until the blessing of death" (*Heart* 49). While the "action" of this bleak, unadorned story deals with an old woman's decision to masturbate to relieve her sexual frustration, its power resides in the fact that it very subtly indicts a society whose mores isolate her and make her feel ashamed of herself for doing nothing more "wrong" than trying to cope as best she can with the demands of her body.

Although Lispector would write numerous variations on this type of autoerotic and psychosexually driven text for her entire career, a famous story from *Family Ties* (1960) takes up another issue, homosexuality, that in a variety of ways would also occupy her attention for years to come. The story in question, "The Imitation of the Rose," deals openly with the twin issues of gender and identity while at the same time subtly intimating that Laura, whose function on the story's most obvious level is to conform to her role as the perfect housewife, may also be sexually attracted to her freer, more unconventional friend, Carlota. Although, as the text makes clear, Carlota, too, lives a life conditioned by gender limitation, she is less repressed than the pathetic Laura, who feels the need to be "submissive to the authoritarian and practical goodness of Carlota, receiving once more her friend's attention and vague disdain . . . [and] perplexed affection full of curiosity" ("Imitation" 54). Keying on images of the female body, especially breasts and hips, the story's text generates a field of repressed desire and deferred pleasure (the erotic analogues of "différance") in which the two women—each subjugated and categorized by the phallogocentric order that envelops them—appear drawn toward a sexual union with each other, one that would seem destined, however, to replicate the same master/slave relationship in which each is already trapped with her husband and with society at large. If one entertains such an interpretation of this story, a reasonable conclusion might be that, as I will argue in Chapters 4 and 5, Lispector is showing us how patriarchal social structures so distort the perceptions and values of everyone involved (the men as well as the women) that no one escapes becoming their victims. The story's fundamental energy derives, therefore, from the muted sexual tension that exists between the two women, the two most obvious victims yet, ironically, the two characters with some reservoirs of passion left. What we may then term the story's erotic subtext deals with the unstated and unconsummated passion that exists between Laura and Carlota, a condition that, exacerbating Laura's already overwhelming sense of frustration and alienation, could be read as providing the final impetus for her mental disintegration.

Another example of Lispector's lifelong interest in the issue of undifferentiated desire comes from *The Apple in the Dark*, a work Gregory Rabassa, its translator, has described as a "high point in the development of Miss Lispector's work" (*Apple* xii), and a text that also invites the reader to wonder whether the two women involved might not be involved in some sort of erotic, though not necessarily sexual, relationship. Although the novel's main character is a man, Martim, and although most commentators have focused on his relationship with each of the two women—Vitória, an unmarried woman in her fifties, and her younger cousin, Ermelinda—the text's thematic opaqueness and ambiguity lead the reader to fill in the gaps and offer some explanation for the numerous unresolved aporias, or moments of "rupture"[8] and undecidability, that structure the relationship between the two women. Exemplary of readings that center around, "questions of sexual difference and of different libidinal economies" (Cixous, *Reading with Clarice Lispector*, 60), *The Apple in the Dark* weaves the ontological issue of love, contextualized constantly as a problem of language, into the very fabric of its structuring. "'Well, then,' Vitória declares at one point late in the novel, 'don't be surprised at what you yourself brought out: my freedom,' and then she was puzzled because she realized that she did not know what she was saying and that she had become lost, playing with words" (*Apple* 280).

The problem of becoming lost in poststructuralism's infinite "play" of words thus establishes itself as the text's primary source of tension and ambiguity, an issue that has a direct bearing on the manner in which the two women, Vitória and Ermelinda, relate to themselves, to each other, to Martim, and to the reader. Early in the novel, for example, the text suggests the existence of a secret, hidden relationship between the two women:

Ermelinda pretended to be so surprised that she looked at the other one with her mouth half-open— . . . : "I was very abrupt," Vitória thought. Ermelinda gave her a fleeting side-glance and . . . it was as if she wished to be so discreet that she would not let the other one see that she understood. Vitória caught it and blushed. A few moments passed. They remained silent, feeling the soft swirl of the breeze around them. Darkness was coming on little by little. For an instant the scent of roses gave the two women a moment of softness and meditation. (73)

The vague suggestiveness of this scene, one replete with sensuous references to the covering mantle of darkness, the scent of roses (echoing "The Imitation of the Rose"), and the "soft," perhaps intimate, proximity of the two women (one of whom inexplicably blushes), makes one unsure about what is transpiring here. Are they sharing, the reader wonders, an amorous secret, a moment of unspoken but shared passion? There seems to be ample textual reason to suspect as much, yet only a few lines later, and continuing on through the remainder of the novel, Vitória, whose authoritative voice and presence (recalling Carlota) dominate their relationship, disdains Ermelinda:

"You always say everything so well!" she said flatteringly.

Vitória was calm. She looked at her deeply, once more immune from everything that the girl was.

"I never would have said that myself. But now that we're living together I've had to learn your language." (73)[9]

It is possible, however, for the reader to imagine a relationship in which Vitória's criticisms of Ermelinda mask an even deeper and unspoken desire for her, a need for her presence and, perhaps, for her body, the body, as we have seen, functioning as one of Lispector's most fundamental narrative building blocks. This interpretation is given further plausibility when we consider that it is Ermelinda who, in contrast to Vitória's very masculine appearance and demeanor, manifests what, as Mara Negrón-Marrero notes, conventional society deems to be appropriate "feminine"[10] expressions of love, the tangled issue that, in relation to the ontological issues of human identity and conduct, orders the narrative. This line of analysis reaches its very subdued climax late in the novel when Vitória, in a long and veiled confession to a confused and enervated Martim, comes close to articulating what she, and perhaps Ermelinda, had come to the isolated farm to find:

"I used to live in Rio. . . . But I came here of my own volition. . . . I'd made a mistake. What was I going to do? . . . I made a mistake like a woman who had been deceived by a man's promises—oh, there wasn't any man, if that's what you mean or at least what you're thinking. (293)

Having implied the issue to this extent, the text then informs us, in a way that again hints at what the reader had earlier suspected about the possibly erotic underpinnings of the relationship between Vitória and Ermelinda:

What had she really come to find? The passion of living? yes, she had come in search of the passion of life, the woman discovered disappointedly; and a drop of sweat ran sadly down her nose. (293)

Artfully maintaining the ambiguity regarding the relationship the two women had, the text thus intimates a sexual attraction—one not necessarily realized—between them while simultaneously offering a plethora of scenes and dialogue exchanges that would seem to make such a relationship less plausible. Yet because love plays such a central role in this novel, as it does in the rest of Lispector's work, it seems prudent for the reader to consider the possibility that Eros can thrive (via language) without being acted on, that the "passion of living," our mind- and body-based, gender-indeterminate erotic impulses,[11] involves failure and (as in the case of Vitória) disappointment as well as success, absence as well as presence, and that to experience this basically poststructural truth about the human condition is, in *The Apple in the Dark* and in Lispector's universe generally, to feel the tragedy of our isolation and the failure of our language to overcome it.

Though it did so early in her career, *Family Ties* was not the first Lispector text to broach the issue of female homosexuality. *Near to the Wild Heart* also takes this issue up, albeit in a more hypothetical and complex fashion. In the earlier 1944 novel, the question of lesbianism arises from two different but related relationships: first, Joana, the protagonist, and Lídia, her husband's pregnant lover, and second, Joana and the nameless woman who keeps house for the similarly nameless man Joana takes for a lover. In the more developed case of Lídia, the text takes pains to connect Joana's early awareness of female breasts (her aunt's and, as we see in the "O banho" ["The Bath"] chapter, those of her own developing body) to her erotically charged consciousness of Lídia's more sensuous body in the crucial "Lídia" section of the novel. It is here, in the powerful and revealing confrontation between Joana and Lídia (whose carnality and basically passive psychological presence elicit pangs of desire in both Otávio and Joana), that we see the homoerotic impulse inherent in Joana's being beginning to stir. Able to envision Lídia as an erotic partner as well as a competitor, and evaluating herself, physically and psychologically, in terms of all that Lídia, whom we can understand as the other, represents, Joana actually suggests that she and Lídia share Otávio sexually, an idea that, though ostensibly shocking to the more conventional Lídia, would, in the context of the narrative's development to this point, only transform into a more female-empowered ménage à trois what is already the triangular relationship involving Otávio, his wife, and his mistress.

The sexual threesome suggested here by Joana, moreover, would only parallel the numerous other triangular relationships that structure this novel (Peixoto, *Passionate Fictions*, 7–8), in particular, the often overlooked one involving Joana, the nameless man she seduces, and her perhaps sado-masochistic relationship with the man's erstwhile lover, who is presented to the reader as if assuming the role of the dominated lover to Joana's role of the dominatrix, a role that links her to the other women of this novel, the "three diabolical graces" (*Heart* 155)—Joana, her lover's former lover, and the teacher's wife. According to Marta Peixoto "[t]he most debased of all the women in the novel" (Peixoto, *Passionate Fictions*, 14), the pathetic woman who is Joana's lover's former lover, is given considerable attention by Joana, who actually envisions the three of them forming a "couple," a relationship that would seem to empower Joana in the same degree that it humiliates the other woman and subordinates the man. As the text expresses it:

> On those first visits to the big house, Joana had felt like asking the man the following questions: Is she now like a mother to you? Is she no longer your lover? Even though I exist, does she still want you to live with her? . . . Meanwhile, the presence of the other woman was so powerful in the house, that the three of them formed a couple. . . . Joana, that woman and the teacher's wife. What was it that finally united them? The three diabolical graces. (*Heart* 154–55)

Binding the two relationships together is the crucial issue of power, which, in a sexually driven yet maternal way (137), Joana finds attractive in Lídia and which, in a darker, more sexually unconventional way, she also finds attractive in "that woman" (154), whose mysterious presence in the novel we understand only in terms of Joana's interest in her.

Implicitly and explicitly, lesbian love also plays a role in the late work *The Hour of the Star*, where the former prostitute turned brothel owner turned fortune-teller, Madame Carlota, advises the desperately unhappy Macabéa to find a woman to love. As Madame Carlota puts it, speaking of her own experience and in a discourse that invites interpretation from a number of different perspectives:

> After he disappeared, I took up with another woman to try and forget him. To be loved by another woman is really rather nice. It would even be preferable in your case because you're much too delicate to cope with the brutality of men. If you can find yourself a woman friend, you'll soon find out how nice it can be. Is there any chance of you finding yourself a woman friend? (*Hour* 74)

Although Macabéa responds in the negative, the seemingly mechanical and unelaborated nature of her response suggests, ironically, that she would indeed respond to anyone, male or female, who showed her some kindness and affection. Whether one reads these lines as a veiled autobiographical statement by Lispector about how she herself may have felt, as a parody of one of popular fiction's most salacious topics (as Peixoto 1994 suggests), or as a feminist statement about the desirability of love between women both as a "chance" for sexual satisfaction and as a form of political solidarity in the face of male violence and oppression (an issue that echoes the conflict in "The Imitation of the Rose" and "The Body"), the reader is struck by the semantic ambiguities of this enigmatic statement as well as by the multiple implications one might reasonably draw from it. Regardless of how one interprets it, however, the reader is reminded of how destabilizing the erotic impulse is in Lispector's world and of how multiform its verbalized manifestations can be.

While later texts like "The Imitation of the Rose," "The Solution," "The Body," and *The Hour of the Star* also suggest the presence of female homosexuality, and while "A Sincere Friendship," "He Soaked Me Up," and "Plaza Mauá" imply or denote male homosexuality, works like "Life au Naturel," "The Message," *The Apple in the Dark*, "Miss Algrave," "Pig Latin," "Better Than to Burn," "But It's Going to Rain," and *An Apprenticeship, or The Book of Delights* emphasize heterosexual relationships. In "The Message," for example,[12] a text that may be considered the first of Lispector's short texts to stress how explicitly words play such a vital role in human relationships, an adolescent girl and boy pass into adulthood by means of what seems to be a metaphorically rendered sexual experience. Presented to the reader in the oblique fashion so characteristic of Lispector on this issue, their sexual and political awakening undercuts itself, however, because, as the final third of the story makes clear, for however much the sexual act—in theory or in fact—has transformed them into "adults," it has also led them to imprison themselves and each other in the chains of radically androcentric sex-role identities. Thus, while their nascent sexuality compels them to change (in their eyes and in the view of their culture), it also seduces them into conforming to the repressive definitions of "male" and "female" that their society demands.

What we understand from a text like "The Message," then, is that while sexuality is an undeniable aspect of our being, there is no guarantee that giving expression to it will lead (as it does for Joana, for G. H., for Madre Clara, of "Better Than to Burn," and for the voice of *The Stream of Life*) to happiness or fulfillment. To the contrary, as we see in "The Message," "Footsteps," "In Search of Dignity," "But It's Going to Rain," *The Apple in the Dark*, or any one of a number of other Lispector works, all too often the formulation and expression of our sexual identity (shaped and given meaning through discourse) leads to the frustration, disillusionment, and repression that characterize life as it is played out under the crippling strictures of phallocentric systems. Apropos of this, as Christine Froula has argued,[13] the boy in question gains entrance into the prevailing male power structure while the girl is exiled from it. What is unique about "The Message" in this regard is that we see clearly how such a system deforms not only the girl-cum-woman but the boy-cum-man as well. While the girl is forced to acquiesce to her "womanly" role of passivity, dependence, and inferiority, the boy is corrupted because, complying with the sex role demanded of him, he has no real choice except to drop his callow innocence and adopt the swaggering posture of the sexual privateer. The great sense of failure that permeates "The Message," then, is that while our sexual urges can and do transform us, they all too often entrap us in the rigidities of psychosexual stereotypes, making us define ourselves not on our own terms (as Joana, G. H., the female presence in *The Stream of Life*, and the characters of "Plaza Mauá" seek to do) but in terms of the conventions that our society demands. And, as we see so poignantly illustrated in "The Message," so long as we allow society to impose its definitions of such key ontological terms as "girl"/"boy," "female"/"male," or "woman"/"man" on us, on our most personal sense of identity, we will always—like Martim and the characters of this story but unlike Joana, Lóri, or the "Burned Sinner"—be more or less quiescent slaves to that society.

Lóri's narrative, in fact, *An Apprenticeship, or The Book of Delights* (1969), paints a potentially more optimistic picture of heterosexual experience. The story of a man (Ulisses) and a woman (Lóri) who find each other by first finding themselves, this very distinctive novel features a frank carnality that goes beyond the sensuality and eroticism of the earlier works. Sexuality becomes a prime mover for both Ulisses and Lóri, but it only achieves the transcendence of love when, in the novel's final mythically charged pages, it paradoxically unites them—as equals—by individualizing them, by leading each of them to see that, honestly and openly dealt with, it has already liberated them, freed them to take on new identities, to be transformed by love, one aspect of which is sexual. Thus it is that (in the novel's climax), when Ulisses and Lóri enjoy not merely sex but the attainment of love and, seemingly, mutual respect as well, Lóri—who initiates their encounter—can declare, first, that "I am yours, you are mine, and we are one" (*Apprenticeship* 112) and then that "I'm a different woman now" (114).

What is problematic in this otherwise gender-effacing and satisfying text is that while we are told that "Lori could finally talk to him [Ulisses] as an equal" (113), she also declares to him that "you seduced me wickedly," and that "[y]ou have transformed me into the woman that I am" (113). As a character, Ulisses, a philosophy professor (like Jacques Derrida), is in full possession of Logos; and indeed, one can easily feel that his numerous explanations, clarifications, and interpretations of their relationship come to dominate the text in a tendentious and, finally, logocentric fashion.[14] This is underscored by the fact that Lóri can state categorically that it is he (and not herself, as was the case with Joana) who has transformed her into the new, suddenly more fulfilled woman that she now is. Yet when she asks Ulisses if he understands what she means, he—in a statement that tellingly undercuts his own authority—says, "I understand. . . . But I don't like to discuss everything" (113–14). Then, in a crucial line that could apply to himself (if, indeed, he too has been transformed by their gender-emancipating love) as well as to Lóri, he says, "Know when to keep quiet so that you don't lose yourself in words" (114), a comment that aptly sums up the poststructural dilemma with which Lispector's characters so relentlessly struggle.

While the problem of becoming lost in words sums up what is the essentially poststructural malaise of Lispector's universe, in *An Apprenticeship* it is offset by the text's open avowal of the positive, potentially liberating power of human sexuality and of language, which, in terms of what our sexuality means to us, is what gives our sexuality significance, what makes it, in fact, a prime signifier. Thus it is that, close to the end of the novel, Ulisses, referring to Lóri's new sense of being, tells her, "Sex and love aren't forbidden to you anymore. You've finally learned how to exist. And this causes the release of many other liberties, which is a threat to your social class" (115). This declaration contradicts the atmosphere of repression and censorship that prevailed in Brazil during the late 1960s. Yet while the text implies that love (achieved and now sustained by means of what seems a virtually tantric form of sex) has transformed (that is, "equalized") both the formerly subservient Lóri and the formerly dominant Ulisses, the work's final, erotically transforming, sexually charged scene is, for Lispector, body oriented and singularly explicit: "She was not startled to feel his hand rest on her stomach. His hand was caressing her legs now. . . . Then she extended her hand and touched his sex organ, which was quickly transformed" (116). More explicitly than in any of Lispector's other texts, *An Apprenticeship* shows us how the transforming power of language and of love (here closely identified with sex) can liberate not only women but men as well[15] (if one interprets Ulisses as having truly liberated himself from his privileged and dominant position).

But if *An Apprenticeship* represents the culmination of Lispector's examination of the complexities and potentialities of heterosexual relationships, a work appearing two years later would lead her into the realm of androgyny, an issue she would also be concerned with for many years to come.

Published in 1971, the short narratives of *Clandestine Happiness* stand out for their utilization of self-conscious first-person narrator-protagonists, the transforming quality of their sexuality, their emphasis on children and adolescents and on the use of female body imagery, their development of hybrid or androgynous characters, and finally, the degree of narrative decentering that takes place within them.[16] A text from this collection that typifies nearly all of these characteristics is "The Waters of the World," an archetypal and mythic tale[17] in which an unnamed woman is presented as a kind of maximal signifier, a magical, mystical being who, as eternal as the sea, "doesn't need communication," being, perhaps, beyond it. In her mystery and polysemic ambiguity, she is portrayed not necessarily as the quintessence of communication but as the quintessence of semantic fecundity or dissemination. Born along by means of closely woven webs of sensuous water and body imagery, the story focuses on the thought flow and bodily sensations of a woman luxuriating in a sea bath. Eventually coming to equate woman

with the sea, but first having the latter serve as a fertilizing and regen-
eratively pansexual force for the former, the lush but enigmatic imagery
that imbues the story with its compelling quality leads the reader to feel
that the woman's communion with the sea (and, through the sea, with
her similarly fluid self) has been a profoundly erotic experience. But,
again typical of Lispector's fundamentally poststructuralist view of human experience, the text cultivates this trend ambivalently, in a way that
undercuts, decenters, and "deconstructs" its own lines of signification.
While, for example, the woman and the sea are implicitly cast as lovers
(much as the girl and her book are on the final page of "Clandestine
Happiness"), and while the woman is further developed as the archetypal vehicle of life, growth, and development, she is also destined (as
the text cryptically tells us) for a mysterious "*naufrágio*" (shipwreck).
Given what we can take to be the primary sociopolitical significance of
Lispector's writings, her lifelong interrogation of phallocentric oppression, I believe we are justified in interpreting this deeply mythic text as
essentially tragic in nature, one that presents woman as a desirable and
desiring life force but that also predicts the disaster (the shipwreck)
awaiting her within the androcentric social structures that envelop her
and from which she will not escape.[18]

But in a move that is once again very characteristic of Lispector's
poststructural consciousness, the final lines of the text decenter the
woman-as-victim thesis not by invalidating it but by both supplanting
and expanding it, as if in an expression of not only "différance" but "supplément" as well, to include everyone, men and women alike. As in "The
Message," the single, rather simplistic argument that women are victimized in innumerable ways in our male-dominated societies is not in any
way rendered untrue but is in fact imbued with the poignancy and
tragedy of a truth of much greater scope: that in any phallogocentric
system, many men will be forced—again by the dictates of social convention—to do things they would not normally wish to do and to "be"
people they might not otherwise choose to be. Thus, at the end of her
narrative, when Lispector expands the concept of "woman" to include,
indeed to epitomize, "the human creature" or even "human existence,"
she introduces the question whether to "be" "woman" (a question here
of both gender construct and biology) isn't better understood not as a
choice between "male" or "female" or "man" or "woman" (Cixous's
"death-dealing" binary oppositions) but as a confluence not only of
these two "oppositions" but of all life-generating, life-sustaining, life-
pleasuring forces (the controlling image of which here is, as elsewhere in

Lispector's work, the sea, or water in general). Read in this fashion, Lispector's "woman" takes on a distinctly androgynous dimension, one that recalls the central image of "the same flesh" that had defined the prephallocentrically gendered identities of the boy and girl in "The Message." Just as they were originally of the same flesh, so, too, are the woman bathing in the surf and all living matter, including whatever we wish to mean when we use such signifiers as "men" or "male." Once again, then (and as we will see in such other texts as "Irresistible Incarnation," "The First Kiss," "Plaza Mauá," "Where You Were at Night," "In Search of Dignity," "A Report on a Thing," and *A Breath of Life*), the question of identity is, at all levels, inextricably bound up in the endless labyrinths of language and desire. It seems, in short, that Lispector intuitively understood life as language, as a semantically ambiguous sign system in which there was potentially limitless free play between signifiers (words like "male" and "female") and their signifieds, their meanings. In such an unstable and amorphous realm, meaning becomes a function of whatever structure can influence it, emerging, finally, as an uncertain semiotic field in which human identity is a ceaseless ebb and flow (like the sea or the act of reading) of physical, emotional, and intellectual sensations and thoughts, in short, of verbal signs and their inescapable "différance." Fluid in both its concept and its gender-bending actualization, Lispector's concept of identity—that it is a matter of ontological hybridism and conflict—is not only inherently language based, it is, in its endlessly productive nature, inherently poststructural.

Epitomizing all these issues is "The First Kiss," a short, underappreciated narrative that ranks among the most brilliant Lispector ever wrote. Showing us once more, and once again in interlocking patterns of lyrically sensual imagery, the pernicious effects of phallocentric gendering on both men and women (with the male figure getting more attention here), Lispector expands an erotically charged interaction between a "thirsty" boy (one reminiscent of the boy in "The Message") and a stone statue—in the form of a nude woman—with water (recalling the life-giving liquid of "The Waters of the World" and anticipating *The Stream of Life*) gushing from its half open mouth[19] into a lushly poetic meditation on the transformative powers of love (particularly erotic love) and language (the mechanism by which erotic love is verbalized and given significance). Here, however—in contrast to what happens in "The Message"—it is the female erotic force (the statue/fountain/woman) that transforms the male force, for just as water (the source of all life) streams freely and steadily out of the mouth of the statue (of the nude woman) so, too, does truth now stream out of him. Springing from out of "an occult fountain" of desire residing deep within him, the boy experiences this revelation only after he drinks of the statue's water—which he does by "kissing" the statue on the mouth, an act that, symbolic of sexual union, represents the culmination of the story's erotic tension at the same time that it allows the boy to be transformed into a fountain of truth.

Undercutting this interpretation, however, as Lispector shows us in the text's final line—"He had become a man"—is the disconcerting suspicion that language (the vehicle of love) relentlessly metamorphoses everything (paralleling the fountain) into ceaseless flow; our lot, as human beings—the language animal—is to learn to deal with realities, identities, and "truths" that change (as seen here in the shift from the nonphallocentric "boy" to the possibly phallocentric "man," as in "The Message," and, conceivably, from the concept of phallocentric "man" to that of possibly nonphallocentric, or "feminized," "man") in accordance with our ever-changing language usage.

Another example of the kind of androgynous or transgendering erotics of reading that apply to Lispector's texts is "Where You Were at Night," from the collection of short narratives published in 1974 under the same title and, in English, under the title *Soulstorm*. The most deliberately and systematically androgynous of all Lispector's many experiments with this issue, "Where You Were at Night" is ambiguous at the very outset, for, given the syntax and punctuation (or lack of same) in the original and in the translation, the reader is prevented from knowing whether even the title is to be read as a statement or a question.

Going beyond the basic ambiguity of the text itself, however, the most striking feature of "Where You Were at Night" is unquestionably the character known, alternatingly, as Ele-ela/He-she and Ela-ele/She-he. Transformed constantly by wave after wave of psychoerotic, cultural, and physiological impulses, and wryly playing out a variety of sex roles and acts, this nakedly androgynous creation exerts a formally decentering force on the text; everything becomes decentered and mixed, an unstable amalgam of the sacred and profane, of male and female, of differing social categories, and of different voices, several of which at times seem to be representing different or changing aspects of the same conflicted psyche. As in a surrealist poem, which, indeed, this oneiric text very much resembles, the welter of conflicting forces that gives structure to it constantly undermines itself, denying the reader a stable, secure critical perspective from which to operate. Achieving something here that is very akin to the kind of free play of signifiers that Derrida speaks of, the language of "Where You Were at Night" effects a structuration that denies the presence of anything even remotely resembling a center, understood by Derrida to refer to "a point of presence, a fixed origin," the purpose of which is "not only to orient, balance, and organize the structure . . . but, above all, to make sure that the organizing principle of the structure would limit what we might call the 'play' of the structure" ("Structure, Sign, and Play," 109). Not possessing a stable thematic or structural center, "Where You Were at Night" functions, therefore, as a dream does, with the reader being drawn into its web of one fantastic, disconnected image after another.

If there were a unifying or structuring force present in this text, however, it would have to be the pansexual eroticism that pervades it. Building initially on images of female breasts, on scenes involving both cosmic sexuality and masturbation, and on what seems to be a general merging of our diverse subconscious urges (chief among which are our sexual urges) with mysticism (which, at one point, is described as, "the highest form of superstition"; *Soulstorm* 121), "Where You Were at Night" ends up obliterating the easy, clear-cut distinctions between things that our ordinary epistemologies lead us to make. Our cultures teach us to see things in terms of absolutes and opposites—truth/falsity, strong/weak, mind/body, or (of particular significance here) male/female—but Lispector's text demands another approach, one both comical (humor, like sex, being a great dissolver of hierarchies and distinctions)[20] and more compatible with the theories of poststructuralism. Indeed, a careful reading of this extraordinary text suggests to the reader that—particularly in its constant syntactic alternation of the She-he/He-she character—"Where You Were at Night" literally embodies what such critics as Derrida, Cixous, and Kristeva speak of theoretically as the need to uncouple the compartmentalizing binary oppositions so characteristic of Western culture and civilization. That Lispector's text so categorically disallows the seemingly unassailable primacy of these oppositions, which are so crucially a part of classical structural analysis, constitutes one of the most outstanding characteristics of her compelling poststructural style.

In a way, moreover, that does not now surprise us (given what we know about the degree to which Lispector practiced a keenly self-conscious brand of autointertextuality in her writing), we can see a direct link between the subversion of phallogocentric gender roles as described in *An Apprenticeship* and their near complete negation or denial in "Where You Were at Night." What Lispector achieves in this latter work, in fact, comes very close to epitomizing the deconstructive strategy of reversal and reinscription that Cixous and, especially, Derrida have made famous. By refusing to allow the reader to know the character only in terms of the "He-she" form (which, as Derrida argues in *Of Grammatology*, privileges the first part, in this case the "He," or male, element), Lispector's text deliberately "deconstructs" itself, denying the reader the luxury of "either/or" thinking and forcing us to understand this character not in terms of being either female or male dominated but in terms of being in flux, of being a hybrid character who is constantly evolving, consciously and unconsciously (via Lispector's use of free indirect discourse) defining and redefining itself in terms of the potentialities and limitations of its language system. The She-he/He-she character, or presence, is thus similar to the Lóri/Ulisses union because, in both cases, each member or element must evolve into the other in order to achieve fulfillment. The difference is that while in *An Apprenticeship* there remains a question about whether Ulisses remains the dominant, or privileged, member of their union, in the later story it is precisely this question of dominance that the text—that is, language—elides (and by means of a clearly deliberate and strategic syntactic maneuver, that of alternately inverting the order in which the terms "She-he"/"He-she" appear). In diverse ways, then, "Where You Were at Night" both represents the culmination of her many experiments with androgyny and gendering (whether of characters or of narrative voice) and epitomizes what one type of Lispectorian poststructural fiction looks like.

But while Lispector certainly devoted a great deal of attention, as we have seen, to the issue of androgyny,[21] she nevertheless maintained her career-long interest in what we might call the erotics of language itself, an awareness of the intimate and symbiotic relationships between language and sexuality. This relationship is vividly depicted in "Clandestine Happiness," a 1971 story in which a coveted book (representing language) is explicitly described as if it were the female protagonist's lover. Embodying a true Barthesian erotics of reading, the text of "Clandestine Happiness" draws to a close with the following sexually charged revelation by the main character: "Sometimes I would sit down in the hammock, balancing myself with the open book on my lap, without touching it, in the purest of ecstasy. I wasn't a girl with a book: I was a woman with her lover" (my translation).

Although, as we have seen, this erotic awareness was present in Lispector's work, if only in nascent form, as early as 1944 in *Near to the Wild Heart*, it grew steadily as a force in her fiction ("Clandestine Happiness," for example) until reaching a climax in *The Stream of Life*, a 1974 text that many readers, male and female alike, have described as being "orgasmic" in nature. While the earlier *Passion according to G. H.* took a more intellectualized approach to language and eroticism, *The Stream of Life*, structuring itself (once again) around the images of water, writing, birth, and the female body, is, without losing its psychic intensity, much more visceral in its handling of this subject. As the nameless female narrator of the 1974 text says, "I'm caught up with the joy of the words, and . . . I feel a voluptuousness in creating what to tell you. I live the initiation ceremony of the word" (*SL* 12). Exhibiting a kind of pansexuality, the text of *The Stream of Life* spills over "into the obscure eroticism of full life" (12) inhabited by, "the voluminous nude bodies of strong women wrapped in serpents and carnal desires of realization" (13). Later, the text's self-conscious voice declares:

> I await the orgasmic apocalypse. . . . What fever: I can't stop living. In this dense jungle of words that wrap themselves thickly around what I feel and think and experience and that transform all that I am into something of my own that nonetheless remains entirely separate from me. I watch myself think. . . . Visceras tortured by voluptuousness guide me. (54–55)

Linking here the transformative power of the body's inherent eroticism as well as that of death, or oblivion ("the orgasmic apocalypse") to the equally transformative power of words (which similarly "transform all that I am"), the text's voice then wonders, in an image that conflates both these concepts, "Could I be having here a real orgy behind thought? an orgy of words?" (70). Interestingly, works like *The Passion according to G. H.* and *The Stream of Life* lend themselves both to Luce Irigaray's study of female mysticism (a controversial issue in regard to Lispector's work) in *Speculum of the Other Woman* and to Julia Kristeva's concept of the "semiotic" ("a pre-Oedipal domain of primary drives and processes associated with a bisexual fantastic Mother and with literary 'gynotexts'"; Leitch 323), as discussed in *Revolution in Poetic Language* (1974). Although in both *The Passion according to G. H.* and, especially, *The Stream of Life* images of the female body tend to predominate, these texts nevertheless do not argue ideologically for any kind of privileging of "femaleness" or for any kind of biological essentialism. Indeed, while there is no doubt that these (and nearly all of Lispector's other texts) derive their basic power primarily from the various images of women that they generate, a close comparative reading of her work suggests that Lispector, like Kristeva, is advancing a new concept of human identity, one that is grounded in what we now understand as a distinctly poststructural sense of language and that therefore would reject as ontologically meretricious any rigidly maintained dichotomy between masculine being and feminine being, these distinctions conceived of more as conventionalized functions of language use than anything else.

This same sense of erotic interaction between language and being (whether textual or human) is expressed in an even more distilled form in *A Breath of Life*, a work that, though actually written by Lispector (in fragments, as was her wont), was ordered by her friend and confidante, Olga Borelli. To the acute consciousness of language's germinating potency that characterizes Lispector's best work, *A Breath of Life* adds (through its three interlocking monologues: one by the character Ângela Pralini; one by the "author," a man, judging from certain features of grammatical agreement; and a portion by this authorial voice that often seems that of Lispector herself) a passionately destabilizing, decentering celebration of language's self-induced and self-inducing eroticism. As Ângela Pralini expresses it:

> I who aspire to the great disorder of desires . . . and [to] the darkness that possesses me in the apocalyptic orgasm of my existence. (my translation)

Soon after this, the (male) authorial voice begins to ponder the nature of the connection between language (words) and the eroticism we say we acknowledge in our bodies (with no distinction—no "dichotomy"—being made between mind and body):

> That illumination of Ângela cannot express itself in words. So the word "olfactory" tries poorly to express what is called "olfactory." (my translation)

Then, striking a distinctly poststructural tone, this same voice concludes, "There are no words pure in and of themselves. They always come mixed together like this: 'I don't know what's happening to me'" (my translation).

Manifesting itself in various forms, then, sexuality is a pervasive force in Lispector's texts, which, as we have seen, are both compelling and mystifying "because they act out the tension between the subject and language, within which the subject is inserted."[22] Whether heterosexual,

homosexual, autoerotic, or androgynous in their characterizational focus, Lispector's texts seldom allow the reader to retreat for long from
the lubriciousness of language, from its capacity to stimulate, arouse,
and transform us. A text like *The Stream of Life* can, in this respect, even
be read as a verbal simulacrum of sexual ecstasy and orgasm, psychological and physiological functions that also relate to Lispector's alleg-
edly "mystical" orientation, to Cixous's concept of "l'écriture féminine,"
to Kristeva's "semiotic" and to the argument Barthes advances in *Le
plaiser du texte*, a theoretical commentary the major points of which
would seem to have prototypical embodiments in *The Stream of Life* as
in parts of *Near to the Wild Heart* and *The Passion according to G. H.*, three
of her greatest achievements. So while they take diverse forms, ranging
from masturbation to androgyny and from heterosexuality to homosexuality, the erotics of language and being that suffuse Lispector's texts
impart to them an intense, destabilizing, and often anguished humanity
that even knowledgeable readers of her work are prone to underappre-
ciate. Far from being tangential to her work, Lispector's psycholinguistic sense of sexuality is integral to it.

CHARACTERIZATIONS, RELATIONSHIPS, AND STATES OF BEING: FEMININE, MASCULINE, ANDROGYNOUS, AND NONGENDERED

Long felt by many to be a weak spot in Lispector's narrative art, her characterizations—when viewed from the critical perspective afforded us by poststructuralism—can actually be shown to rank among the most powerful, compelling, and surprising though it may at first seem, deeply humanizing aspects of her work. Indeed, one can argue that it is precisely through her diverse yet prototypical characters that Lispector succeeds in putting a human face on the often abstruse and, for some, even dehumanizing theories of poststructuralism. Crucial to this process are the ways her always language-grounded characters see themselves and the ways they deal with the relationships—with self and other—in which they evolve. As Lispector herself wrote in a *crônica* (24 July 1971), "The mystery of human relationships intrigues me" (*DW* 480).

Encompassing a surprisingly wide range of characters, whose identities engage such issues as gender, sexuality, age, race, class, and power, Lispector's narrative relationships feature women, men, God, androgynous beings, degendered (and sometimes seemingly autobiographical) voices, and animals who, for all their diversity and conflicts, have one feature in common: their identities (whether they are conscious of it or not) are, at bottom, language based. From a nameless presence like G. H. or the narrator of *The Stream of Life* to the pathetic and abandoned elderly "street-woman" of "Journey to Petrópolis," Lispector's characters come to life as functions—"structurations"—of language. This does not mean, as we shall see, that they lack sociopolitical significance or that they are somehow "excessively mystical";[1] only that, as literary creations in the poststructural mode, their most definitive problems of identity spring from out of the interminable play of language that defines them and from which they cannot escape. The familial relationships we see in *Family Ties*, for example, can thus be interpreted as simultaneously liberating (because of strong family ties we have the kind of support we need to become whatever we wish) and oppressive (because of the numbing weight of convention and stunting effects of sexism, ageism, and class consciousness these same family ties also impede us from becoming something "different").[2] And because such family ties are overwhelmingly functions of language, as is the concept of family itself, the paradoxically liberating and oppressive position they place us in parallels the endless semantic conundrums and paradoxes that, for poststructuralism, constitute the most defining feature of human existence. Although later of Lispector's characters—Martim, G. H., or the voices of *The Stream of Life* and *A Breath of Life*, for example—would more self-consciously present themselves as acutely sentient creatures whose essential identities were defined in and by language, this same linguistically circumscribed condition is, to varying degrees, characteristic of all her personages.

As suggested earlier, Lispector's characters show a greater diversity than even someone well-read in her work might at first think. For purposes of discussion, however, it is useful to divide them into five categories: her female characters (who constitute the largest group), her male characters, her androgynous characters, her nonhuman characters (supernatural beings and animals), and God. In nearly all cases, however, these characters develop in relation to what Derrida calls "the play of signifying references that constitute language" (*Of Grammatology* 7), the quicksilver verbal play that metamorphoses the various relationships existing not only between them but within them. The two polarities of Lispector's characterizational process, the economy of exchange that takes place between a fragmented and constantly mutating self and an uncertain other, typically coalesce to become a monologue rather than a dialogue, a site, as poststructuralists term it, where what used to be thought of as a single, stable "subject" is seen to lose its sense of control and of rational consciousness, to become, in short, what Lacan views as a "fiction" or a construct (*Écrits* 293–329).

Lispector deserves the recognition she has received for the inventiveness, imagination, and intensity that she brings to her female creations. Although the majority of Lispector's female characters are middle-aged and middle- to upper-class Brazilians, and although (as Giovanni Pontiero has noted) they are often best understood as "states of mind,"[3] there are several notable exceptions, including the fifteen-year-old girl of "Preciousness," the homeless old woman of "Journey to Petrópolis," the old and violent matriarch of "Happy Birthday," the aged widow of "Footsteps" (who resorts to masturbation to alleviate her sexual torment), the sixty-year-old woman of "But It's Going to Rain" (who, in one of Lispector's best comic tales, takes—"buys"—a nineteen-year-old boy as a lover), and finally, Macabéa, the tragically disadvantaged protagonist of one of Lispector's greatest achievements, *The Hour of the Star.*

In virtually all her female characters, however, from the early ones (like Laura, of "The Imitation of the Rose," whom "pleasure" made "blush") to the late ones (like Macabéa and the presences in *A Breath of Life*), a powerful though repressed erotic impulse, structured by means of a poetically rendered psychosexual sensitivity to language, is the animating force. In reading these narratives carefully, however, one is not led to assert confidently that they express either an exclusively female ontology or an overt sexuality; rather, one comes away feeling that while they are compelling and, at times, brilliant portraits of particular women (who may, nevertheless, as in the case of Laura or Macabéa, be regarded in some sense as social types), the sexual aspects of their characterizations often seem less exclusively female than human, a kind of "fe/male" pansexuality that, however it becomes shaped, or gendered, by social forces, can be viewed as another view of the all-inclusive eroticism that permeates Lispector's work.

One especially revealing example of how social roles define (and also frustrate) this basic human urge is, again, that of Laura, whose severely restricting and preestablished role as the model housewife (and, potentially at least, mother)[4] neuters her development both sexually (by forcing her to exist only in terms of a monogamous heterosexuality) and socially (her identity exists only in terms of her status as the perfect middle-class wife). Beyond these two modes of existence, as the surface discourse of this calm, smooth text tells us, Laura has no real place in the world, no options that are hers to take. The question of her "madness" can therefore be seen in terms of its constituting a very complex semiotic sign, one that involves the crushing defeat of her more passionate but as yet silenced inner world (the world of her desires) by the weight of propriety and convention.

The great decentering or "deconstructive" subtext in this narrative is therefore the sexual attraction that may exist between Laura and Carlota, her more self-assured friend. The relationship that exists between Laura and Carlota, indeed, is perhaps the most fascinating of the entire story, which, as Diane Marting has observed, develops around a tangle of human relationships and the commitments they entail (Marting, *Clarice Lispector: A Bio-Bibliography*, 58–59). Subtle and multifaceted, the relationship between Laura and Carlota can, for example, be read as merely a matter of social etiquette (they are both middle-class wives who, along with their husbands, are about to have dinner together), as a psychological presentation of two friends with very different personalities (one, Carlota, is dominant while the other, Laura, is passive), or as a psychosexual portrait of two married women whose interest in each other may transcend the ordinary and the acceptable. But whether it is sexual or not, the relationship between Laura, the story's protagonist, and her friend, Carlota, certainly serves to underscore the more basic conflict between order (perfection, Logos) and chaos that infuses the story. Anticipating the dinner she and her husband, Armando, will enjoy later that evening with Carlota and her husband, Laura, as early as the story's second paragraph, begins to think about how dinner will go—an event she conceives of almost entirely in terms of her relationship with Carlota:

> [S]he would talk to Carlota about women's things, submissive to the authoritarian and practical goodness of Carlota, receiving once more her friend's attention and vague disdain, her natural abruptness, instead of that perplexed affection full of curiosity—watching Armando, finally oblivious of his own wife. (FT 54)

So although it is clear that Laura will talk with (not to) Carlota about "women's things," it is also certain that she sees herself as "submissive" to her friend, a reference suggestive of an as yet unexplored aspect of their relationship. Initially emphasizing what can be taken as the socially conventional part of their friendship, however, this scene, coming at the very outset of the story, then expands (some two pages later) into an intimate consideration of the differences between the two women:

> The reactions of the two women had always been different. Carlota, ambitious and laughing heartily; Laura, a little slow, and virtually always taking care to be slow. Carlota, seeing danger in nothing; and Laura ever cautious. (55)

With Laura and her "horror of disorder" (55) or confusion, and her passion for order and routine (55–56) representing what we might think of as the structuralist worldview, and Carlota, who is not bothered by "confusion" and who (described in basically male terms) defies established norms and codes of conduct, representing a kind of subconsciously poststructural mode of being, the nuanced story of Laura and Carlota continues to evolve, becoming, in fact, the story's sexually charged subplot, the tension of which, building on the interplay of desire and frustration, parallels Laura's larger relationship to the world around her. We learn, for example, in a brilliant moment of Lispector's famous "style indirecte libre," what Laura would do if ever her "friend" were threatened:

> Not that Carlota had given cause for any scandal, although Laura, were she given the opportunity, would hotly defend her, but the opportunity had never arisen. She, Laura, was obliged reluctantly to agree that her friend had a strange and amusing manner of treating her husband. (61)

What is surprising in this scene is the revelation that passive, ostensibly very proper Laura is prepared not just to defend Carlota (as a "friend" might be expected to do) but to defend her "ardently," as, perhaps, a lover would.

The submerged sexual tension that, potentially at least, animates the relationship between the two women seemingly intensifies two pages later, reaching its maximum, though still oblique, expression. Coinciding structurally with the surface story's turning point (Laura's phenomenological "discovery" of the "perfect" roses), Laura suddenly has "an idea which was in some way highly original" (62), a reference that catches the reader's attention because the same adjective, "original," had been used earlier by Laura to describe Carlota herself; Laura, we now learn, will send the roses to Carlota "de presente" ("Laços de família" 46), as a gift. This thought, which gives Laura intense pleasure and satisfaction, immediately generates an imaginary scene in which Laura is clearly anxious to please Carlota with her gift, one that, given the traditional symbolism of red roses (passionate love, beauty, perfection), functions semiotically as a barely restrained expression of the love or passion Laura "ardently" feels for Carlota, a love or passion she cannot openly express. Such a reading of the roses (that, in sublimated fashion, their giving represents the consummation of the sexual act) allows us to interpret them as the symbol of Laura's passion for Carlota and all that Carlota represents: strength, confidence, daring, unconventionality; in short, a kind of being different from her own and capable of fulfilling her as yet inchoate desires.

Such an interpretation would also explain why the impulsiveness of Laura's decision to give Carlota the roses is so stressed. Laura, for example, imagines herself saying to Carlota, "Oh, no! no! It is not because of the invitation to dinner! It is because the roses are so lovely that

I felt the impulse to give them to you! Yes, if . . . she had the courage, that was exactly what she would say" (FT 63). Both the unexpectedness of Laura's idea and her fantasy-like embracing of it lead one to speculate whether Laura's desire to give Carlota a gift of roses is not a "Freudian slip," the loosing of an unexpected welling up of a sexual desire long-repressed but, once uttered, now "ardently" desired. If so, it would be consistent, seemingly, with the reaction to her overture that Laura imagines (hopes?) Carlota will have:

> And Carlota would be surprised at the delicacy of Laura's sentiments—no one would imagine that Laura, too, had her ideas. (63)

This last clause, with its key final word, is telling, as is the fact that the entire scene is imagined by Laura to be "pleasurable" (63). Although a prototypical example of how Lispector cultivates an artfully poised ambiguity in her work, this line also strongly suggests something like a climax in terms of Laura's relationship to Carlota. Having already imagined that, on accepting the roses (and all that act would imply), Carlota will say that such things are not necessary between them, the "narration from within" that gets the reader inside Laura's mind to "overhear" the free flow of language through it leads one to wonder whether Laura's "ideas," or "ideiazinhas" (which no one except Carlota would imagine poor, timid Laura had), are not the passionate fantasies she secretly harbors for Carlota? That they are seems a quite plausible interpretation of this justly famous story.

The final piece in the interpretive puzzle surrounding the relationship between Laura and Carlota is the intense self-interrogation that Laura engages in immediately after articulating the idea (wish fulfillment?) of giving the roses to Carlota not because of the invitation to dinner but in full recognition of the fact that she simply had to do so, that the roses possessed such extreme beauty that she could not resist the perhaps erotically driven impulse to give them to her:

> And also because that extreme beauty disturbed her. Disturbed her? It was a risk. Oh! no, why a risk? It merely disturbed her; they were a warning. Oh! no, why a warning? (62)

If one reads "beauty" as also meaning "love" (an interpretation justified by the traditional symbolism of the rose), then it requires no great distortion of the text to speculate that the "extreme beauty" that so attracts Laura would, given the conventions of her status as a middle-class wife, also "disturb" her. Struggling, in this climactic scene, to accommodate her conflicting impulses, Laura senses that her desire to send the roses to Carlota constitutes both "a risk" and "a warning."

The word "warning" is wonderfully apropos of Lispector's exceptional ability to develop a scene (in this case, a very complex and perhaps sexually repressed human relationship) by means of ambiguity, by employing a diction and a syntax that make a number of different interpretations simultaneously viable. Although the Portuguese term *advertência* can, indeed, be translated into English as "warning," it could (in a less vernacular mode) also be "advertence," which, reflecting its Latinate roots, implies "giving attention" to or—in a way especially significant for the love between Laura and Carlota that may be expressing itself here—"heedful of." Thus, the single word *advertência*/"warning" conveys both the sense of danger that Laura feels about her intentions and the exhilarating sense of excitement and recognition that she derives from them. It is this psychosexual tangle of desire and fear, of "extreme beauty," the destabilizing force of love, and the act of risking both personal rejection and social condemnation by heeding her burgeoning passions, that is then woven into the similarly ambiguous but crucial term *ideiazinhas*, a diminutive that possesses a multitude of meanings, one of which, in this context, could well be that Laura might feel herself attracted to Carlota not only as a friend but as a lover.

But whether realized, imagined, or desired, the (perhaps) sexually charged relationship between Laura and Carlota comes to an end at this point, with Laura, her passion for Carlota and the roses receding, casting herself once again as "Laura, the one with the real lace collar, dressed discreetly, the wife of Armando, . . . who no longer needed to think about his wife" (63). As she loses her nerve, and as she vacillates wildly over whether she should follow through on her urge to present Carlota with the roses or keep them herself (attracted as she is to their Christlike perfection), Laura feels herself becoming increasingly undone, a pathetic creature caught between the demands of both propriety and desire:

> She looked at them, so mute in her hand. Impersonal in their extreme beauty. In their extreme and perfect tranquility as roses. . . . Vacantly, sorrowfully, she watched them, distant as they were at the end of her outstretched arm—and her mouth became even dryer, parched by that envy and desire. (67)

At this point, Laura's maid, Maria, takes the roses from her (with part of her still wanting to call Maria back and thus prevent her, superego-like, from delivering the roses to Carlota) and proceeds, presumably, to deliver them to Carlota, whose real reaction to getting them is unknown as the story of Laura and Carlota and their relationship ends inconclusively. By interweaving Laura's seduction by the "tempting perfection of the roses" (67) with the perfection symbolized by Christ (who, she believes, "was the worst temptation" (55), and with both of these temptations linked to her possibly psychosexual attraction to the dominant and more self-assured Carlota (whose feelings toward Laura are concealed from the reader, except insofar as Laura interprets or fantasizes about them), Lispector deftly embeds the mysterious story of Laura and Carlota in the larger story, which can be summed up as Laura's self-destructive quest for perfection (the word "perfection" emerges as a basic motif of the story) in a highly imperfect world.

A final, poignant irony is struck when Laura, late in the story, decides to imitate the roses: "she tried for an instant to imitate the roses deep down inside herself. It was not even difficult" (69). The result is that, in achieving "perfection," she finds herself totally isolated from everyone else around her, everyone, that is, except perhaps Carlota, whose presence, like the roses (and the passionate love they symbolize), was still keenly, if problematically, felt:

> In her heart, that one rose, which at least she could have taken for herself without prejudicing anyone in the world, was gone. Like something missing. . . . An absence that flooded into her like a light. (68–69)

The final step in this particular reading of what could be considered the epitome of the kind of small-scale human tragedy Lispector specializes in would be that after Laura overcomes her timidity and debilitating self-denial and actually sees the roses sent to Carlota, she then falls prey to a self-induced isolation, one that, generated, ironically, by the roses/Christ/perfection/beauty/love amalgam, may or may not be overcome—by Laura or by Carlota, should the latter respond as Laura seemingly hopes she will (that she accept the "warning," that is, Laura's offering of the roses, and that she respond as desired to her *ideiazinhas*). This interpretation receives one additional bit of credence in that, at just this moment, her husband looks at her and finds himself "mortified by his wife's shamelessness as she sat there unburdened and serene" (71).[5] The reader wonders whether Armando's curious reaction implies that he has long suspected some sort of attraction between the two women and that now, when Laura has seemingly acted on it (and for that reason is "serene" because she has now "unburdened" herself by releasing her long pent-up and, for Armando, "shameless" desires concerning Carlota), he is "mortified." But in the story's final line, with Laura depicted, via a striking metaphor, as being "once more alert and tranquil as if on a train. A train that had already departed" (72), the text itself offers no definitive clue; ambiguity, at all levels of signification, reigns supreme, and the relationship between Laura and Carlota, the compelling subtext of the story, remains a suggestive mystery.

Because Lispector's middle-aged and middle-class women characters are often portrayed as being trapped in unhappy marriages (where satisfaction, whether psychological, sociopolitical, economic, or sexual, is rarely forthcoming), it is not surprising that their stories often read as indictments of marriage as an institution, as a politically signifying act mandated by social convention, and not (necessarily) as a loving human relationship. This interpretation would certainly apply to the unnamed woman in the early short story "Flight," and to the prototypical case of Joana in Lispector's first novel (*Near to the Wild Heart*), but it would also be valid for the presentations of the female characters in several of Lispector's later works, including *The Apple in the Dark* (where Vitória and Ermelinda have a relationship that, recalling D. H. Lawrence's novel *The Fox*, could be read as paralleling the Carlota/Laura relationship), *An Apprenticeship, or The Book of Delights*, "Plaza Mauá" (where Luisa the housewife finds sexual and economic fulfillment only when she transforms herself into Carla, an exotic dancer at a Rio sex club), and the gender role–reversing females of "O relatório da coisa" and "Life *au Naturel*." Of these texts, however, only *An Apprenticeship* presents the female character as seeming to have real prospects of finding satisfaction and fulfillment within the confines of marriage, which, as a social, legal, and psychological structure (one built, however, on certain words defined in certain ways), generates its own conflicting set of "family ties." Yet just as the term marriage comes, potentially, at least to mean something new in *An Apprenticeship*,[6] so, too, does it reveal its inherent potential for the abuse of power both within the relationship and without, as the repressive forces of society are shown to be aligning themselves in opposition to the "freer," more "honest" and "equal" ways the man (Ulisses) and woman (Lóri) want to live.

In certain ways, however, Lóri (the female protagonist and the character who commands the reader's attention) can be interpreted initially as being a fairly conventional type, an intelligent and sexually active (but unfulfilled) young woman who "finds herself" only by pairing off with a mentorlike man, Ulisses. From a poststructural perspective, several destabilizing tensions arise from out of this text, one unique in all Lispector's work:[7] Lóri, for example, does, in fact, go to Ulisses (though only when *she* is "ready," when *she* chooses to do so), which, for all her (and Ulisses's) talk about how they could really "come together" only when each had become sufficiently unshackled so as to be able to make such a choice "freely," leads the reader to wonder if the barrage of high-sounding words laid down (chiefly) by Ulisses (a philosophy professor) doesn't end up further ensnaring both Ulisses and Lóri rather than liberating them. Do the very words they use to emancipate themselves end up deceiving and misleading them as they do with so many of Lispector's characters? Or do their words (Ulisses's words primarily) truly free them? And, as a female character, how does Lóri compare to a Joana, a G. H., or an Ângela Pralini?

An even more revealing comparison exists between Lóri and the middle-aged couple in "The Obedient Ones," a story published in 1964, five years before *An Apprenticeship* appeared. While Lóri, whatever her justification may be, opts for a kind of sanctioned security (the sanctioning stemming not from the legal status of marriage but from the idealistic verbal relationship she and Ulisses have built up through their [his?] discourse), the unnamed woman and man of the earlier story both indict the stifling weight of the vast phallogocentric system that manipulates their lives by expressing what is basically a destabilizing worldview. She, for example, declares, "Each thing appeared to be the sign of something else, everything was symbolic" ("Obedient" 85), while he—also a victim of this perverse system—feels himself similarly trapped by a maze of signs and symbols he cannot understand and by the "anguished masculinity" (85) of his existence. Thus, if what this man and woman have come to realize—that we live in a language-structured world in which everything is merely "the sign of something else"—then even what appears to be the self-liberating and scrupulously careful language use of Lóri and (especially) Ulisses turns out to be just another cell in the prison house of language. If this is so, however, it would be a cell that the later female voice of *The Stream of Life*, the most complete expression of Lispector's poststructural worldview, would transform into a universe that is at once linguistically driven and both infinitely expanding and infinitely contracting. We can therefore understand the *texte* that is *The Stream of Life* to be the epitome of Derrida's "différance," the force of semantic "difference" or "deferral," inherent in all language use, that functions as a counterbalance to the false security of the logocentrism that so many of Lispector's characters unknowingly seek.

In summary, then, at least three qualities typify Lispector's female characters. First, they constitute by far her largest single category of characters. This does not necessarily mean, however, that we should label Lispector a "feminist" writer ("feminist" being a term—a label—she did not use to describe herself),[8] for there are grounds for arguing that Lispector's extensive use of women characters does not so much reflect a feminist ideology as a subject matter that she personally—and imaginatively—knew best, a point that is not, of course, inconsistent with one of feminism's most powerful defining principles. A second key feature of Lispector's numerous female characters is that they reflect a considerable variety in terms of age, social class, strength (some, like Joana, are determined and aggressive; others, like Ana [of "Love"], are timorous), and sexuality (which pulsates as a powerfully self-affirming—and constantly decentering—force in her strongest characters). The full range of Lispector's female creations becomes apparent only after reading her stories, where a greater diversity is achieved. Third, Lispector's females are nearly always cast in terms of being in flux, caught in the throes of a fluctuating and unsatisfactory relationship. Although this relationship typically involves another person (male or female), it nevertheless never avoids a continual confrontation with self, or with the manifold aspects of one's being, the latter an issue that comes to the fore in her most seminal works. It is in this relational context (with both other and self) that the word "love" should be approached in Lispector's work. Undercutting and decentering conventional ideas about what is "properly" romantic, amorous, or erotic in a relationship, the word "love" (often presented in terms of its "other," "hate") appears time after time in Lispector's texts as an ontological problem peculiar to human beings, as a sounding of how language use and variations in meaning affect and effect our existences. Far from being merely a question of highly stylized characterizations, Lispector's female characters make us realize, viscerally and intellectually, the extent to which it is language that, at every moment (the "moment" being yet another key motif of her work), shapes and transforms our identities.

In many ways, G. H., the female protagonist of Lispector's fifth novel, *The Passion according to G. H.* (1964), can also be read as an essentially language-defined character. Wealthy, privileged, and (the sociopolitical implications of her mysterious inner "experience" aside) very bourgeois, G. H. is not a character one can warm to easily. Yet regardless of how the reader feels about her, G. H. and her text, as we shall see, embody the poststructural condition. Epitomizing the basic conflict between the binary ordering so characteristic of structuralism and the anarchic disorder we associate with poststructuralism, part of G. H.'s sense of identity seeks order and stable form while another part questions this very desire. As G. H. herself expresses it:

> I've always liked putting things in their places. I think it's my only true calling. By ordering things I create and understand at the same time. . . . Ordering is finding the best form. . . . Ordered form itself? (*Passion* 25)

Yet as G. H. relates her story, which is her attempt to understand the epiphany-like experience she has undergone, the reader begins to see another G. H., one not canceled out by the first and who has begun to confront the fundamental mutability of the universe—and who has consequently begun to deal with our human desire for order and control and the diversity and riot of existence, a chaos that undermines our wish to control it:

> I'm terrified of that profound disorganization. . . . Am I disorganized because I have lost something I didn't even need? . . . Up to now, finding myself was having a ready-made person-idea and mounting myself inside it: I incarnated myself inside that set-up person and didn't even sense the great construction project that living was. The person-idea that I had came from that third leg of mine, the one that held me fast to the ground. But now . . . will I be freer? (3–4)

Having now lost the enslaving dependency, the "third leg" of her being, G. H. goes on to declare (of her newly discovered sense of being):

> If I'm brave, I'll let myself stay lost. But . . . I always want the guarantee of at least thinking that I understand, I don't know how to just give myself over to disorientation. How do I explain that my greatest fear is precisely in relation to . . . to being? (4–5)

Wrestling with the central ontological dilemma posed by poststructural thought—how should one live one's life when the very nature of existence seems to deny our efforts to control it?—G. H. then declares:

> And my struggle against that disintegration is just that: is just trying to give it a form. A form gives contours to chaos, gives a construct to amorphous substance. (6)

This line of poetically tangled, inner rumination, dealing, as it does, with the language-based and closely interrelated issues of truth, meaning, personal identity, and doubt, inexorably develops G. H. as a deeply human poststructural hero, a radical, acutely self-conscious and self-questioning skeptic whose development as a character is marked by her growing consciousness of the role language plays in life and, as a consequence of this, her learning to question and challenge established, conventional verities. G. H. is thus seen to be in quest of what she sees, metaphorically and linguistically, in the remains of the crushed cockroach: "what I saw was life looking back at me" (49), she declares, seeking now, in the "horrible, brute raw matter," the "dry plasma," and the ancient "mud" of prehuman existence, "the roots of my identity" (49).

But, the reader wonders, of what does this "raw matter," this primitive "life," really consist? Are we really to understand it as the sacred "mud" of a more pure time, or even as the protoplasm that oozes from the roach's body (and that, as living matter, links G. H. to primordial life)? Although the text certainly presents these readings as being plausible, a more satisfying interpretation might be that the "raw matter," the "mud," and the "life" referred to here are metaphors for language, for the various processes of signification by which human beings define themselves (by establishing their various identities) and, by naming things and thereby differentiating them within the "raw matter," attempt to impose order, form, and meaning on the ambiguity of existence. Such an interpretation of these images would be consistent with what we can regard as Lispector's most basic theme, the role language (the sacred "mud" of existence, its real "raw matter") plays in the ebb and flow of our identities. As a character, G. H., whose existence is otherwise (that is, in conventional terms) as empty as the charcoal sketches she discovers in her maid's quarters, exists by, through, and in language; G. H., whose narrative epitomizes the poststructural malaise, not only lives language, she is language. Further, it is precisely her claustrophobic but ultimately unresolved quest to "understand," to possess Logos itself (a quest that, as the text makes clear, takes place entirely within the context of language), that marks her as a poststructural character. One of Lispector's most complex creations, G. H. represents, however, only one of the Brazilian author's many characters who seek, in diverse ways, to come to grips with the simultaneously stabilizing and destabilizing force that language exerts on human existence and reality.

Although numerically fewer in number, Lispector's male characters are often powerful, if pathetic, creations. With only a few exceptions (the boy in "The Message" and in "The First Kiss," the man in "The Obedient Ones," and Ulisses, for example), Lispector's male characters fail to connect with the kind of boundary-blurring and poetically expansive language use that animates her most memorable female characters. A consequence, perhaps, of Lispector's sensitivity to the affective interplay of language, gender, and being, this failure gains a poignant human face in characters like Otávio (from *Near to the Wild Heart*); Antônio (the husband in "Family Ties"); the husbands of "Obsession," "Flight," and "Beauty and the Beast, or The Wound Too Great"; and Martim (of *The Apple in the Dark*). While these characters vary in regard to the extent to which they are actively present in their texts (Otávio and Martim being crucial to theirs while the husbands are hardly there at all except as symbols of a particular sociopolitical institution), what they have in common is a curious but well-known paradox: although highly "trained" (Otávio is a lawyer; Martim an engineer), these men are nevertheless "ignorant," lacking in the awareness of the relationship between language (they are instead possessed of an overweening faith in stability, epistemological certainty, clear distinctions, and hierarchies—in a word, Logos) and being that would allow them to deal with the vagaries of the relationships that envelop them and that elude their best efforts to control and determine them.[9]

Different though it is in regard to the issue of power, the case of Otávio, the male figure in the love triangle that dominates and shapes the novel, embodies the phallogocentric order. A man who seeks "[t]he consolation of Order" (*Heart* 115), Otávio is writing a book on civil law in order "to get away from that horrible world, so repugnantly intimate and human" (79), a shifting verbal world personified by Joana, who creates new realities by inventing words (like "lalande") and by using old ones in new combinations. For Joana, a poststructural protagonist who succeeds, via her "intimate and human" relationship to language, in constantly re-creating herself, her growth—her self-emancipation from all that Otávio represents—made it natural for her to desire to go beyond "that zone where things have a set form and edges, where everything has a solid and immutable name" (179), the world, in short, represented by Otávio. Increasingly, the reader learns, Joana "sank into that fluid region, quiescent and unfathomable, where clouds hovered, indistinct and fresh like those of dawn" (179), because for her, like "an embryo that remained moist amidst the parched and burning rocks" (181), "words are pebbles rolling in the river" (179).

But in keeping with the poststructural ethos that pervades this work, Lispector does not present Joana and Otávio as being "binarily" opposed as characters; rather, each gains in complexity because each recognizes in the other (though not necessarily in equal or static proportion) something of value, something that is desired. Though in profound and irrevocable conflict with each other, they are not diametrically opposed; indeed, they are attracted to certain qualities possessed by the other. Thus, Joana appreciates (at the same time that she loathes) the power that Otávio wields and has access to, while Otávio, for his part, desires (but also fears) the lethal potency of Joana. It is worth noting, moreover, that although both Otávio (the upholder of the legal code) and Joana (the self-liberating verbal anarchist) possess the same words, they understand them in radically different ways. While Otávio fears and is repelled by what he correctly senses as the inherent anarchy of language (a condition he cannot abide), Joana ardently embraces it, sensing in it the key to the creation, the birthing, of her own multiple identities—this in contrast to the single identity that Otávio and all he represents would impose on her. Thus, the fundamental difference between them has to do with how each relates to language, whether it is understood as a phallogocentric system that makes clear distinctions between things and that maintains the established power structure (Otávio) or one that exposes the fluidity and arbitrariness of our lives and the conventions that govern them (Joana).

An additional, and very important, decentering element in this affair is the relationship between the fecund, sensuous Lídia, whose "ample" breasts are "solemn, restful and pale" and in whose belly "there is even room for a child" (133), and Joana, whose "impoverished" being/body can only boast of breasts that are "futile" and who has misgivings about becoming pregnant (144). Had she been a more orthodox writer, it would have been easy for Lispector to develop some clear bond of solidarity between these two "marginalized" (by virtue of being women in a sexist society) women, but she does not do this. Rather, even though the text makes it clear that while they are "two women" who "could form an alliance and provide for humanity," "a child may be born in the womb of all women" (133), Lispector's text implies that it is not biology but language that determines gender, a point that, in a variety of ways, she uses to explore the concept of androgynous or nongendered being. Moreover, as the enigmatic scene between Joana and Lídia implies, the differences between individual women in terms of their psychological and sociopolitical identities are often as great as those that separate men like Otávio from women like Joana.

Summing up their complex relationship, Joana thinks (to herself): "I am a feathered creature. Lídia is covered in hair and Otávio is lost between us, defenseless" (133). Although the text has highlighted the differences between these two women (one embodying the stereotype of woman in a very phallogocentric society, the other in rebellion against it) and brought into sharp relief the nature of the conflict between them (power, its source, utilization, and consequences), it also shows Otávio, deceived and trapped by the speciousness of the phallogocentric system he represents, as being pathetic and "impotent," "lost" and "defenseless" between the very different powers possessed by the two women. For Lídia, this power is sexuality, which leads to control of Otávio via the highly structured sex and gender roles of their culture (he could easily keep Lídia as his mistress); for Joana, it is an intellectual and emotional power that grows and evolves through its linguistic fecundity. While Lídia exists chiefly through her body and all it represents to Otávio's culture, Joana lives through both her body and her language, with, indeed, the latter coming to expand her consciousness of the former.

Deftly combining a desire for both female sexual pleasure and female power[10] with the issues of birth and motherhood, Joana both complicates the nature of her character (which is the source of the text's power) and exposes, metaphorically, the lot of women in an androcentric society:

> Do you think I'm sterile? Not one little bit. I haven't had any children because I didn't want them.
>
> I can feel myself holding a child, Joana thought. . . . But after I've given him milk from these delicate and attractive breasts [the change in the way Joana describes her breasts is crucial to charting her psychosexual evolution], my child will thrive on my strength and crush me with his life. (144)

Then, in a devastating critique not only of the nature of motherhood in such a system but of the role of power in human existence in general, Joana concludes, discoursing on the future of her imaginary child and on the nature of their relationship, "He will distance himself from me and I shall become his useless old mother. I won't feel cheated. But simply defeated" (144). As this last scene's final line—"I shall utter no other word for truth will bring comfort to my arms" (145)—suggests, however, Joana's tormented but now resolute being is, at bottom, a function of the arbitrary and ephemeral linkage between the "word" (Logos) and "truth." If Lídia epitomizes the power of sexuality as inscribed within the possibilities and constraints allowed by androcentric society (that is, her sexuality derives from her bodily presence and is permissible only in terms of her role as a mistress), Joana, the epitome of a militant "différance," exudes another kind of power, the "plaisir du texte," as Barthes might say, the pleasure of language itself.

Prefiguring the Laura/Carlota relationship of "Family Ties," the potential attraction between Joana and Lídia, which the reader is apprised of almost entirely through the perspective of Joana alone, is neither complete nor perfect. Yet, at least in terms of Joana and her desires, it is a constant presence in the text, animating it at several key points and expanding its range of semantic possibilities. For example, with Lídia's "nascent pregnancy" now "penetrating" her, Joana has become keenly aware of Lídia as a "beautiful woman," one possessed of the full, sensuous lips "of someone who is not afraid of pleasure, who receives it and without remorse" (130–31). Comparing herself, bodily as well as psychologically, to her rival, Joana then muses about the "power" an "alliance" between the two women might have, an alliance that, as seen from the reader's perspective at this point in Joana's disquisition on her relationship with Lídia (who is described primarily in physical terms), might easily involve a sexual dimension, one that would not necessarily have anything to do with love, however. The potential for such a sexual liaison is further developed when Joana, entering, seemingly, into a psychological state of free association, sees herself wanting to spend time watching Lídia and being with her in intimate surroundings. "Was this," Joana asks herself, perhaps unconsciously merging her desire to be nurtured with her sexual desire, "what had always been missing in my life?" (137). Then, imbuing this already suggestive question with even more of a sexual charge, Joana, thinking of Lídia, asks herself, "Why is she so powerful?" (137). Joana then proceeds, albeit indirectly, to answer her own question, but to do so in such a way as to further sexualize the entire fantasy-like image that is developing in her subconscious mind: "I want . . . a woman who is ugly but wholesome with large breasts. . . . A woman who will give me a warm bath, dress me in a white linen nightdress, braid my hair and put me to bed" (137). The psychoanalytic overtones of this brilliant and compelling scene are hard to ignore, with the crucial issue being that Joana, in a revealing moment of gender transference, could be interpreted to be making sexually driven references to her absent mother, or to a female mother figure.

The potential for a sexual relationship between Joana and Lídia is also suggested in a later passage when Joana, denouncing the boredom of married life by striking yet another powerfully suggestive sexual metaphor (that of two people "eating the same tasteless bread day after day" and seeing their "frustration" mirrored in their partner's habits), seems to imply that she is now ready, psychologically speaking, to seek out something different, perhaps even a sexual experience involving Lídia or some other woman "with large breasts" who will both "put Joana to bed" and satisfy her sexually and provide her with the mothering that has been lacking in her life.[11]

But if, in contrast to Joana, Otávio, the prototype of one of Lispector's two main categories of male characters, chooses to continue clinging to the chimera of authority, legitimacy, and control that his privileged position affords him, then Martim, whom Gregory Rabassa describes as "a perfect antihero" (*Apple* xii), represents her other category, the one in which men either reject authority and power or misperceive and mishandle them, both these avenues being, again, functions of language. Referring to Martim, for example, Rabassa notes that "he hopes for some kind of regeneration as he loses language. . . . He wants language, but he also rejects the form in which he has known it. His struggle for language is one symbolic track of the futility of his rebirth and rebuilding as he goes back to what he had before" (xiii–xiv). A dense, lyrically structured text[12] that, through its endlessly self-referential meditations on language, knowing, and being, features "a story with no sure future, no definitive accomplishments, with everything still doubtful at the end for all the characters concerned" (xiii), *The Apple in the Dark* can, in a sense, be read as an extended metaphor of the tensions that exist, not infrequently in a comic mode,[13] between structuralism and its controversial progeny, poststructuralism. By this interpretation, Martim, in his rather muddled desire for language (more precisely, his vague desire for what a perfect language would be able to do) and his equally confused desire to reject the forms (the structures) through which he had previously known it (language in its binary structural sense), comes to epitomize the poststructural condition, one in which a great malaise, stemming from his becoming engulfed in the semantic and self-referential flow of language, has rendered him hopelessly entangled (a "prisoner of a ring of words"; 37) and incapable of decisive action. Like Ana, of "Love," Martim, having once rejected it, seeks to return to the security and stability meted out by the tightly structured phallocentric world, one characterized by the insurmountable operation of a vast, all-encompassing system in which everyone is given (via its hierarchical structures) a place, a role, and an identity. Lispector opts here for an obvious displacement of gender-based power roles (another manifestation of her penchant for reversing and reinscribing binary oppositions) in that she creates a character, a man and a therefore privileged member of the hierarchy, who, though semicognizant about experiencing the ontological vicissitudes of language, proves unable to regenerate, or "rebirth," himself through it. It is on this point that we feel the great gulf that separates a male character like Martim (or, for different reasons, Otávio) from a female character like Joana (or from a host of other Lispectorian characters, including G. H., Rodrigo S. M., and the voices of *The Stream of Life* and *A Breath of Life*).

An alternative approach to this issue can be found in a number of Lispector's texts, however, exemplary among which are "The Message," "The First Kiss," *An Apprenticeship, or The Book of Delights*, and *The Hour of the Star*. In the first three works, there is a sustained linguistic interaction between the female and male characters. I say "linguistic interaction" instead of "communication" because it is precisely this concept that is at issue. Does an exchange of language (speech, in the sense that we understand dialogue as "spoken" language) necessarily result in "communication"? Lispector's texts almost inevitably lead the reader to answer this question negatively; indeed, after moving us to question what we mean when we use the term "communication," her texts then show us that it can never have a single, stable meaning, that, in fact, the word "meaning" itself gains and loses semantic significance only in terms of other words that are, in terms of their meanings, inherently in flux, whether spoken (as in dialogue, of which there is relatively little in Lispector's world) or written. The written word is, for Lispector as for Derrida, the more primal, the more complex, the more compelling form of expression. Moreover, because Lispector's major texts are, even works like *The Stream of Life* and *The Hour of the Star* that ostensibly "shout" to us,[14] overwhelmingly texts in which written language predominates, they are best approached as being poetic and philosophical discourses on writing and being. Thus, as we see in such texts as "The Message" and "The First Kiss," this issue involves not the issue of whether there is or is not "communication" between the characters (male and female) but how one word relates to those that came before it and that will come after, their syntax, punctuation, structuring, and semantics underscoring what Derrida has in mind when he speaks of "différance," "supplément," and "dissemination" as natural but unavoidable aspects of even ordinary language use.

As Christine Froula has shown (Froula 197–220), the issue of gender plays a prominent role in "The Message," a 1964 text (first appearing in *The Foreign Legion*) that must certainly rank among Lispector's greatest achievements in the short fiction form. Although it seems quite likely true, as Froula suggests, that the boy of the story does indeed gain admittance to the culture symbolized by his father (while the girl does not), one also senses in this opaque, uncertain tale perhaps the most powerful single presentation of the case for androgynous or nongendered being that Lispector ever made. A close reading of "The Message," as we shall now see, reveals no fewer than six separate yet organically linked representations of this issue.

Employing an image (that of mixed genders) that will echo throughout the narrative and that will literally tie the end of the story to its beginning (the presence of the mother), the text describes the boy in terms that, at the outset of the tale, evince the gender-blurring ethos we associate with the more explicitly developed presentation of androgyny that occurs later on in the tale: "he who from a woman's heart had received no more than a maternal kiss" (*FL* 31). Surprised that only with this girl could he finally talk about things that really matter, the boy (whose seemingly open-minded and still gender-free acceptance of the girl is subtly destabilized by the power that is implicit in his decision about how to treat her) "began treating her as a comrade" (31).

At this point, the narrative broaches the theme of androgyny a second time; this mention is much more explicit than the first and seems, for this reason, a definite marker of the issue's role in this story. Speaking at first of her alone as "a new sex" (31), the narrative then, in the same sentence, expands this now sexually charged frame of reference to include both the girl and the boy, each of whom is seeking out the other:

> Hybrids—who so far had not chosen a personal life-style, who so far had not acquired any distinctive handwriting and took notes in class with a different lettering each day—Hybrids, they searched out each other. (31–32)

If one reads the clause "who so far had not acquired any distinctive handwriting" as an image suggesting that neither the boy nor the girl (both of whom, at this point in the narrative, are presented as "comrades," even having entered into a mysterious "pact"; 35) as yet possesses a separate, individualized, differentiating identity (a "definitive calligraphy," a "distinctive handwriting"; 31), one can then interpret the remainder of this metaphor (that they "took notes in class with a different lettering each day") as suggesting that, being "hybrids," the boy and the girl presented different identities ("different lettering") to the daily routine of life ("class"). Deftly linking language (and specifically the act of writing, their "distinctive handwriting") to being, Lispector merges here her great theme, the ontological centrality of language to human existence, with another great concern of hers, the extent to which language determines our identities, including, as we see so trenchantly rendered in this particular narrative, the psychological, sexual, and cultural implications of gender.

Struggling from this point on to hold fast to their "hybrid" identities in the face of the growing pressure to conform that "the *others*" [15] exert on them, the boy (who is sixteen) and the girl (who is seventeen) are both in conflict with what society demands a "man" and a "woman" to be. The fact that she is older than he functions as an additional destabilizing force in the orthodox power structure of their relationship, which, as seen from the conventional perspective of "*the others*," is, at all levels, presented as being unconventional and therefore not acceptable.

The boy and girl find their unique relationship, their radical alterity, even more featured in the text's third expression of androgyny, where, in a deft reversal of conventional gender roles, he is described as "pale," "gentle," and "uncertain" (36) while, in contrast, she is portrayed as being "agressiva" (aggressive; my translation). "Unformed," as they are then further described (in reference to their personal senses of gender), the text tells us that, in such a state, "they found everything possible, and sometimes they even exchanged certain qualities . . . she became virile, and he acquired the almost ignoble sweetness of a young girl" (36).

With their, as yet, "unformed" qualities constituting, along with their seemingly easy and unconscious interchange of gender traits, a narrative thread that more and more carries the story along, the text then moves quickly to present its "turning point" scene, the one in which the reader, who is here forced to decide for herself or himself just what has happened here, senses that a great if still mysterious transformation has taken place; the "he" of the tale is no longer a "moço" or "rapaz" (boy) but an "homem," (man), while the "she" is now a "mulher" (woman). Significantly, Lispector ties their gender transformations together by repeating the motif of randomness (and therefore of ontological uncertainty), first for him, then for her: "Now and then, when his need was greatest, he became a man" (40); and "For, now and then, she was a woman" (41).

More significant, however, than the move suggested in this key scene toward the kind of rigid, mutually exclusive, either/or gendering demanded by society ("the *others*") and social conventions (he must now "be a man," with all that term carries with it, while she must now "be a woman," with all that category of being carries with it) is the powerful suggestion that this socially imposed gendering has damaged not only the girl-cum-woman (which is only what one would expect given the codes of conduct germane to a male-dominated society) but the boy-cum-man as well. When the boy/man lights a cigarette (which he had not done before), we learn, in a revealing clause, that he does so "as if he were the *others*, taking advantage of the gestures of the freemasonry of men provided for his support and guidance" (40). The implication is that we are now dealing with power, the power, specifically, that accrues automatically to boys on becoming men and that, as we see so poignantly in the painful, sexually based images that describe the girl in this scene, also inescapably involves the exercise of that power, the abuse (here, seemingly, psychosexual) of others, especially females.

Previous to this decisive scene, the boy and girl—while clearly not possessing a perfectly harmonious relationship—did enjoy a positive, mutually beneficial and supportive relationship; after this scene, however, their androgynous, pregender bond is broken, never to be regained. At this point, having finally accepted the rigidly gendered roles society has forced on them, they find they can no longer deal with each other as equals, as "comrades" who had "made a pact" (32). With more than a hint of tragedy, the text suggests that, as far as relations between women and men are concerned, it is society, with its power-obsessed cultural codes, that turns us against each other, that dehumanizes and debases us all, males and females alike. This latter point is dramatically driven home in the closing scenes of the narrative, when the boy/man, struggling to privilege his new, socially endorsed (albeit cruel and abusive) treatment of the girl/woman (formerly his "comrade") over his former, more innocent attitudes and actions, watches her, with "pornographic eyes," as she runs toward the departing bus and imagines that she is "like a monkey wearing a short skirt" (42).

"Imprisoned in his kingdom of man" (42), the boy/man then discovers, ironically, that he needed her, that, indeed, "[h]e hungered after her in order never to forget that they were made of the same flesh" (43). This fourth reference to androgynous being then gives way to its fifth and penultimate expression, one that also links the conclusion with the original reference to the boy as having a woman's heart and having received his mother's kiss: "Now, alone at last, he was defenseless and at the mercy of the hasty lie with which the *others* tried to teach him to be a man. But what about the message? . . . Mummy, he said" (43).

Because the boy/man chooses to stay at the house, which can be understood as the seat of the financial and proprietary power he commands, while the girl/woman runs "in desperation" (42) so as not to miss the bus (which can be understood as the only means at her disposal by which she can evade this suddenly and dramatically deteriorating situation), we can, in the context of poststructural thought, understand the house as symbolizing the solidity and power of Logos while the bus, representing movement, changing structures, and fluidity, symbolizes "différance," the means by which Logos is offset, or at least "deferred." While she (momentarily) escapes, in symbolic terms, what may have already become for her a drearily prototypical scenario—a "man" asserting his masculinity by forcing a "woman" to be his sexual slave—he does not; lost, ironically, "no seu reino de homem," where, having now done what society expects him to do, he will never imagine how he himself could be "imprisoned" by his culture's gender imperatives, how, indeed, he, in his newfound loutishness, may be as much a victim of it as the girl is.

The story's conclusion is thus poignant for two reasons, then; first, because both the pregendered (that is, androgynous) boy and girl suffer a loss of innocence by being forced to enter the exploitative world of adults, and second, because, with the passage of time, the here nascent chasm between the "man" and the "woman" will become ever greater, a fact that in symbolic terms augers ill for the healthy development of their society. As Lispector's story frames it, then, the pernicious and socially divisive forces of gender overwhelm the forces of peace, mutual support, and wholeness represented by androgynous being (with "being" understood here as a social construct).

A sixth poignant touch emerges from the two concluding pages of the text as the boy/man, now alone (the girl/woman having left or "escaped" him) in his dominion, is described in the following terms: "Now, alone at last, he was defenseless and at the mercy of the hasty lie with which the *others* tried to teach him to be a man. . . . Mummy, he said" (43). As the language of this unsettling final line suggests, although the boy/man has assumed the power and disdain his role as a man in an androcentric culture bestows on him, he also feels the pain of his loss of innocence (recalling the male adulterer of "The Burned Sinner and the Harmonious Angels") and a degree of shame at now being required to uphold the "lie" of his corrupting patrimony, the most ironically revealing sign of which is his calling out for his mother, women being the very class his power and arrogance will degrade.

In texts like "The First Kiss" and "The Message," then, this issue of semiotic ambivalence is the force that generates the dynamic interaction between the male and female characters (one of which, in the former story, is the statue of a nude woman). In each work, Lispector presents human reality as an infinitely interconnected and ceaselessly changing verbal structure in which language use constantly transforms everything. In the mind of the boy in "The First Kiss," for example, even a stone statue (or, as in "Clandestine Happiness," a book) can become a lover, one who erotically alters his sense of being. The physical act that is the kiss has no "meaning," the text shows us, until we animate it through language. Human existence, Lispector thus implies, is endlessly discursive because an endless skein of meanings emerge, ineluctably, from the words we use, including the very ones we use to define the others. This explains, I believe, the sense the reader of a Lispector text often has of being engulfed in a torrent of words—words, moreover, that seem to have no clear-cut external referent and that do not coalesce to project some clear-cut "main theme" (unless, of course, we regard the semantically murky nature of language itself to be such a theme). Not surprisingly, the characters who inhabit such a world are quite likely going to be unique, a quality that, from Joana and Lucrécia Neves[16] to G. H. and Rodrigo S. M., aptly describes those created by Clarice Lispector.

Rodrigo S. M., in fact, can be said not only to be a singular literary character but to vividly encapsulate Lispector's relentlessly destabilizing approach to writing. The self-conscious male narrator of *The Hour of the Star* (and possibly an alter ego for Lispector herself),[17] Rodrigo muses metafictionally on a multitude of vintage Lispectorian issues: the elusive nature of meaning,[18] writing as an act of birthing[19] (thus is the image of motherhood evoked), the close proximity of reading and writing,[20] the relationship of a narrative voice to the text, and finally, the relationship of the author and the reader, both real and implied, to the text. What Lispector gives us in *The Hour of the Star* is therefore a profoundly self-conscious work written by a woman but narrated (and in that sense, "birthed") by a verbally astute man (Rodrigo) who, in turn, creates a virtually illiterate woman, Macabéa, to be his principal character. Of all Lispector's characters, Rodrigo (even more than the male "author" of *A Breath of Life*) is the most troubled by textual authority. As he says:

Remember that, no matter what I write, my basic material is the word. So this story will consist of words that form phrases from which there

emanates a secret meaning that exceeds both words and phrases . . .
the word is the fruit of the word. (*Hour* 14–15, 20)

Rodrigo's faith in his ability to harness the anarchic power of language and direct it to the attainment of some larger social good—namely, equality between men and women—makes him one of Lispector's most complex characters. More incisive than the befuddled Martim and more perspicacious than Ulisses, he, once again, faces the poststructural dilemma: Given what, after Saussure, we know about language (its arbitrary and differential relationship to both material and nominal reality and the relativity of meaning), how should we live our lives? How should we relate to ourselves and to other people? On what basis or justification do we make our decisions? It is here that, often couched in terms of lushly metaphoric, yet painfully self-conscious language use, that Lispector's characters—nearly all of her women but, as her writings evolved, increasingly her men as well[21]—evince their powerful ethical implications.

Although these concerns make Rodrigo similar to such characters as Joana, G. H., or the voice of *The Stream of Life*, he is in other ways quite different from them. Because, given his authoritative position in the text and because of words he utters about this role, the source of this difference would seem to involve the issue of authority or control, one wonders whether the question shouldn't involve not only gender and biology but the nature of language itself? Such an interpretational approach, which would be consistent with Lispector's penchant for a kind of border-blurring, even androgynous epistemology, would provide at least one answer to the fascinating question about this superb late work: Why, after creating such extraordinary female characters as a Joana, G. H., and the presence that animates *The Stream of Life*, did Lispector elect here (in the last work she would see published in her lifetime)[22] to select a man to narrate her tale?

One answer is that in creating a man to tell a woman's story Lispector is offering her reader a "realistic" picture of the "real world." Though this argument is plausible, it is not entirely convincing, however, primarily because of the nature of Lispector's previous work and because of her own understanding about the relationship between art and reality.[23] An alternative though related explanation would be that for all their differences—of class, of sex, of opportunity—Rodrigo (the master) and Macabéa (the slave) have two conditions in common: Neither has a satisfying identity, and both are "marginals" (Macabéa because she is a woman, poorly educated and nearly destitute, and Rodrigo because, as a freethinking and iconoclastic writer, he is a pariah),[24] people who pertain to society in only tangential ways. As the reader comes to learn, Rodrigo, as author, wrestles (very much like Lispector herself) both with the problem of truth (or meaning) in language and with its ontological corollary, the symbiotic relationship between language and being (his as well as that of his character, Macabéa). Although Macabéa's "presence" certainly dominates *The Hour of the Star*, a deeper struggle is the one that exists between a person writing (Rodrigo, again like Lispector, disavows being a "professional writer"; 17)[25] and that person's sense of writing as a mode of existence. As Rodrigo says:

> As I write—let things be known by their real names. Each thing is a word. And when there is no word, it must be invented. . . . Why do I write? First of all because I have captured the spirit of the language and at times it is the form that constitutes the content . . . when I write I do not lie. (17–18)[26]

If we consider the possibility that Macabéa and Rodrigo share these two features (their marginality and their identity problems), then we can also speculate about a third—and closely related—interpretation, one fully consistent with Lispector's other work: the implicit challenge to phallogocentrism that permeates her narratives. Viewed from this perspective, interestingly enough, both Macabéa and Rodrigo turn out to be victims; Rodrigo's gendering does not save him, primarily, the reader feels, because his personal ontology is built on an acute consciousness of language's inherent unreliability. True to what I believe is her essentially poststructural sense of life and writing, Lispector does not, however, allow this powerful text to split, thematically speaking, along binary, female/male lines. To do so would be to convey an egregiously oversimplified sense of human existence, and this no Lispector text has ever done, including *An Apprenticeship, or The Book of Delights*, which is conspicuous in Lispector's oeuvre for its portrayal of an at least potentially successful love affair between a "man" and a "woman."[27]

Yet while it is easy to understand the pathetic Macabéa as a victim, how can the privileged Rodrigo be so viewed? The answer to this question springs from two sources: first, the characterizational trajectory that runs from Otávio, through Martim, the boy in "The Message," and Ulisses, to Rodrigo; and second, what we can take as Lispector's most fundamental theme, the ontological primacy of language, the degree to which language makes us who and what we are, yet while also changing us moment to moment.

Of the first source, we can conjecture that in terms of their relationships to authority and language—to Logos (or, more precisely, to phallogocentrism)—Otávio and Rodrigo are very different, and this difference (as in *A Breath of Life*, where it has a parallel) is crucial to our better understanding of Lispector's development as a writer. Where Otávio, the male chauvinist lawyer who upholds the legal code and all it represents, sees language as a mechanism that he would dominate in order to further consolidate his power and authority, Rodrigo, a writer, perceives of language as a fluid semiotic system that controls him and that both creates and undercuts his sense of being and his sense of authority. For Otávio, words are instruments of control; for Rodrigo, however, they are the signs of the epistemological anarchy within which he must attempt to create an authentic existence for himself and his characters. As he puts it:

> [T]he word is the fruit of the word. To attain the word is my first duty to myself. The word must not be adorned and become aesthetically worthless; it must be simply itself. (20)

It is in this metafictional and ontological sense, then, that Lispector's male narrators—like her female narrators—can also give birth to themselves and create new identities that, freed from the stultifying and oppressive structures of phallogocentric thought (as symbolized by Otávio and, to a degree, Lídia), bring to light new ways of being. If we view this summary as being an accurate description of Rodrigo's position within the text he is so self-consciously creating, we can interpret his character as a kind of alternative to the warping power of phallogocentrism, as proof that we can learn to live differently and that it is our consciousness of language that will enable it to happen. Interestingly, then, Rodrigo—the male author—is simultaneously privileged and marginalized; privileged because of his gender, history, and socioeconomic status but marginalized because of what he knows about language and its anarchical power, all of which leads him (as it would have never led either Otávio, Martim, or Ulisses) to declare:

> I belong to no social category, marginal as I am. The upper classes consider me a strange creature, the middle classes regard me with suspicion, afraid that I might unsettle them, while the lower classes avoid me. (18)

But while Rodrigo here presents himself ("With stiff, contaminated fingers I must touch the invisible in its own squalor"; 19) in ways that his three male predecessors could not, he does so in ways that make us think of him as a male G. H., as a privileged male narrator whose old textual authority has been transformed, or undermined, by his new awareness of language, the inexorable force that, embodying poststructural ethos, ceaselessly births and rebirths us all. As Rodrigo expresses it:

> I am holding her [Macabéa's] destiny in my hands and yet I am powerless to invent with any freedom: I follow a secret, fatal line. I am forced to seek a truth that transcends me. (20)

Then, in a revelation that might well serve as Lispector's personal and artistic credo,[28] Rodrigo declares:

> I write because I am desperate and weary. I can no longer bear the routine of my existence and, were it not for the constant novelty of writing, I should die symbolically each day. (21)

We can see, in summary, that while Lispector's female characters greatly outnumber her male characters, the latter are by no means ignored. There are, indeed, grounds for thinking that, as we see in works like "The Message," "The First Kiss," *An Apprenticeship, or The Book of Delights*, and *The Hour of the Star*, she created a series of male characters who, like so many of her females, could be transformed by gaining a heightened consciousness of language. While the lyrical and erotic female voice in *The Stream of Life*, for example, may differ tonally from the male voice of Rodrigo in *The Hour of the Star*, both works suggest that in terms of characterization, language—more than any other concern (including very real questions of sex, gender, race, age, and class)—was Lispector's major concern, the prime mover of her texts. Like Barthes's concept of "le degré zéro de l'écriture,"[29] her novels, stories, and *crônicas* do not tend to cultivate the conceits or the preciousness of "literary" language; rather, her characters are beings whose existences, identities, and self-conscious meditations are, for however much they possess sociopolitical ramifications, based on the plurisignation and ambiguity of language, their common bond being the fundamentally poststructural epistemologies that they either embrace (like Joana, G. H., or the animating presence in *The Stream of Life*), struggle to comprehend (like Martim, Lóri, or Ulisses), or reject (like Ana and Otávio).

But, as we have already seen, Lispector does not limit herself to female and male characters; she also offers the reader several different kinds of androgynous beings, characters who, implicitly and explicitly, merge female and male modes of existence.[30] Though present even in Lispector's first novel (where, with characteristic ambiguity, we learn that "Joana was man like this, man. And so she became a woman. . . . She believed herself to be very powerful. . . . That's how Joana grew, man," *Heart* 158), her interest in the creation of gender-bending characters reaches a climax in the oneiric "Where You Were at Night," which features the strange and captivating character He-she/She-he:

> He-she was already there at the top of the mountain, and she was personified in the he and he was personified in the she. The androgynous mixture had created a being so terribly beautiful, so horrifyingly stupefying, that the participants could not look at it all at once. ("Night" 114)

Charged by an androgynous or pansexual eroticism, the text then tells us:

> Ecstasy was reserved for He-she. Who suddenly experienced a prolonged exhalation of the body. She-he said: Stop! For she was being driven mad by feeling the pleasure of Evil. All of them were taking pleasure through her: it was the celebration of the Great Law. The eunuchs did something it was forbidden to see. The others, through She-he, received, quivering, the waves of orgasm. (122)

This extraordinary tale, more a surrealist poem than even a lyrical narrative, is perhaps the supreme example of Lispector's vision of a totally mixed—and mixing—universe, a way of being that denies efforts to divide and segregate and in which nothing stays the same.[31]

But when, in addition to these two texts, we consider the other of Lispector's works ("Obsession," "In Search of Dignity," "The Departure of the Train," "A Report on a Thing," "Soulstorm," "Irresistible Incarnation," "The First Kiss," "Better Than to Burn," "Plaza Mauá," and "Life *au Naturel*") that deal with sex- and gender-role reversal or displacement, we see just how pervasive her interest in androgyny was in her work, where, after 1972, it became more and more prominent. It is important to note, however, that in none of these works (not even in the prototypical "Where You Were at Night") does Lispector ever explicitly advocate androgyny as the ideal mode of being. Rather, she consistently presents it as another possible form of existence, an approach to the subject that parallels her technique of creating texts that generate a profusion of meanings and that lead her readers to consider as many interpretations as they—or the texts—are able to generate. It is in this semantically mercurial context that we can see why Lispector's androgynous narratives deal not with physiology (the orgasm of "Where You Were at Night" notwithstanding) but with gender, with sex roles, and with the all too often pernicious effects they have on the social roles both men and women are regularly forced to endure, on relationships, and on the creation of satisfying self-identities.

Long overlooked even by critics well versed in Lispector's work, questions concerning her utilization of God also demand our attention. From a poststructural perspective, God, in Lispector's texts, invokes more the question of ultimate authority, the "Law"—indeed, of an ultimate form of phallogocentric authority—than of any orthodox religious sentiment,[32] though this, too, as Giovanni Pontiero suggests (*DW* 26), may be applicable to Lispector. Either way when one reads all of Lispector, it becomes clear, moreover, that there is a great deal of concern about who or what God is, about the nature of our human relationship to God (and to the very idea of God), and fascinatingly, even about whether God, physiologically or conceptually, is male or female.

It is this latter point, which comes up tangentially in "A vingança e a reconciliação" and literally in "Day by Day" (*Soulstorm*), the latter a spare text that vividly broaches the issue of God-as-salvation-or-as-ultimate-phallogocentric-oppression, that connects with a number of other Lispector texts and that leads the reader to differentiate between the various presences God has in Lispector's narratives. On telling her brother that he looks like a woman (after which, as if to affirm male violence and male revulsion at looking like a female—itself a form of gender interrogation—he kicks her), a girl sardonically declares, "[d]on't worry about it, God is a woman!" ("Day" 46). But then, in a wry statement that decenters her previous utterance (itself phallogocentrically decentering), she adds, softly, "I know that God is a man, but I don't want to get beaten up" (46). The story "ends," however, with the self-conscious narrator (possibly Lispector herself) invoking an unexpected and startling demonstration of female violence ("Grandma gave me such a slap I got knocked cold"; 46), the effect of which is to destabilize the easy condemnation of male violence the reader had been led to make only a moment before.

One comes to the conclusion that, for Clarice Lispector, God (a constant and unsettling motif in her work) appears in basically two modes: as the keeper, arbiter, or symbol of the state of perfection, grace, or transcendence (often taking form as a kind of mystical ecstasy) that we humans seek, and as a symbol of authority, of God (nearly always depicted as being male) as the ultimate phallogocentric power, the latter point common to such poststructuralists as Derrida, who see God identified with Logos and imbuing it with a kind of divine final authority. Although the former category finds representation in nearly everything Lispector wrote (*The Passion according to G. H.* being a prime example), it is the second utilization of God, the more contentious and problematic one, that elicits the most challenging representations and that, in fact, occasionally transforms the concept of God into God-as-character, an all-powerful but capricious being with whom Lispector's protagonists must contend. In *Near to the Wild Heart*, for example, we learn of Joana, whose entire existence involves a struggle with authority, that "her body had never needed anyone, she was free . . . . she had abolished God, the world, everything" (*Heart* 177). Later, however, in yet another anti-logocentric declaration (one that, in addition to invoking Derrida's key concept of the constantly evolving "center that is not the Center," nevertheless "decenters" her earlier statement about abolishing God), we hear Joana declare:

> God, God, God, come to me, not to save me, salvation should be in me, but to smother me with Your heavy hand, with punishment, with death, because I am powerless and afraid of dealing that tiny blow which will transform my whole body in this centre which longs to breathe and which is rising, rising . . . the same impulse as that of tide and genesis, genesis! (184)

Also wrestling with the problem of all that is inherent in the concept of God is G. H., who can speak of both "the profound abyss of God: absorbed into the core of an indifference" (*Passion* 114) and "the immense magnitude of God" (115) while also broaching the question of phallogocentric authority:

> I was uselessly on my feet before Him, and it was once more a nothingness that I was before. . . . I now understood that I had not sold it [my soul] to the devil but much more dangerously: to God. . . . For He knew that I wouldn't know how to see whatever I saw: the explanation of an enigma is the mere repetition of the enigma. . . . I had lost myself in a labyrinth of questions. (127)

A similar position is taken by the narrator of *The Stream of Life* who, though acknowledging her ardent desire to know the perfection, ecstasy, and transcendence that God represents, also asserts that "God is a monstrous creation" (*SL* 76) and, casting God as her great antagonist, that

I rebel against "God." . . . I'm not going to die, do you hear, God? . . . Don't kill me, do you hear? . . . [E]verything returned to nothingness, returned to the Force of what Exists and is sometimes called God. (78)

Then, continuing to situate both God-as-antagonist and God-as-divinity in the context of the maddeningly paradoxical human condition, this same anguished voice intensifies the accusation: "Because it's infamy to be born only to die not knowing where or when" (78). Thematically linking the endless act of writing-as-being that constitutes the text with an image that captures the destabilizing self-referentiality of all linguistic expression, the female voice of *The Stream of Life* also declares:

Everything ends but what I write you continues on. . . . Still, the best hasn't been written. The best is between the lines. . . . What I write you is a *this*. It won't stop: it continues on. (78–79)

Finally, and in an utterance that fuses Lispector's career-long concern with language and writing with her equally fundamental struggle with the issues of creation and being, the "autor" of *A Breath of Life* declares, "Eu inventei Deus— . . . Deus é uma palavra?" [I invented God— . . . Is God a word? (my translation)] (126). To paraphrase Heidegger,[33] the "limits" of Lispector's world would indeed seem to be the "limits" of language.

Not theological in the traditional sense of the word, Lispector's complex inscribing of God into her texts seems more than anything else an attempt by her characters to come to grips with the philosophical problem of death and with the problems of meaning and authority in life. But because Lispector's texts so relentlessly portray meaning and authority in terms of language and language use, the reader comes to understand that, for Lispector, God—a word, the ultimate symbol of the power and arbitrariness of (phal)logocentrism—comes to function in her texts as a symbol of the totalizing, either/or, and restrictive mode of thought that Derrida and others have challenged and that Lispector, through her characters, interrogates. Semiotically, then, Lispector's utilization of God is consistent with her overall sense of language as a seductive, self-referential, and ultimately mysterious web of signs, one that emphasizes both language's ceaseless semantic mutability and our dependence on it, our desire for stability and certainty.

Two other of Lispector's important characterizational categories must at least be noted; one of these, her extensive use of animals, has been widely commented on, while the other, her creation of what we might best think of as supernatural beings, deserves more attention. While the former group figures prominently in such works as "The Chicken," "The Crime of the Mathematics Professor," "The Buffalo," "Monkeys," "The Egg and the Chicken,"[34] "The Fifth Story," "The Foreign Legion," "Dry Point of Horses," "Uma esperança," and "A Story of Such Love," the smaller, latter group would include works like "Miss Algrave," "The Way of the Cross," and, in a sense, both "Where You Were at Night" and *The Stream of Life*. Critics have long felt that, for Lispector, animals represented some form of "primitive," prehuman (and therefore prelinguistic) existence against which, as in "Animals" (I & II), "The Crime of the Mathematics Professor," and "The Buffalo," women and men can orient and define themselves.[35] In addition to functioning as characters, animals (particularly horses and chickens) often appear as motifs in her work (the grazing horses in *The Besieged City* and their relationship to the novel's protagonist, Lucrécia Neves, being a prime example),[36] or the symbolic functions of chickens in such stories as "The Egg and the Chicken," "The Chicken," "A Story of Such Love," *Laura's Intimate Life* (1974), and *Almost True* (1978).

Lispector's usage of supernatural beings is much more limited; only Ixtlan, the creature from Saturn who comes to Earth "to love" (*Soulstorm* 11) Miss Ruth Algrave (who, through her experience of sex, is humorously transformed as both a person and as a politically conscious worker), and She-he/He-she develop as major characters in her work. Although other strange, mythical creatures are conjured up in both *The Stream of Life* and "Where You Were at Night," and in the children's stories, *Laura's Intimate Life* and *Almost True*, they do not serve as characters in the ways that He-she/She-he and, especially, Ixtlan do. An interesting variation on this question of supernatural beings, however, is "Little Flower," the tiny (but otherwise "normal") woman of "The Smallest Woman in the World," a droll tale from *Family Ties* that can be read as an allegorical indictment of how we exploit each other or, more specifically, as an allegorical indictment of how society regards women,[37] the latter being one of Lispector's predilect themes. In general, Lispector's infrequent usage of supernatural creatures allows her both to slip the bonds of realistic narrative (a kind of writing she found "boring" and which she discusses in "The Unreality of Realism," 20 January 1968, and "The 'True' Novel," 22 August 1970) and to inject a degree of ironic humor into her texts, humor playing a more substantive role in her work than one might expect (Lastinger 1989).

Finally, however, we must take note of an easily overlooked—but, I believe, absolutely essential—aspect of Lispector's characterizations: The fact that they are always rooted in relationships, or, more to the point, to the changes that are inherent in relationships, including one's apprehension of the multiple, fragmented self. Although Lispector's most powerful characters, like Joana, G. H., the voice in *The Stream of Life*, and Macabéa, initially impress the reader as iconoclasts, loners, or misfits, on reflection they all suffer and exult in terms of some kind of relationship, either with another being (male or female, animal, human, and even nonhuman) or with evolving aspects of their own personalities, different identities (sexual, psychological, or sociopolitical), and evanescent degrees or levels of awareness. It is in this relational or social context, in fact, that the reader most fully appreciates the extent to which Lispector's texts humanize the poststructural condition by addressing such language-sensitive constructs as gender, sexuality, class, race, consciousness, and being.

Moreover, Lispector's characters are disturbingly human because, like poststructuralism, they force us to confront one deeply disconcerting fact of human existence: that even when we are in a relationship, we are alone; for all that we manipulate language to strengthen, weaken, or otherwise alter our relationships (with self and other), we cannot escape our isolation. It is precisely because these most basic dramas of human existence are framed in and played out through language that Lispector's narratives generate their unique and compelling power. Indeed, for Lispector the drama of language is, to paraphrase Benedito Nunes, inevitably the drama of existence, this being a sine qua non of her work that finds its maximum expression first, in *The Stream of Life*, second, in *The Passion according to G. H.*, and third, in *The Hour of the Star*, the three works that, ironically, appear at first glance to be the stories of totally isolated protagonists. As we shall now see, however, G. H., Rodrigo S. M., and the protagonist of *The Stream of Life*—like many of Lispector's other characters—all project their experiences into not only the private sphere but the public one as well.

An issue that continues to swirl about Lispector's work is to what degree and in what sense does it possess a political dimension? A response to this important question leads us to consider not only the ancient relationship between literature and life but, as I will now try to show, the relationship between poststructural theory and the dynamics of social change, specifically in terms of how Lispector's characters view themselves, their relationships, and their place in society. Although many commentators have regarded poststructural thought as being nihilistic, endlessly reductive, and incapable of saying anything meaningful about the plight of millions of women, men, and children on our planet, a thorough and open-minded examination of its premises and implications shows that it need not be any of these things; indeed, one can argue that precisely because poststructuralism *is* so concerned with language (the possession of which is said to define us as human beings), it must rank among the most innately human, even humanistic, of all our various systems of thought. From this, one can reasonably infer that, since human society is a collection of individual beings, poststructuralism should be capable of speaking meaningfully not only to individuals but to the group, to society, as well.

And it does, though not easily or obviously. The problem is threefold: the content of the message (or messages) that poststructural thought delivers; the nature of the medium (language) in which the message is delivered; and finally, what we humans, as the makers and users of language, will do, individually and collectively, with both the content (that we can never express or know anything perfectly) and the medium (the constantly changing and relentlessly ambiguous system of self-referential tropes that language is). From linguists like Peirce, Chomsky, and above all, Saussure, to philosophers like Wittgenstein, Carnap, Ayer, and Derrida, the relationship between language and reality, and therefore between what we know and how we know it (and what we mean when we say we know something), has been at the heart of twentieth-century literature and thought. Yet while Clarice Lispector, who cultivates these issues and who also considered herself a "committed" writer (*DW,* 30 December 1967), is very much a twentieth-century writer, what is not so clear is exactly how such esoteric literary and philosophical concerns translate into sociopolitical concerns. How, to return to my initial question, do the seemingly hermetic and arcane texts of Clarice Lispector generate any sense of physical awareness? How do they escape what, on the surface at least, appears to be a kind of all-consuming solipsism, the endless ruminations of agonized and acutely self-aware consciousnesses?

Approaching this question from not entirely different directions, two critics, Daphne Patai and Carol Armbruster, have questioned whether Lispector, at least the Lispector of *The Passion according to G. H.* and *The Stream of Life*, two of her best known works, offers us any viable sociopolitical message. Patai, for example, writes (of G. H.) that "she rejects her fellow human beings," that "she struggles to find a fixed position for herself via her own idiosyncratic definitions of what life in the world is like," and finally, that her ruminations are merely "ideological pretexts for avoiding the specifically human, the confrontation with one's fellow human being, with all that this implies of uncertainty and change."[1] Taking a similar stance, Armbruster, citing what she sees as the danger of "mysticism" in *The Passion according to G. H.* and *The Stream of Life,*[2] writes:

> Mysticism can lead to true Otherness, but it can also lead to the most extreme self-centeredness. Depersonalizing and dehumanizing oneself in order to enter Otherness, take it on, and then speak for it is nothing short of self-deification. (Armbruster 157)

Pursuing this line of thought further, Armbruster then concludes:

> The decentered subject scattered throughout a text finds the cosmic, unites with it, and then speaks its difference. The body, the unconscious, sexuality, women—all lose substance, dissolving into the beatitude of the "néant," which we understand is nothing. Is this what we want? (157)

Although there is much to sustain such interpretations (particularly if one is working with critical assumptions deriving from orthodox notions about literary realism), there are other ways of reading these same self-questioning, language obsessed texts. A poststructural reading, for example, interrogates whether in fact G. H. "rejects dynamic human existence for the static world of her own projections" (Patai 133). Indeed, a reading of *The Passion according to G. H.* as a text that exemplifies the theoretical issues dealt with via poststructuralism leads us to feel that the "projections" of G. H., self-consciously based as they are in the irresistible ebb and flow of language, constitute neither a "static world" nor the establishment of "a fixed position for herself." The referent for the discourse of both G. H. and the voices in *The Stream of Life* and *A Breath of Life* is not a "fixture" in the external world but the nature of language itself, language being the most "specifically human" of all our attributes as well as the one that most profoundly, elusively, and mysteriously leads us to an endlessly evolving "confrontation with one's fellow human being, with all that this implies of uncertainty and change." One could argue, moreover, that G. H.'s language-based discourse epitomizes—at the deepest levels of being—the inherent uncertainty and mutability of the human condition. The life that G. H. embraces, then, is poststructural life, human existence as defined by language, a kind of being that emphasizes the epistemological problem of knowing and that foregrounds the anxieties deriving from our inability to know with certainty who and what we are in a world of changing signs we can neither decipher nor control.

Such a text would seem to lead naturally to various forms and degrees of self-consciousness, much as lyric poetry does; whether it also leads to the dangerous, "self-deifying" "mysticism" that Armbruster warns us of is another question. The problem here would seem to be the term "mysticism" itself, and what we understand it to mean. If, in fact, we feel that Lispector's texts are "mystical," in what sense is this "dangerous"? In what context is mysticism a problem? To be specific, does G. H.'s discourse truly cause "[t]he body, the unconscious, sexuality, women" to "lose substance," to dissolve "into the beatitude of the 'néant'," into "nothing"? I think not. Again, read from the critical perspective that self-consciousness about language (and everyday language use) results in a continuously evolving ontological self-portrait (one that undermines rigidly fixed boundaries and borders), *The Passion according to G. H.* can be more satisfactorily explained, I believe, from a poststructural perspective, that is, as a text that dissolves neither the body, the unconscious, nor the sexuality of women (indeed, it affirms these things) but the various power structures that limit our potential for growth and development. This, to posit an answer to Armbruster's question, is very much what we want, and we see it in Lispector's texts when we see how profoundly they themselves undermine, decenter, and desacralize[3] these same structures (which are themselves revealed to be functions of language usage in which power and control are the primary goals).

Of all the Lispectorian texts that elicit a political response from the reader, however, few are more beguiling than her "children's story," "The Mystery of the Thinking Rabbit" (1967), suggestively subtitled "Uma estória policial para crianças" ("A Detective Story for Children"). Published in 1967, three years into the military dictatorship that had begun in 1964, this short, seemingly "simple" text can easily be read as an incisive political allegory, one in which the fat and content white rabbit, Joãozinho (who serves as the story's protagonist), can be understood as Brazil's bourgeoisie, especially in its relationship to the social and economic order imposed by the generals. Termed a "tale of confinement and flight" (Rosenstein 160) that, because of its sociopolitical overtones, has adult implications, "The Mystery of the Thinking Rabbit" features a preface that may be understood as instructions about how to read what follows:

> Since the story was written exclusively for domestic use, I left out all the reading between the lines work [the interpretations] for the oral explanations. I ask forgiveness from the fathers and mothers, uncles and aunts, and grandparents for the forced contributions they will be obliged to give. . . . Besides, that "mystery" is more an intimate conversation than a story. (my translation)

By interpreting "domestic use" to mean both "in one's home" and "Brazil" (Lispector's home), one can then easily react to the story that follows from the perspective of a Brazilian intellectual living under the heel of the "ditadura" in the late 1960s. When the narrative voice (presumably that of Lispector herself) says that, in writing this story, she dropped or omitted all the "entrelinhas" for "oral explanations," she is reiterating a revealing point made three years earlier in the *crônica* "Miraculous Fishing" (from *The Foreign Legion*, 1964) about how she understands the deeply entwined processes of writing and reading: that both occur "between the lines," that is, with the reader reacting to the plethora of possible meanings that arise from words by entering into their semantic webs and, in the act of interpreting them, by producing even more. In a very guarded fashion, then (as would be appropriate for someone about to criticize the dictatorship), Lispector seems to be alerting the reader, understood here as the "fathers and mothers, uncles and aunts, and grandparents" to another, more politically conscious way of reading this superficially benign story. As good Brazilians, their "contributions" (their politically charged interpretation) will be something that they "will be obliged to give," presumably because the text will be so structured that, as careful readers, they will not be able to avoid doing so.

Gradually becoming aware that the *casinhola* (hutch or hovel) he inhabits has become less of a "home" than a prison, an indictment of life under the military regime, Joãozinho gets an idea: he will try to get out or escape whenever there is insufficient *comida* (food) available to him. Because Joãozinho is characterized as being fat, happy, and none too aware, the hunger he seeks to satisfy is likely not the physical hunger that Lispector writes about so often in her *crônicas*, the hunger that marks the potentially disastrous schism between the very rich and the very poor that afflicts modern Brazilian society. Joãozinho's hunger, one feels (at this point in the story), is either for a liberty and freedom now lost or for the material trappings of affluence that came to Brazil's middle class via the Brazilian "economic miracle," the existence of which was the trump card of the dictatorship; so long as the bourgeoisie's demand for more goods and services could be appeased, the generals could more easily suspend civil rights and place Brazilian society under what amounted to martial law. Read in the light of these social and political circumstances, certain of the story's key lines take on added meaning. As if learning better how to control their charge, for example, the "authorities" who would apprehend Joãozinho in his escape attempts realize that if they kept Joãozinho's "plate full," he would be content, supportive of the political and economic system that provides him with the things he wants.

When they begin to do this (which we can think of as the economic benefits that accrued to the wealthy during the years of the "economic miracle"), the narrative voice then tells us, "And life, for that white rabbit, came to be very good. Food was not what he lacked" (my translation). The "between the lines" message here would seem to be that while the Brazilian people could be pacified with food and the material accoutrements of an aggressively marketed but antidemocratic consumer society, it was freedom that they needed and wanted, what they really hungered for. Thus it is that Joãozinho's *donos* (his masters, that is, the generals), suspecting that he was not entirely satisfied with what he was being given, "became angry with him." But as the text notes (in a way that captures the patronizing attitude the generals had toward the Brazilian people), "they became angry as fathers and mothers become angry with their children," with "children," of course, symbolizing those Brazilians who spoke out against the severe political repression of the *ditadura*, especially that of its fanatically anticommunist *linha dura* (hard-line) faction.

The apex of the story's political significance comes only a few lines later, when we get an "explanation" of how the fat, content, and none too "aware" Joãozinho comes to be not just another "rabbit" but a "thinking rabbit":

> At times, Joãozinho would also escape just so he could get a good look at things, since no one would take him out for a walk. It was at those times that he would become a thinking rabbit. (my translation)

Symbolizing (perhaps) the gradual realization of the Brazilian citizenry about what was happening to them and their country, Joãozinho's transformation into a "thinking rabbit" then allows the narrator to bring their political subtext to closure by saying, in a way that serves as a warning to all people about the need to pay attention to what their political leaders do: "In his flights, he also discovered that there are things that it's good to smell but that aren't good to eat" (my translation). Things, in other words, are not always what they seem, and while they (government edicts, for example) might be made to appear beneficial (that is, "smell good"), their real effect may well be detrimental (not "good to eat"), for individual citizens as well as for nations.

Originally composed in English (and later translated by Lispector herself into Portuguese), "The Mystery of the Thinking Rabbit" (1967) deserves more attention (as does her "children's" literature in general) than it has received. Beyond its extraliterary context, this short, allusive narrative offers us a prime example of what Lispector took the crucial reader's role to be in the production of a text's meaning, specifically our need to work "between the lines" in an active, engaged effort to contemplate the multiplicity of meanings that any language structure generates. More than a simple "children's story,"[4] "The Mystery of the Thinking Rabbit"—like much of the popular music of the period—can easily be read as an indictment of Brazil's political situation circa 1967 and a telling exposition of how even an ostensibly "simple" narrative has unexpectedly complex and "mysterious" connotations—at least for a "thinking reader."

Lispector's political consciousness makes its presence felt even in a fantastic, oneiric story like "Where You Were at Night." This is at first surprising since, as David Jackson observes, this entire collection of short narratives, *Where You Were at Night* (1974), continues to plumb the depths of the theme of absence, which, in relation to being, is "congruent with" Barthes' concept of "writing degree zero," where writing, one of Lispector's most definitive preoccupations, "is made to reflect on its own instrumentality in a return to origins" (Jackson 105). But while "Where You Were at Night" might at first glance appear to possess little or no political commentary, a close reading shows that on one point— our sense of identity and the relationships that arise from out of it—this singular story actually conveys a powerful and dramatically rendered political message, one that links a consideration of human sexuality to the larger issues of language and both public and private being.

To begin with, there is the possibility that the androgynous being (whose identity, He-she, alternates, as we have seen, with the form She-he throughout the text) expresses not only Lispector's implicit suggestion that, as Plato discusses it in *The Symposium*, androgyny is a superior form of existence but that language, the fluidity of which is exemplified in the constantly alternating She-he/He-she figure, is the most androgynizing, or "degendering" of all human creations, the one tool we have that truly can change the various identities people claim for themselves. We are, Lispector's texts seem to tell us, what we say we are, or, to paraphrase Sartre's existential credo, language precedes not only our existence but our essence as well.

In "Where You Were at Night," the political ramifications of this position are tremendous, even revolutionary in import. By having She-he/He-she considered early on as "a beacon" (*Soulstorm* 115), the text establishes the possibility s/he is to be understood as a "guiding light," a model, as it were, of a more socially desirable kind of being, one free of the prejudices and inequalities sustained by society's current norms. With the verb "to mix" playing a key role in the development of this theme, the text, stressing the need to deny repression by seeking freedom through (as in G. H.'s story) a quest for the "prohibited," then broaches the issue of revolt by creating an image in which the "She-he" figure will "devour" its "brother," all of which can easily be read as the symbolic destruction of patriarchal society:

> On moonless nights, She-he turned into a screech owl. You will eat your brother, she said in the thoughts of others. (119)

This same image is then repeated, in an intensified, more emphatic version, only a few pages later, when we read:

> And then She-he said:
> "I will eat your brother, and there will follow a total eclipse and the end of the world." (123)

Given Lispector's consciousness of the pressures exerted by the weight of gender and the forces of power in human society, it is not impossible to interpret the "total eclipse" and the "end of the world" as the end of a particular kind of sociopolitical organization and of the gender-biased power structures that go with it.

But true to Lispector's characteristic approach to writing,[5] this entirely plausible reading is decentered, expanded ("supplemented," Derrida might say), by another quite reasonable interpretation, one that (as symbolized in the androgynous figure He-she/She-he) actually brings women and men together as allies in a common cause, as human beings who, working together, must overcome the structures and forces that divide and exploit them. The image that generates this interpretation appears between the two that depict the devouring of the brother and establishes itself as the most dramatic, most compelling, and yet most enigmatic image of the entire story:

> The women who had recently given birth squeezed their own breasts with violence, and from their nipples a thick, black milk squirted forth. A woman spat hard in the face of a man, and the rough spit dripped from his cheek to his mouth—avidly he licked his lips.
>
> They were all cast loose. The joy was frenetic. They were the harem of the He-she. ("Night" 121)

Since the He-she figure has just been described (a page earlier) as their "Lover," one senses that sexuality, an omnipresent if elusive force in this underappreciated narrative, plays once again a uniquely destabilizing role in human existence, undercutting our efforts to erect rigid boundaries between different identities and modes of being. Sexuality, Lispector's texts often imply, is thus the great lubricant of being, the seductive force that, shaped and reshaped through language, effaces boundaries and facilitates change. As Lispector demonstrates in the She-he figure, sexuality, like Kristeva's "semiotic," is not an issue germane only to women, though it is more often through her female characters that Lispector dramatizes its decentering role in human existence. By thus politicizing sexuality, and making it speak to the ways we define ourselves and structure our society, this text—and especially its patterning of these images—leads the reader to speculate that while women (as an oppressed/repressed group; cf. 62) may elect to engage in violence (and especially sexual violence) to make their grievances known (hence, the violence of the breast imagery employed here) to men (spitting in the man's face), the story's final three sentences and images imply a sense not of rancorous division but of amicable unity, one that arises from a realization that we must all—men and women alike—free ourselves from the corrupting, perverting pressures exerted by phallocentric structures:

> The joy was frenetic. They were the harem of He-she. They had fallen into the impossible. (121)

By casting both men and women into the role of sexual acolytes of the androgynous or gender-evolving He-she, "Where You Were at Night" effectively undermines conventional ideologies about "correct" or "proper" sexual conduct, suggesting, instead, a new approach to sexuality, one directed toward a degendered and communal sense of identity and being, yet one nevertheless seemingly "impossible" to attain in the "real," that is, phallocentric world, a point acutely sensed by the reader at the end of the tale, when the person in question awakes and the dream vanishes. Put another way, the "fall" (read "growth") into this newly conceptualized mode of being (which, in this story, can be understood as the "free play" of the textualized Lacanian subconscious) cannot be achieved except through language, that great dissolver, in consort with sexuality, of rigid distinctions, boundaries, prejudices, and hierarchies.

As if awakening from a deep sleep, the text thus comes to an end with the light of day, understood metaphorically as reason or consciousness reasserting its primacy and authority over the unfettered free play of the unconscious and making the weight of its logocentric presence known once again: "He-she had vanished long before in the air. The morning was crystal clear like something recently washed" (130). Yet the narrative voice that then offers us the epilogue subtly undercuts the authority of reason by suggesting that while everything the s/he has written here is "true" and that it "existed," it is also guided (as was the narrative voice) by "a universal mind" (130), a mysterious entity or force that the reader can understand as either God, rational consciousness, or language. In the context of the story, however, and given the nature of Lispector's other work, one feels drawn toward reading this "universal mind" that "guides us" more as language, with its endlessly interlocking and decentering chains of signifiers, than as God or reason, which, as concepts seem inescapably locked into Logos, the desire to establish and maintain what one group has declared to be the perfect, unchanging, and totalizing system of Truth.

Interestingly, it would seem to be this very conflict between the semantic anarchy of language and the perfect authority of God (a conflict rendered more complex, for Lispector, in the religious concept of the Word and in the typically masculine gendering of God) that leads the narrative voice to ask what turns out to be the key philosophical question of the entire text: "Where were you at night?" (130). Functioning as a reference to the unfettered energies and desires that we possess in the "darkness," or "night," of our repressed subconscious, this decisive question also frames the story by establishing a contrast between its context (being as the writing of the "night, that is, the subconscious) and the dawning of a new day (consciousness) that ends the narrative. Directing this query, moreover, at the reader (whose collaboration in determining the text's potential meanings has been established at the outset), the narrative voice then undermines its own question by saying, "No one knows. Don't try to answer. For the love of God. I don't want to know your answer. Adeus. A-deus" (*Soulstorm* 130). With the "A-deus" (literally, "to God") functioning here much as Derrida's "différance" does,[6] the reader is justified in thinking that the narrator says this because the response (that the world as we know it [our epistemologies], indeed, our very being) is itself a function not merely of language but of language's inherent "slippage" and arbitrariness, its self-questioning elusiveness. Perfect, unchanging meaning, authority, and origins (Logos and God) are illusions, this phantasmagoric text suggests, manifestations of a particular use of language. We are, the epilogue leads us to suspect, lost in a repressive and exploitative sociopolitical construct where even our concept of God—our yearning to go "to God"—reveals itself to be a function of language. To change this situation, the text implies, we must rethink who we are and what, as individuals and as a society, we wish to be.

Although it is highly unlikely that she would have ever put it in quite these terms, Lispector's work clearly reveals a lifelong struggle to undermine what we can now see as phallogocentrically established gender roles (Barbosa, *Clarice Lispector: Spinning the Webs of Passion*, 11, 94–95), this quality undoubtedly being her greatest single response to those who demand a socially committed "dimension" to her literature. Indeed, it would not be an exaggeration to say that Lispector's texts manifest what can be described as the epitome of sexual ideology in the poststructural age. As Elizabeth Lowe notes, "Despite her protest that she is unable to answer to social issues, social inter-relationships are the very fabric of her fiction. She deals sensitively with interfamilial relations, social mediocrity and the psychology of the modern, urban woman" (Lowe

1979, 34). Relentlessly working and reworking the sundry power rela-tionships that exist between women and men, and yet simultaneously charting the tangled process (always linguistically derived) by which women especially come to hold certain kinds of identities, Lispector of-fers her reader both a new vision of fe/male existence (one that is both sexually emancipating and economically pertinent at the same time that it is subversively political) and a unique vision of several different kinds of relationships (female/female, male/male, and female/male), a vision that at every point links the development of one's complex and often changing personal identity to the larger sociopolitical sphere. This is no mean feat, and though it is not always immediately obvious in Lis-pector's narratives, it is always there. We can, in a sense, interpret this effort as constituting an attempt to degender human experience, or to free it from its rigidly gendered expectations, and, as such, it could be said to rank as not only Lispector's most telling political statement but poststructuralism's greatest triumph as well.

One of her most intriguing forays into this area is the 1974 collection of stories entitled *The Stations of the Body*, which, though earning a mixed response from the critics when it first appeared, can now be seen as pointing toward a new line of development for its author, one that, as Nelson Vieira and others have argued, reveals a keen awareness of the plight of Brazil's lower and middle classes. Featuring an overt if re-strained sexuality, a stripped-down style that eschews the lyricism of earlier works (including *The Stream of Life*, published only the year be-fore), a self-consciousness that invites readerly participation, and a utili-zation of the fantastic or the improbable, these short, wryly humorous narratives parodically undermine many of the assumptions and conven-tions of androcentric society (Peixoto, *Passionate Fictions*, 73). By making sexuality (and in particular female sexuality) a common denominator of these stories, Lispector positions herself to deal with a number of sup-posedly "taboo" topics, including homosexuality, masturbation, bisexu-ality, rape, and geriatric sex. Yet in no case does this essentially subver-sive female sexuality ever assume a lurid or gratuitous presence; rather, it is presented as a natural, though powerfully fundamental, aspect of human identity, one that is ignored, denied, or repressed only at great personal and social cost.[7]

It would be a mistake, therefore, to believe that *The Stations of the Body* is primarily "about sex," for it is not. A particular manifestation of love, a subject that is conflictively endemic to Lispector's fiction, human sexuality does indeed possess a powerful presence here, but in nearly every case it is presented as the most destabilizing, decentering force of all in human existence. Dissolving the boundaries that otherwise separate social classes, genders, races, and attitudes (particularly in regard to what it means to be "female" and to be "male"), sexuality, more than any other single signifier, puts everything into play. For Nelson Vieira, for example, the potent female sexuality of *The Stations of the Body* is a form of empowerment, one that combines an open cultivation of desire with self-realization and economic struggle.[8] As Vieira reads it, *The Stations of the Body* reflects Lispector's increasing identification with the struggles of Brazil's disadvantaged classes, a trend that he sees developing simultaneously in the *crônicas* that she was writing at the time for the *Jornal do Brasil* (Vieira, in *Clarice Lispector: A Bio-Bibliography*, 149–52). When read in this context, Lispector's introductory "Explicação" can be understood as her effort to relate to the reader her intention to question all forms of patriarchy, particularly as it manifests itself in our all too often rigid and oppressive thinking about human sexuality, gender, marriage, parenting, and motherhood, the latter an issue that figures prominently in her Saturday newspaper column. In this sense, as Vieira observes, the "Explicação" "sets the appropriate tone for the . . . subversive nature of these stories" that "undermine absolute notions about sexuality as well as gender, marriage, heterosexual/homosexual love, parenthood, and particularly motherhood" (150).

One of the collection's most brilliant examples of this kind of writing is the endlessly self-decentering story "Plaza Mauá," in which a transvestite, Celsinho (who has adopted a four-year-old girl), turns out to be a better mother than his married but childless colleague, the erotic dancer, Carla, who dotes on her cat. Not only does Celsinho prove himself to be a superior mother to the child, sacrificing his own time, energy, and money for her happiness and welfare, he eventually declares himself to be more of a woman than Carla as well, Carla being cast, from the reader's perspective, as the epitome of what society expects a "real woman" to be. When he screams at her, in the story's climactic moment, "You . . . are no woman at all! You don't even know how to fry an egg! And I do! I do! I do!" (PM 57), the reader understands the ironic reversal of gender roles that has taken place. An additional irony is that Celsinho's successful venture into motherhood/womanhood is built on utterly conventional assumptions about what constitutes a "real mother" (or a "real woman"), that is, someone who can "properly" prepare an egg, someone, in other words, whose identity is much less a question of biology than of gender, a term still understood only in the context of established patriarchal norms. Suddenly and unexpectedly transformed by Celsinho's gender-bending outburst back into her other existence as Luísa, the effectively disenfranchised and conventional married woman (whose economically oppressed and sexually repressed existence she had escaped by becoming Carla, the dancer at the Club Erotica), Carla, as if she were extinguishing the heat and fire of her life, crushes out her cigarette and leaves the club, alone, in the dark, and facing an untenable future.

Another story from this singular collection, and one that generates a telling indictment of the violence toward women that characterizes patriarchal society, is "Pig Latin,"[9] a spare, enigmatic tale about two rapes, one seemingly "real," the other either narrowly and ingeniously avoided or imagined, the result, perhaps, of a tangled and repressed sexuality. Although, on the surface, the story leads the reader to feel that its primary focus is on the "real" rape that Cidinha, the young female protagonist, manages to evade, another reading suggests something very different, that the entire episode may be nothing more than a figment of her tortured imagination. Yet this reading is itself undercut, in vintage Lispectorian fashion, by Cidinha's discovery, near the story's conclusion, that a rape did indeed take place on the train on which she had been riding and that it involved the same girl who had disdained her, ironically enough, for the very whorish behavior that, apparently, had saved her life.

But given the class consciousness and violence that permeates these narratives, one also feels that while Cidinha may or may not have been on the verge of being attacked by the two men on the train, she most certainly does live in a culture that tolerates rape as a "normal" aspect of existence. The most important political dimension of "Pig Latin" may therefore not stem so much from what we fear is about to happen to Cidinha as, by way of extension, what truly does happen to Cidinhas everywhere, the character, Cidinha, in this interpretation becoming a metaphor for female existence in general. The story's final line, "Fate is implacable" (62), would seem to reinforce this interpretation, the sense that the story's primary thematic thrust has less to do with what may or may not be happening to this particular Cidinha than with all the Cidinhas of the world, who are all too often reduced to having to live lives that are repressed, socially and sexually, or to living in fear of being raped and murdered. Either way, their fate is sealed, this conclusion constituting a powerful indictment of the ways society is structured, as we see in the ways the male authorities deal with Cidinha, and of the ways this structuring permits the systematic abuse of women, an issue that has echoed as a basic theme of Lispector's work since "The Burned Sinner and the Harmonious Angels."

Lispector's work is, then, intensely ideological because, as a proto-typical form of poststructural writing, it shows, as Terry Eagleton observes, that "the binary oppositions with which classical structuralism tends to work represent a way of seeing typical of ideologies" (Eagleton 133). By relentlessly undercutting and displacing these oppositions (male/female, for example), Lispector's texts, in a way that parallels Derrida's own working method (as in *Glas*), "show how texts come to embarrass their own ruling systems of logic" (133). Her basic technique in this enterprise is to construct narratives that, structurally speaking, are essentially self-questioning chains of aporia, moments of undecidability or impasses of meaning when the text seems to contradict itself or, at least, to tantalize the reader with plausible interpretations that seem both consistent and inconsistent with others that stem from it. Although "Pig Latin" epitomizes this essentially deconstructive technique, it is present in virtually everything else that Lispector wrote.

Not surprisingly, then, Lispector's sociopolitical concerns also often surfaced in her nonfiction works, especially in those that appeared in her Saturday column for the *Jornal do Brasil* between August 1967 and December 1973. Although, as befits the genre, these *crônicas* (which she described as her "Saturday conversations") vary greatly in terms of style, tone, and content, and many of them are political in ways both implicit and explicit. A careful review of these fascinating texts, many of which are very personal in nature, reveals Lispector's often pungent irony, her droll sense of humor, her insightful reflections on her own work as a writer, and the idiosyncrasies of her life (including her life as a mother) and outlook. Rather quickly, however, the reader of these columns comes to regard Lispector as a socially conscious writer, one who considered herself to be both committed and "engaged." As we read in "Literature and Justice," for example, Lispector regarded herself as "engajada" (engaged), as a writer who felt her work was very much connected to the world in which she lived.[10] Never strident or obvious, Lispector's political voice is yet always present, acutely conscious of the terrible inequities that afflict Brazilian society and giving the lie to the widespread myth that she was somehow indifferent to Brazil's urgent social, political, and economic problems. Noting, in a 30 December 1967 *crônica*, that she "would like to see a socialist government in Brasil" (*DW* 82), Lispector goes on to say that although the political aspect of her own fiction may or may not "become more powerful one day" (84), the need to provide food to people who are starving is of more urgent concern; as she points out, this concern involves "the latest Papal Encyclical which defends armed rebellion as a last resort against dictatorships" (84). As Giovanni Pontiero has aptly summed it up, while Lispector's "political voice may have been understated, her note of censure discreet," "her solidarity on behalf of Justice and human dignity was beyond question" (30).

As we have seen, Lispector's texts are characterized by their play of varied, often contradictory forces, which, in Lispector's world, emerge as something akin to Kristeva's "semiotic" (Mathie 121–34), the disruptive, pulsational pressure within language itself.[11] The particular tropes, moreover, that so distinguish Lispector's work—semantic ambiguity, narrative disruption (or decentering), silence and absence—express their poststructural sense of destabilization even more directly than do her characters and themes, which, given the densely poetic nature of her style, tend to find themselves disseminated among her interweaving of images and rhetorical conceits. As evidenced in the syntax that relates to her characters, however, Lispector's view of our need for change in our social structures (defined, at its base, by changes in relations between people) parallels Kristeva's argument in *Revolution in Poetic Language*. In both cases, the pressure for social change is expressed in a language that disrupts, subverts, or offers an alternative to the various discourses of authority. For both Kristeva (in theory) and Lispector (in practice), the "desire" inherent in poetic language extends the subversively decentering "semiotic" into the authoritarian power structures that define society's closed, symbolic order.

Many of Lispector's major texts, however, also demonstrate what Kristeva seems to have in mind when she uses the term "semanalysis," which is understood by poststructuralists to refer to a critical approach to literature in which a text is viewed as a dynamic psychic battleground in which the language of the speaking/writing subject, driven by desires and fears only partially understood, reacts to the sociopolitical and economic forces of culture and history. As Kristeva outlines it in *Semeiotiké: Recherches pour une sémanalyse* (1959), this interpretive approach to the literary text allows us to perceive its inherent "productivity," its tendency (more pronounced in Lispector's post-1961 texts) to displace, decenter, suspend, or otherwise destabilize the ideological orthodoxies of a given culture by using its language in unorthodox, disruptive, and "forbidden" ways. It does this in order to emphasize the semantic "slippage" and uncertainty that come into play when we attempt to definitively connect a signifier with its alleged signified. The result of this approach to literature (to writing, reading, and understanding), as we see vividly expressed in virtually all of Lispector's novels and stories, is the textual production of what Kristeva understands as polysemic "negativity," a semantic free play that undermines our facile, programmed acceptance of such oppositions (and their concomitant sociopolitical structures) as truth/falsity, good/evil, right/wrong, and (of particular importance for Lispector) male/female. Such an interpretation (or such writing) thereby "opens up" not only a text's endless potential meanings but also the diverse—and often conflicting—cultural discourses that inscribe them. Accurately reflecting the particular political consciousness involved in the evolution of structuralism into poststructuralism (with the issues of gender, power, and sexual ideology leading the way), the narratives of Clarice Lispector, which deal so relentlessly with the ways men and women conceive of themselves and of each other, are thus political in ways that are both profoundly personal and broadly public. Her poetic, introspective texts lead their readers (male and female) to reflect on how we should live our lives, on what it means to engender an identity for one's self within the context of a society whose power structures—whether familial, social, political, sexual, or economic—are so often oppressive. It is here, therefore, in the liberating, humanizing confluence of poststructural thought and feminism,[12] that we see the true nature of Lispector's political significance.

Written, according to Olga Borelli, concurrently with *The Hour of the Star* between the years 1974 and 1977, Lispector's posthumously published novel, *A Breath of Life: Pulsations* (1977), exemplifies this vital linkage between language, being, and identity (both individual and cultural), a linkage that had characterized such earlier works as *The Passion according to G. H., An Apprenticeship, or The Book of Delights*, and *The Hour of the Star*, the latter a text with which it has much in common, particularly in regard to the role played by the two male narrative voices and their relationships to the female characters they "create." In a larger sense, *A Breath of Life* also involves the reader in what we might call the dialectic of language, the ongoing struggle "in which," as Susan Canty Quinlan observes, "people engage with themselves and with society" (in *Clarice Lispector: A Bio-Bibliography*, 145). Returning once again to the issues of gender and power, as these relate to both human and textual relationships, *A Breath of Life* features a self-conscious male narrator/ author who, for Maria José Somerlate Barbosa, functions (like Rodrigo S. M., of *The Hour of the Star*) as the focus of a subversively parodic text, one that challenges and, eventually, offers an alternative ontology to the prevailing logocentric power structure, or "system" (as Lispector tended to refer to it).[13] As the male "autor" of *A Breath of Life* declares, at one point: "I note with surprise but with resignation that Ângela is commanding me. She even writes better than I. Now our modes of speaking are crossing and becoming confused" (my translation). And later, this same male "autor," at this point frustrated with the growing independence and authority of his creation, the character Ângela Pralini,[14] begins to contemplate the creation of a new woman:

> I'm going to invent a woman, one who's organized and logical, who has the propensity of a [female] surgeon. Or she might be a lawyer. And who in bed is limpid and without sin. I'm going to live with her. There would be more security than with Ângela. (my translation)

Then, in another example of the kind of unexpected undercutting that is so characteristic of Lispector's writing, the "autor" realizes that he needs Ângela (and all she represents) much more that he needs his "organized and logical" woman (who, in yet another case of ironic gender displacement, can also be said to represent the female appropriation of the same phallocentric order that the text seeks, on another level, to subvert):

> What can I do if she's anarchical?
> Except imitate her since she is stronger than I am: I am a product of a thought, she isn't a product: she's everything. She broke my system. She is my ancestor and so pre-historically mine that she's becoming inhuman, even though she writes with a false order.
> Ângela is my aphrodisiac . . . (she) is freer than I am. (my translation)

By creating a text that, through the decentering interplay of its various narrative voices, challenges its own veracity, *A Breath of Life* effectively undermines our ordinary notions about power and control with a convincing implementation of what Rita Terezinha Schmidt terms "feminine discourse," "a kind of writing (and consciousness about both writing and reading) that, as practiced by Clarice Lispector, effaces the conventional distinctions between such institutionalized dichotomies as male/female, self/other, and truth/falsity" (Schmidt 59–67). In short, Lispector's texts, from the beginning of her career to the end, interrogate the unstable and unsettling process of signification that characterizes poststructural theory in its sociopolitical context.

Apropos of this, as works by Chris Weedon (*Feminist Practice and Poststructuralist Theory*, 1987) and Mark Poster (*Critical Theory and Poststructuralism: In Search of a Context*, 1989) show, two aspects of poststructural thought (both of which apply to Lispector's texts) have established themselves as being especially significant in the sociopolitical context: its powerful critique of language as an ontological force, and its view of human identity as being the product of linguistic practices that are constantly experiencing historical and cultural change. Language, like the various ideologies and technologies that relate to it, inexorably alters the phenomenological experience of each subject,[15] which is why it is misleading to think of G. H.'s narrative world, for example, either as being "static" or as losing "substance" and "dissolving into . . . nothing." It is true that while the reader must extrapolate the sociopolitical significance of texts like *The Passion according to G. H.* and *The Stream of Life*, in many other works, including "The Burned Sinner and the Harmonious Angels," "Family Ties," "The Smallest Woman in the World," "Beauty and the Beast, or The Wound Too Great," *An Apprenticeship, or The Book of Delights*, or *The Hour of the Star*, this same sociopolitical potency lies much closer to the surface.

The story of Macabéa (*The Hour of the Star*) is, in this regard, especially illustrative of Lispector's late political consciousness. Chronically malnourished and so bereft of training that she is virtually incapable of surviving, economically and socially, even in a culture of no more than rudimentary technological sophistication (she is an incompetent "hunt-and-peck" typist), Macabéa, like so many other Lispector characters, is a victim of language, a point poignantly underscored by her virtual inability to type, to "process words." So utterly overwhelmed is she by the world of business, telecommunications, and data processing that her pathetic sense of self actually derives from her relationship to those very technologies and from her equally disempowering human relationships with Glória (her "friend" and workmate) and Olímpico (her "lover"), as well as with the larger discourses and power structures that sustain them all. Indeed, Macabéa's plight can easily be taken as a metaphoric representation of late-twentieth-century Brazil, a culture whose passion and commitment to technology and development is undercut both by its deeply rooted, institutionalized, and dehumanizing social inequities and by its poverty, which (as we see in this novel) has a real psycholinguistic coefficient in the character of Macabéa.[16]

A Marxist critic, however, like Fredric Jameson or Catherine Belsey, might well question this point, arguing that if indeed it was Lispector's intention in *The Hour of the Star* to indict the kind of society that spawns not just Macabéa but the "thousands of girls like this girl from the Northeast to be found in the slums of Rio de Janeiro" (*Hour* 14), then she should have been much more explicit about doing so. As it is, however, *The Hour of the Star* does indict this kind of unfair and inhumane social organization, but it does so obliquely, in ways that the reader intuits primarily from the abusive, meretricious, and exploitative relationships that Macabéa can neither escape nor avoid.

As the text makes clear, nevertheless, the first and most basic of all these relationships—one that precedes even the economic relationships—is that of the individual human being and language, which emerges in this novel as an ontological web that forwards itself by means of the symbiotic relationship between (seemingly) Lispector herself, her acutely self-conscious male author/narrator (Rodrigo S. M.), Macabéa, and, finally, the reader (real and implied), whose active interpretational involvement in this work should not be underestimated. As the male narrator makes clear, for example:

> Remember that, no matter what I write, my basic material is the word. So this story will consist of words that form phrases from which there emanates a secret meaning that exceeds both words and phrases. . . . In no sense an intellectual, I write with my body. (14–15, 16)

Later, when Macabéa is struck and killed by a yellow Mercedes (an event that, with trenchant irony, fulfills the prophecies outlined by the fortune-teller, Madame Carlota), the narrator asks:

> What was the truth about my Maca? It is enough to discover the truth that she no longer exists: the moment has passed. (84)

At this point, as if to summarize his cognizance of the creative but elusive process that is writing and reading, the narrator declares:

> Macabéa has murdered me. She is finally free of herself and of me. . . . I have just died with the girl. . . . Suddenly it's all over. Macabéa is dead. The bells were ringing without making any sound. I now understand this story. She is the imminence in those bells, pealing so softly.

The greatness of every human being.
Silence. (85)

Macabéa, then, trapped by her penury and ignorance and symbolizing not only the victimization of one class by another but the destructive operation of systems and structures that are beyond control, ranks as one of Lispector's most compelling and most overtly politicized characters, one who suffers the failure of language as viscerally as she suffers the hunger that gnaws at her belly and the pain that racks her body.

Yet for however much Macabéa's plight does offer the reader a singular opportunity to approach one of Lispector's most powerful texts in terms of class conflict and economic exploitation, a less obvious form of conflict comes to the fore in many of her other works: the problems inherent in attempting to develop a viable, honest, and satisfying identity in a society that both segregates and categorizes people on the basis of such issues as race, class, age, and gender, and that then denies them an opportunity to change. Linking all of this together, however, is the question of language, which, as in so many of Lispector's texts, deals with the problem of power, of authority. In *The Hour of the Star*, as we have seen, Lispector shows us that inasmuch as power is a function of social, political, and economic structures external to us, it is also a function of individual identities and human relationships, both of which are defined in terms of language use.

That Lispector, a woman writer fully cognizant both of the socioeconomic situation of women in Brazil[17] and of its terrible social inequities, creates a man, Rodrigo S. M., to tell the story of a fatally disadvantaged woman, Macabéa, is not as revealing of Lispector's most basic concern as is the metafictional nature of the male narrator's discourse itself; for all that he is empowered in other ways (class, age, gender, resources), Rodrigo cannot dominate language, and because he cannot there emerges a sense in which he cannot dominate even a virtually languageless creature like Macabéa. Such control as he has is illusory, if not pernicious, a facet of the text that the reader can interpret as "an undermining of the dominant language of sexual indifference—the phallocentric language—which is responsible for the oppression of Brazil's Macabéas (and Lispectors, too) and for the failures of the linguistic sign."[18]

While this merging of Marxist, feminist, and semiotic interpretations (Gálvez-Breton 63) clearly distinguishes *The Hour of the Star*, a similar impulse runs throughout Lispector's work. In *An Apprenticeship, or The*

Book of Delights (1969), for example, a work dominated by dialogue between a man (Ulisses) and a woman (Lóri), the question of dominance (as a function of language) arises from out of the relationship that Lóri and Ulisses create for themselves, a relationship unique in all of Lispector's work.[19] Writing intensely from the body, the text emphasizes that language is simultaneously our gift and our curse, that it cannot express what we wish it to express, even as we use it, paradoxically, to deal with the silence that both goes beyond language and lies within it:

> How to come within reach of that profound meditation of silence? Of that silence beyond the memory of words? . . . Sometimes you recognize silence in the very middle of the word. . . . There's a great silence inside me. And that silence has been the source of my words. . . . Know when to keep quiet so that you don't lose yourself in words. (*Apprenticeship* 19, 21, 46, 114)

Yet the text also makes it clear that although Lóri and Ulisses suffer from the frustration and uncertainty that stem from language's instability, they cannot avoid their predicament, for the language that fails them is, in their quest for perfect union, for perfect love, precisely the same force that compels them to seek something better. Eventually, Lóri and Ulisses will have to confront a society that will not easily accept the new and "revolutionary" identities they desire to forge into a new (and, to a degree, androgynous) union, one that they feel will transform them both. The revolutionary dimension of Lóri's character is, ironically enough, not fully perceived until the very end of the novel, when she (and the reader) suddenly find themselves contemplating a society structured in ways that even Ulisses might find difficult to accept, especially if he has not really changed as much as he says he has (he is, after all, still interrupting Lóri even in the novel's final line in order to impose his interpretation of the events that have transpired between them). Recalling that the mythic basis of Lóri's name evokes the legend of the Lorelei, the reader realizes that the very profemale sociopolitical structure Lóri may have in mind at this point in the novel (when she has, effectively speaking, liberated herself) would, if enacted, spell the end for patriarchal culture (for example, no more interrupting of female empowerment), just as the Lorelei lured ancient boatmen to their deaths.

So while Ulisses talks a great deal about how he has already begun—through a new awareness of language—to create a new identity for himself, it is the story of Lóri, seen, as in *The Hour of the Star*, largely from the (dominant?) perspective of a man (Ulisses), that commands the reader's attention, however. This helps explain why, late in the novel, Lóri must ask Ulisses the hitherto submerged sociopolitical question: "What's my social value, Ulisses? I mean right now?" (115). To which Ulisses, who, like Rodrigo, enjoys certain privileges, responds: "That of a woman, a marginal member of Brazilian society's middle class today" (115). As a socialist who claims to be trying to forge a new identity for himself (and, presumably, for his society) by valorizing semantic relativity and flux—that is, the silence that, as Eduardo Portella notes ("O grito do silêncio," introduction to *A hora da estrela*, 9–12), is paradoxically inherent in all language use—Ulisses stands in relation to his text (which, as a male professor of philosophy, he tends to dominate) in a way that is similar to the way Rodrigo relates to his, and in a fashion slightly more self-effacing than occurs in *A Breath of Life*. The difference is that while Ulisses is aware that he is "inevitably humble" when he writes (*Apprenticeship* 64), Rodrigo knows that he can never control language, that the full presence of his references and meanings will always elude his desire to control them.

Although the overall thrust of *An Apprenticeship, or The Book of Delights* is, on its most obvious level, toward the "perfect fusion," the "entire unification," of Lóri and Ulisses, their slowly evolving love story is subtly undercut by several factors, chief among which is the problem of power, of control. As the reader slowly comes to realize, the evolution of the protagonist's relationship deconstructs itself in a way that is prototypical of Lispector's poststructural conception of language and life. Although at their surface level the words of the narrative lead the reader to anticipate a "perfect fusion" for Lóri and Ulisses, one that would be based on a new and "revolutionary" (102) equality between them, the careful reader begins to wonder whether the differences in power that separate them will allow such a union. And while *An Apprenticeship* does, in fact, progress, structurally speaking, on the strength of many scenes, images, and parallel phrasings ("The desire to be Ulysses' and for him to be hers," for example; 86) that imply ontological interchangeability (even to the point of their gendering), it also manifests a progressively greater discrepancy between what the words (especially Ulisses's words) *appear* to mean (their orthodox denotation) and what they may *also* mean, especially to the reader and to Lóri, whose relationship to self and to the other (Ulisses) hangs in the balance.

This powerfully decentering, semantically destabilizing technique, which exemplifies both Lispector's style and her poststructural worldview, attains its maximum expression precisely in the narrative's climactic scene in which Lóri and Ulisses finally engage in sex, the one element of their relationship that, as if it were the embodiment of Derrida's "différance," has been "deferred" until this moment. Having ostensibly "unified" their hitherto separate existences, and having symbolically exchanged orthodox gender roles in the process, Lóri and Ulisses now talk, with Lóri uttering what may be considered the text's most socially significant lines:

> I'm learning along with you, although you think that I've learned from your instruction. But that's not true. I've learned what you didn't dream of teaching me. (115)

Implying, as they do, that what Ulisses (and, perhaps, the reader) had thought all along was the case in regard to Lóri (that he was the "master" while she was the "apprentice") is now not necessarily so, these lines suddenly suggest that what Lóri has really learned from Ulisses may be quite different from what he thought he was teaching her. Thus, the text unexpectedly opens itself up, creating in the process one of the moments of aporia, or undecidability, that form the warp and woof of Lispector's narratives. As befits a poststructural writer, the elusive nature of language itself emerges here as the primary complicating factor; what Ulisses's words appear to mean (that he truly desires Lóri to be "free," that she come to him only when she is "ready") stands in ironic contrast to the actual and often surprising effects his words have on Lóri. By continually interrupting and correcting her, for example, Ulisses effectively "colonizes" Lóri, remaking her, God- or artistlike, in his image, rather than truly "liberating" her, which is what he seems to wish to do. Speaking to Lóri, Ulisses, in fact, declares at one point: "I thought that I could work with you the same way some artists do: conceiving and creating at the same time. . . . [T]o conceive and create is the great privilege of a few" (31).

When, at the conclusion of the novel, Lóri observes that what she has learned from Ulisses he never dreamed he was teaching her, she reveals the great irony that, stemming from her name, leads the reader to reconsider the power structures—some seen, some not seen—that are altering the relationship between them. Reinvoking her mythological heritage, Lóri (or Lorelei) suddenly reveals herself to the reader as much less of a siren, whose seductive song leads sailors to their death, than does Ulisses, the would-be liberator and "revolutionary" whose own siren song (which does, by her own admission, seduce Lóri) can be said to effectively uphold the very phallogocentric power structures he claims he wants to subvert. The reader comes to feel that Ulisses's seemingly attractive but ultimately authoritative voice (his language) eventually emerges, ironically, as the greatest threat to Lóri—and to anyone who seeks a genuinely equitable, mutually supportive and harmonious relationship.

But even this interpretation is rendered uncertain by a further consideration of Ulisses in this same context. Insofar as he can be taken to be a pedantic, self-possessed, and occasionally fatuous intellectual, Ulisses does not come across as either malevolent or deliberately deceitful (though, significantly, Lóri does contemplate this latter issue: "Lóri had only one fear: that Ulisses, the great Ulisses . . . might deceive her. Like her father"; 109); indeed, the reader feels that even in the full presence of his pretentious verbosity he is basically sincere in his love for Lóri and in his determination to wait for her until she is "ready," until she is able to "advise herself," for, as he himself says, "I don't give you any advice. I simply . . . think that all I do is wait. Wait perhaps for you to advise yourself" (32). Interpretationally, the reader's problems with regard to Ulisses are thus twofold: First, to what extent, if at all, does he perceive the discrepancy that exists between the language he uses to guide or instruct Lóri in her supposedly liberating "apprenticeship" in life and the ironically imprisoning effect it has on her? They are equal, for example, only when he remains silent; when he speaks, his language—his masculine discourse—overwhelms her. Indeed, as Ana Luisa Andrade has argued, *An Apprenticeship, or The Book of Delights* can easily be interpreted as a deeply parodic work in which Ulisses's "masculine" writing is undone and re-dressed (as if in women's garb) via the "feminine writing" of Lóri (Andrade 1988, 47–54), which, in its fluidity, expansiveness, and semantic fertility, stands in animating and, as we have seen, truly revolutionary contrast to his language.

The second uncertainty with respect to Ulisses' character—and especially as it manifests itself in the conclusion—is to what extent he sees himself as a victim, or at least a product, of the same androcentric culture that, symbolically speaking, has "emasculated" Lóri, rendering her "passive" and quiescent and (for purposes of the narrative) necessitating her "apprenticeship" and her subsequent "transformation" into "a different woman" (*Apprenticeship* 114), the one who emerges in the conclusion, the one whose relationship with Ulisses is, for the reader, suddenly rendered moot, perhaps most especially to her. In ways clear to the reader, but, apparently, not clear to him, Ulisses is what he is because, for all his talk about having undergone his own "liberating" "apprenticeship" (102, 104), he still upholds, in his relationship to Lóri, the very sociopolitical structure from which he says he wants to free her. Hence, the discrepancy between what his words seem to mean and the imprisoning effect they may be having on Lóri (and, again, ironically, on him).

This would explain why, again in the very complex conclusion, although Ulisses twice tells Lóri that they should get married (marriage being a legal status that, in 1969 Brazil, would, again in symbolic terms, have also made Lóri very much a prisoner, much as Joana was in *Near to the Wild Heart* and that the woman in "Flight" was), she remains silent, the self-affirming flow of her burgeoning female language already carrying her, perhaps, down a different, more revolutionary path: "The quavering light of dawn was breaking. For Lóri the atmosphere was miraculous. She had reached the impossible in herself" (116). The reader can easily infer from these poetically charged words that Lóri's "final" transformation was sweeping her into a state of freedom that, surprisingly and unexpectedly, transports her beyond even that of the perhaps well-intended but still trapped Ulisses, who, as the text indicates, is about to launch into yet another "masculine" discourse ("What I think is this: . . ."; 116), one that "ends" the narrative by simultaneously (and ironically) implying that while his condition will continue on as it is, hers—and society's—may have only just begun to evolve. This particular response to the manifold openness of *An Apprenticeship, or The Book of Delights* thus destabilizes what we have seen are the novel's most cogent sociopolitical lines (in which Ulisses tells Lóri that, as a woman, she is a marginal member of Brazil's middle class), and it does so chiefly by legitimizing Lóri's sexuality:

> [Y]ou've just come out of prison as a free agent and no one can forgive you for that. Sex and love aren't forbidden to you anymore. You've finally learned how to exist. (115)

This learning how to exist, the apprenticeship of life that springs from the confluence of language, gender, power, and being, thus takes on implications for Lóri/Lorelei that Ulisses, the "master" who would speak the words of instruction and guidance to her, is not aware of and that he cannot, as yet, see the relevance of for his own existence. The reader comes to feel, at the end of this novel, that if human society is truly to become more equitable, for men, for women, and for relations between them, the Ulisseses of our world, who possess power, must learn to wield it differently, whether in love, in apprenticeships, or in marriage, none of which exist outside of language. So while as early as 1940 and "Flight," and "The Burned Sinner and the Harmonious

Angels" (written between 1948 and 1949), Lispector was linking the se-miotic fluidity of language and the politics of discourse analysis to the situation of women (and of men) in a society ruled by oppressive phal-logocentric value systems, this intensely sociopolitical theme would be dealt with again and again by her, becoming, finally, one of the defining thematic features of her work.

Although *An Apprenticeship, or The Book of Delights* is undoubtedly the most famous of the several Lispector works that deal with this issue, another text that very effectively demonstrates Lispector's concern with the issue of gender and its sociopolitical implications is "The First Kiss," a story first published in 1971. Replete with a number of prototypical Lispectorian motifs, including the complexities of love, the problematic relationship of words to reality, and interlocking images involving water, animals, the body, and truth, "The First Kiss" charts the transformation of a callow "boy" into a "man," a state of being once again circum-scribed, as the text shows, by feelings of aggressiveness, isolation, power, anxiety, and pride.

One of the relatively few Lispector texts to feature a male protagonist, "The First Kiss" is also unique in that it utilizes a nascent sexuality as the force that transforms the main character. But because the images that convey his final metamorphosis are so negative, with his newfound "aggressiveness" given particular emphasis, the reader is led to wonder whether the "boy" is really any better off for having "become a man" (*DW* 435). If to "become a man" means one must also accept aggressive-ness, isolation, anxiety, and pride, among other seemingly undesirable attributes, then the process by which our cultures define what it means to be a "man" is called into question, as it is in "The Message," a story that, as we have seen, deals in a most striking way with a similar theme. In "love" with a "girl" but suffering from a great "thirst," one that per-vades his entire being and that "had been there for years" (434), the boy comes across a statue of a nude woman, from whose open mouth a steady stream of water gushes forth. By "firmly" pressing his lips, "to the orifice from where the water was emerging" (435), the boy, in effect, makes love to the "woman" and receives from her the life-giving water. As he real-izes that he has "pressed his lips to the mouth of this female statue," the reader learns that "[l]ife had streamed from those stone lips, passing from one mouth to the other" (435).

Quickly moving from this epiphanic moment to one that, driven by a powerful though muted eroticism, initiates the boy's confusing trans-formation into "manhood," we then read:

Intuitivamente, confuso na sua inocência, sentia intrigado: mas não é de uma mulher que sai o líquido vivificador, o líquido germinador de vida. . . . Olhou a estátua nua.

Ele a havia beijado. (515–16)

[Confused in his innocence, he intuitively felt perplexed: it is not from woman that life-giving semen comes, that germinating sap of life. . . . He stared at the naked statue.

He had kissed her. (435)]

Absent in the original but rendered overt in the translation, this oblique reference to semen, which, appearing in a number of Lispector texts can be taken as another case of Lispector's "writing the *male* body," then immediately leads into the story's pivotal scene, one that bespeaks the boy's disruptively burgeoning sexuality:

He felt a tremor which was outwardly invisible and which started deep down inside him, possessing his entire body as it finally exploded and caused his cheeks to burn (435).

Implying, through suggestions not only of penile erection but of ejaculation, that the boy's new consciousness is profoundly sexual and body based, the narrative then concludes this crucial though ambiguous scene by telling us that the boy, "[p]uzzled and apprehensive[,] . . . could see that part of his body which had always been so relaxed, and which had now become aggressively tense. This had never happened to him before" (435). Linking images of this newly discovered sexuality to male aggression, the text then tells us now that for this "boy," "[l]ife was completely new, different, a fresh discovery which left him uneasy" (435), for, as the reader realizes, "[h]e had become a man" (435), the latter an ontologically and politically dubious state of being in Clarice Lispector's uncertain, opaque universe.

A telling sign of this uncertainty is that beyond its possible focus on the sexually driven transformation of a "boy" into a "man," "The First Kiss" can also be read as a story of rape, of violation, abandonment, and isolation. Seen from this perspective, these same lines take on very different meanings, a feature that is fully characteristic of Lispector's best work. As if not wishing to "see" (that is, to understand the implications of what he is doing), the boy closes his eyes before pressing his lips "firmly" (435) on the "orifice" from which the water pours. Why, one feels compelled to ask, does Lispector employ the modifier "firmly" ("ferozmente" in the original), which, among other possible meanings, certainly suggests an "aggressiveness" on the part of the boy, an "aggressiveness" that could be construed as denoting a symbolic act of rape? In doing so, he is, in a sense, forcing himself upon the statue/woman, violating her in selfish fulfillment of *his* great psychosexual need, *his* inner "thirst." One wonders, too, why he presses his lips "firmly" against an "orifice"; surely this particular diction choice on Lispector's part expands the range of semantic possibilities to include the sexual. Once finished with his "drinking" of what the statue/woman "offers," or represents, he opens his eyes and "sees" that "her face" (435) was "almost," but not quite, "touching his" (435); in other words, there was no union of male and female, as was so powerfully suggested in *An Apprenticeship, or The Book of Delights*, only the violation of one by the other and the resultant separation and estrangement. In a key line for this interpretation, the text tells us that when the boy had "taken that first sip" (commenced the violation, literally or figuratively), "something icy had made contact with his lips, something," we learn, that was "colder than water" (435). What does he feel that is "colder" than the "water" he seeks to slake his raging "thirst"? Could it be his aggression, the cure for which lies in the quick repetition of this attribute as it epitomizes, albeit disturbingly, his nascent manhood? This would explain why, as he begins to sense the implication of what has happened, he became suddenly "confused in his innocence," and why "he intuitively felt perplexed," for he had been gendered to believe that "it is not from woman that life-giving semen comes, that germinating sap of life" (435), which, in this context, is perfectly paralleled in the image of the woman/statue's "life-giving" water, and which can also be described as "that germinating sap of life." When, as in the poststructural universe of Clarice Lispector, human existence is understood in terms of language, women can possess semen/water and men can "give birth" to new states of consciousness and being, to new identities, to texts (as authors), and most important of all, to lives understood as texts, as verbal relationships that are fluid, mutable, and generating diverse interpretations.

Presented as the bane of human existence, aggression surfaces in Lispector's world as a destructive, exploitative force, one that, though more typically seen as a prime feature of what society ("the others" of "The Message," for example) chooses to call a "man," clearly has a pernicious effect on the ways both women and men see themselves, each other, and their relationships, which constitute the basic units of our societies. One solution, Lispector's gender-conscious texts suggest, is to reformulate our accepted biological, psychological, and cultural definition of what it means to be a "man" or a "woman." In Lispector's world, being—in terms of our consciousness of it—reveals itself time after time to be a function of language, which, in its myriad manifestations, runs the gamut from the broadly public (as when Lóri, of *An Apprenticeship, or The Book of Delights*, asks Ulisses what her "social value" is) to the deeply private (as in the lyrical stream of life/language presented in *The Stream of Life*). One of Lispector's most brilliant stories, "The First Kiss" demonstrates the extraordinary range of her semantically shifting, politically contextualized, and erotically charged narrative world.

One of her later works that went even further in this direction was *The Stream of Life*, a 1973 "fiction" that has been described by Elizabeth Lowe as a narrative that "initiates a whole political process that lives beyond the text" and that "has to do not just with sexual politics but . . . a holistic vision of an evolving society."[20] Focusing on Lispector's life-long preoccupation with the silence that envelops and permeates words, Lowe goes on to say that the Brazilian writer "wages her revolution with silence, creating spaces around words that allow her protagonist to follow her own text" (82). Exemplifying Derrida's theory of signification, these "spaces" constitute a primary source of the poststructural ethos that so pervades her work. Based here, as elsewhere in her writings, on a self-reflective and probing dialogue with the issues of language, gender, and power, *The Stream of Life* rejects "the dominant male, the law and its male-imposed order" in the creation of "a new transsexual language" (Lowe 1990, 83). As the nameless female narrator, who wants "the breast," and its "thick milk" (*SL* 28), declares:

> It suddenly occurred to me that it's not necessary to have order to live. There's no pattern to follow and there's not even pattern itself: I am born. I'm still not ready to speak of "him" or "her." I point to "that." (28)

The silence that permeates this "transsexual" language is thus neither totally positive nor totally negative; an evolving combination of diverse elements, it transforms itself in relation to the other signs that surround it. Expressing both the fecund wellspring of true communication and, paradoxically, the failure of language to communicate, silence emerges as one of Lispector's most integral motifs,[21] one, moreover, that erodes barriers between differing modes of being (the masculine and feminine, for example) while seeking at the same time to harmonize them in an all-consuming affirmation of life freely lived in a state of maximum consciousness.

A work that had earlier moved in this direction was *The Passion according to G. H.* (1964), a novel featuring yet another self-conscious female narrator trying to come to grips with existence and her place in it. Concentrating once again on the relationship between language and being, the narrator (a woman known only by her initials, G. H.) comes to realize herself in terms that are both private and, less obviously, public. Surprisingly, however, the telling linkage between her public and private world occurs almost at the outset of her story, where its political significance is easily missed. Expressed in the form of an unusual metaphor, this critical linkage is presented as a "third leg" that G. H. says she is missing:

> Something's missing that once was essential to me and is so no longer.
> I don't need it anymore, as though I had lost a third leg. (*Passion* 3–4)

The politically decisive element here is that G. H., reflecting on the meaning of the experience she will describe in the remainder of her text, clearly apprehends that this now lost "third leg" had previously kept her from "walking" (that is, seeing, understanding, or becoming something different) by making her a "stable tripod" (4), an image that is essential to the early development of G. H. as a character. The key to deciphering G. H.'s predicament in this crucial opening scene is to understand this "third leg" as representing the phallogocentric system. If we interpret her missing "third leg" in this fashion, we can see not merely that G. H. is, through the run of her narrative, a woman profoundly transformed by her encounter with language, but a woman being granted a new vision of how she might now deal with other people, how she might now function differently in society.

Fascinatingly, however, this interpretation of the text as reflecting the birth of a "new" G. H. is itself undercut by other events. Coming late in the narrative, as she is emerging from her reverie, G. H., suddenly making plans for what she will do that evening, appears to choose to go out with her friends to the "Top Bambino Club," a decision that, seemingly, suggests that, like Ana (of "Love"), she is returning to the ways of her former, pre-epiphany self. Sensing, perhaps, that as a social being she is unable to live an authentic existence in the inauthentic world of sociopolitical structures, G. H. may here be retreating, in part or in whole, from the unsustainable insights and revelations that precede this moment. To do so does not necessarily invalidate what she has experienced and realized; indeed, it expands it, showing us in the process the perhaps unresolvable tension that exists between our "authentic," and tumultuous, inner worlds and our "inauthentic" but inescapable "now." G. H.'s transformation thus involves her growth from the secure but restrictive "stable tripod" identity she knew in a world where she passively accepted the norms and roles apportioned her by society to the relatively free and unfettered (if "disillusioning" and "horrifying") existence she is living in the novel's "now," when she has divested herself of the immobilizing "third leg." Couched in other terms, G. H.'s metamorphosis moves from the stability afforded by structuralism and its neatly interconnecting systems to the messy flux of poststructuralism and its denial of the all-encompassing and comforting systems of knowledge symbolized by G. H.'s "third leg."

Although in 1964 G. H. (like Clarice Lispector) did not have the lexicon of poststructuralism available to her, this remarkable *texte* fully engages the destabilizing, decentering experience of language play that poststructuralism involves, including the anxiety we feel, having lost or rejected our conventional sense of self and of our "proper" place in the universe, at having to face the uncertainties and sense of arbitrariness that characterize the poststructural worldview. As G. H., keenly conscious of her own evolving persona, expresses it:

> Up to now, finding myself was having a ready-made person-idea and mounting myself inside it. . . . The person-idea that I had came from that third leg of mine, the one that held me fast to the ground. (4)

But just as poststructuralism, for all its semiotic free play, cannot escape the endless systems of structuralism, neither can G. H. escape the systems that, paradoxically, structure the (relative) "freedom" she now feels is imminent:

> But now . . . will I be freer?
>   No! I know that I'm still not sensing freely, that once again I'm thinking because my goal is to find . . . (4)

Then, evincing the distrust of totalizing systems that is a hallmark of poststructuralism, G. H. declares:

> I always want the guarantee of at least thinking that I understand, I don't know how to just give myself over to disorientation. . . . Maybe disillusionment is the fear of no longer fitting into a system? (5)

G. H. concludes her tangled rumination on being-as-language by both "writing and speaking" (10), an act that, recalling Derrida's reservations about "phonocentrism," momentarily "privileges" the first term ("writing") of this yoking only to "de-privilege" it a moment later:

[L]et me have the great courage to resist the temptation to invent a form. . . . I'm afraid I'll start "making" sense, with the same meek madness that up to yesterday was my "healthy" way of fitting into a system. (7)

By reading this "system" as the phallogocentric Weltanschauung, replete with its self-sustaining sociopolitical organization, we can interpret G. H. as a character suddenly confronted with the freedom to begin living differently, to make different choices, and to act on the strength of new insights and outlooks; in short, G. H. presents herself as having the potential (if not the will) to change in accordance with her sudden and destabilizing experience of language, her experience of "living language" as opposed to merely "using it" as a tool of rational discourse. As *The Passion according to G. H.* shows, the great ground of Lispector's fictional universe is always language, and G. H., one of Lispector's most memorable characters, develops by, through, and in language usage:

I don't have a word to say. Why don't I just stay quiet, then? But if I don't force myself to talk, silence will engulf me in waves. Word and form will be the plank on top of which I shall float over billows of silence. . . . [N]ow, in my disparagement of the word, perhaps I'll finally be able to start talking. (12, 14)

We can infer from this that what G. H. experiences is a vision of a new kind of human existence, one that, through its written form, affords us a more honest (if imperfect and disconcerting) understanding of our selves and of the unstable, uncertain worlds we make with our language. G. H. concludes her narrative, in fact, by coming to the realization that while language is the mercurial mechanism we humans use to seek knowledge and understanding, these can never be "fully" or "perfectly" attained because there is no "transcendental signifier," no ultimate source; words, G. H. comes to discover, "mean something," or signify, only in terms of other words. G. H.'s dilemma, then, is the poststructural dilemma: to understand is a function of language, the semantic fecundity of which is impossible to stop, control, or evade. As G. H. expresses it:

The world interdepended with me—that was the confidence I had reached: the world interdepended with me, and I am not understanding what I say, never! never again shall I understand what I say. For how will I be able to speak without the world lying for me? How will I be able to speak except timidly, like this: life is itself for me. Life is itself for me, and I don't understand what I am saying.[22] And, therefore, I adore . . . (173)

The ellipsis that actually "ends" G. H.'s narrative (by generating in the reader yet another thought or expression), however, thus implies that even though we cannot, in any perfect way, understand life (that is, reality and the ways we use language to shape, frame, and interpret it), we can, reverentially and erotically, still adore it. Indeed, what we "adore" most of all about the interplay of language and life is (as with G. H.) our newly acquired awareness that, insofar as it is a linguistic construct, life is what we say or write that it is; language shapes, and, in some cases, literally creates, reality. Things happen in the world, of course; people, whether out of love, hate, or some combination or permutation of both, have sex. Violence is done. Hunger hurts inside bellies. And love is (sometimes) attained, created, or lost.

But while things do happen, how we define them and how we imbue them with meaning[23] are inescapably problems of language use: Whose language? With what intent? Under what circumstances? With what consequences? Or meaning? Why? These are the questions that Lispector's characters lead us to ponder as we experience their stories, which gradually lead us to confront the possibility that what we all too easily speak of as "human reality" is, to an extraordinary degree, profoundly verbal in nature, an amalgam of language-based systems—like our legal codes, our moral codes and religions, and our political structures—that, while we may wish them to be perfect and stable, are nonetheless inherently fluid, imperfect, and in a process of constant change. What we must not do is shrink from the tremendous moral responsibility such a liberating worldview places on our words (and the actions that derive from them) and fall back (as characters like Ana, Martim, and G. H. do) on the comfortable but imprisoning "third leg" of a meretricious phallogocentrism that has too long oppressed us all. On balance, then, one feels that even in perhaps "mystical" or mystically inclined texts like *The Passion according to G. H.* and *The Stream of Life*, the world created by Clarice Lispector is, as Elizabeth Lowe says, full of "tremendous energy and hope" (Lowe 1990, 84). At every step, and in a way true to Lispector's always language-conscious vision, it is up to the reader to transform the conceptual vicissitudes of the poststructural *texte* into concrete forms of political action and being.

The more one reads Lispector's texts, the more one feels compelled to interpret her work from a psychoanalytic perspective. Repression (especially of a sexual nature), anxieties about identity and being, frustration, and death are the issues that emerge most in this context, the issues that drive the Brazilian author's endlessly probing narratives. Indeed, once this interpretive tact is taken, the reader is tempted to speculate on the psychology of Lispector herself, to interpret or psychoanalyze her through her work, which, it can be argued, possesses a unique relationship to the development and expression of her personal sense of self. This, certainly, is one of the traditional techniques of psychoanalytic criticism, and though its viability here is as questionable as it is anywhere, I believe it can have a valid role in assessing Lispector's often tormented and perhaps self-expressive texts. As I will try to show in this chapter, these texts lend themselves to analysis particularly in terms of the fragmented Lacanian Subject and Lacanian desire and in terms of both Kristeva's concept of the "subject-in-process" ("sujet en procès") and her theory of the conflict between the semiotic (which, breaking with Lacan, she views as a pre-Oedipal and maternal drive that functions as a point of resistance, or subversion, to all forms of patriarchy) and the symbolic (which, following Lacan, she associates with phallocentric, rule-bound Order).

In psychoanalytic terms, then, the tension that animates Lispector's work may be said to derive from two basic sources, the sexual and the philosophical, with the ontological anxieties of the latter often stemming from the frustrations and complications of the former. From the early story "Flight" to the late "Beauty and the Beast, or The Wound Too Great," but especially from *The Stream of Life* to *A Breath of Life*, Lispector gave birth to narratives in which, seemingly, she sought, through the struggles of her diverse characters, to reveal, define, and valorize herself through the act of writing. For an author so concerned with writing as self-realization, it is not difficult to speculate that Lispector might also have understood writing, and language use in general (particularly in its epistemological function), as our definitively human mode of understanding not only the other but, of more psychoanalytic moment, the splintered, conflicted, and mercurial self as well.[1] It is in this therapeutic, self-creative sense, then, that I believe we are legitimately led to consider the autobiographical dimension of Lispector's *écriture* from a psychoanalytic perspective. Of unique utility to us in this endeavor, moreover, is, as several critics have already noted,[2] an approach to the texts of Lispector from the perspective of modern, and especially Lacanian, psychoanalysis. I seek to expand the critical implications of this approach because of Lacan's application of poststructural thought to his own discussions of psychoanalysis. If there is validity to my argument that poststructuralism represents the best overall theoretical approach to Lispector's texts, then we should be able to see these same issues manifesting themselves in the psychoanalytic terms that Lacan and, in an important way, Julia Kristeva, have elaborated.

As it pertains to poststructural theory, modern psychoanalysis rests heavily on the work of Jacques Lacan, who, as we know, has recast traditional Freudian theory along the lines of Saussurean linguistics. The result—as a number of people, including Jacques Derrida, Hélène Cixous, and Julia Kristeva, have noted—was a new and uniquely language-based explanation of how the human mind works. Central to their description, and an issue that figures prominently in the texts of Clarice Lispector, is the concept of the "speaking" or (more appropriately for Lispector) "writing" subject. For Lacan, who believes that human beings are born into a kind of "pre-existing system of signifiers which take on meanings only within a language system" (Selden 84), a speaking or writing "I" cannot be monolithic and stable; it must be multiple and fluid, changing, if only slightly, in accordance with changing circumstances. As the linguist Emile Benveniste has shown,[3] the "I" who actually enunciates (or writes) a self-referential statement like "tomorrow I will play soccer" cannot be perfectly identical to the "I" of the sentence, which linguists refer to as the "subject of the enunciation" (to distinguish it from the flesh and blood human being who actually makes the statement). Thus, language—even ostensibly self-referential language—can never entirely be that to which it claims to refer, even when it seems to refer to a particular self, a problem any number of Lispectorian protagonists face.

An unalterably symbolic system of signification, language can, however, "be" its own kind of reality; that is, the world of words, of language use, that surrounds us and that identifies that dimension of human existence that sets us apart from the other animals actually constitutes, as for Martim, G. H. or the volatile presence in *The Stream of Life*, a form of reality that exists in and of itself. As a critical theory based on an acceptance of language's inherent ontological potency and on its semantic variability, poststructuralism focuses attention on the relationships that exist between these various subjects, or, as Clarice Lispector presents them, these various aspects of a single (though not unified) subject, a single yet multidimensional character. And because, from Joana to the personae in *A Breath of Life*, Lispector's characters tend to develop from out of their own silent written discourse, they can easily be seen as the loci of the unresolvable conflicts of the unconscious and as the conscious processes that are identified with the chain of unstable signifiers (words) that, linking together, give form to the constantly evolving identities that fill the pages of Lispector's work.

In contrast, then, to what has been called the "old" psychoanalysis, which scoured literary texts in search of vaginal and phallic symbols, Lacanian psychoanalysis is language based, viewing the unconscious not only as being a product, or function, of language, but as being structured like language. As it applies to literary analysis, this "new" psychoanalysis thus has a good deal to say about how texts actually work, how their various constituent parts relate to each other, how they generate their various meanings, and how their readers respond to them. Although in reading Clarice Lispector's work one is led to feel that her life would seem to call for a thorough, psychoanalytically based biography,[4] our task here will be limited to a discussion of what appears to be the most salient psychoanalytically based aspects of her work: sexuality and repression, Thanatos versus Eros, Oedipal relationships (developing, as in an Electra complex, primarily from a female perspective), dreams, and the Subject as site of protagonal conflict.

Seen from the perspective of psychoanalysis, the issue of human sexuality, whether expressed or repressed, deeply affects who and what we are. In the texts of Clarice Lispector, however, sexuality emerges, albeit obliquely, as a force that is absolutely fundamental to our sense of being while at the same time seeming often repressed and troubled, in conflict with established social codes and mores. Yet from *Family Ties* to *A Breath of Life*, we have seen how Lispector's texts are permeated by a strong, if often latent, sexuality, one that stems both from a keen and vital awareness of the body and from the often subversive ways language shapes our realization of the erotic impulse and our understanding of it. Strikingly close to Lacan's theory of language as a pulsating network of signs that totally envelops us and that functions, unconsciously and, at times, consciously, as "a libidinal dynamism" of desire ("The Mirror Stage," *Écrits*, 2), a narrative like *A Breath of Life: Pulsations* does, indeed, "pulse" with desire, which, as always in Lispector's work, develops as a force that is simultaneously "structuring" and "destructuring" itself, that is, undermining, challenging, or otherwise subverting its own conventional laws of conduct and those of readerly interpretation.

Nowhere, however, in Lispector's work is this tension more clearly in evidence than in the story "Plaza Mauá," where, as we have seen, an erotic club is the scene where both men and women can throw off their suffocatingly gendered existences and, giving free rein to their desires, transform themselves into the persons they have wanted to be. Yet even in this powerful tale, the need to express one's sexuality itself is undercut by what could be taken as an authorial reluctance to write, explicitly at least, about sexual expression, about the ontologically signifying nature of the sexual act itself. In short, the sexual potency of "Plaza Mauá" is muted, perhaps even repressed, at the same time that the need to express and recognize a sexually based identity is dramatically brought into focus. The result is that this story vibrates with both a pathos and a humor that make it unique in Lispector's work.

While at this juncture it would seem appropriate to speculate about how Lispector viewed sexuality—her own as well as that of others—it is beyond the scope of this study to do so. Nevertheless, it is interesting to note that Lispector, who is said to have enjoyed at least some forms of pornography (Marting, *Clarice Lispector: A Bio-Bibliography*, xxx) and whose most successful texts pulse with a powerful sexuality, was loath to write even "sexy," much less pornographic, literature, an issue she guardedly discusses in her preface to *The Stations of the Body*, one of her most sexually "explicit" books. What we can do, however, is examine this perhaps revealing story more closely in terms of the sexually charged tension that informs it, a tension deriving from the conflict that, recalling Kristeva, exists between our need to give vent to our sexuality and our knowledge that society prohibits us from doing so. And while this problem affects both men (who, Lispector's texts repeatedly show us, are also forced into rigidly gendered and repressive roles) and women, it is more germane to women, who constitute the great majority of Lispector's protagonists.

In the case of "Plaza Mauá," for example, Luísa, a frustrated housewife, frequents a cabaret known as the Club Erótica, where, once inside, she becomes Carla, an exotic dancer who "stripped," "unfolded," "undulated," and "gave all of herself" (PM 54) in an erotic show that is simultaneously public and private in terms of the transgressive play of desire it engenders. Read on one level, "Plaza Mauá" shows us that for men who possess both power and money, sex is a prized commodity, and at the Club Erótica it is bought and sold freely, as is appropriate for the use of sex as a poststructural signifier. What is less clear, however, is exactly who is doing the buying and selling, and it is here, in this vague, disputed area of libidinal economy, that Lispector's *texte* develops itself. Fully illustrative of Lispector's poststructural outlook, even a seemingly simple text like "Plaza Mauá" possesses, on closer consideration, aspects and relationships that are puzzling, inconsistent, and often contradictory. Implicit both in its socioeconomic implications and in the structuring of the text itself, however, is the possibility that, again in the erotically emancipating space, or site, that is the Club, even hitherto conventional women, too, become free not only to buy and sell sex but to empower and enjoy themselves through sex: "Many mothers and housewives," we are told, went to the club "for the fun of it and to earn a bit of pocket money" (57).

The surface innocence and naiveté of this line of interpretation masks a deeper, darker struggle, however, one that the text itself subtly comes to feature by focusing on the psychosexual drama of Luísa as she slides, like one of Lacan's desire-laden signifiers, in and out of her identity as Carla and as she relates to the male character, Celsinho, who, as a popular and successful transvestite/transsexual of the Club, becomes her rival for the affections of "a tall man with broad shoulders" (57) who enters the Club one evening presumably for reasons that are not only sexually motivated but ambiguous in terms of their sexual orientation. This interpretation is quickly reinforced by Celsinho, who, we are told, took hormones to gain more shapely hips and breasts, who wore lipstick and false eyelashes, and who was a favorite of the sailors, who, the text wryly notes, paid for his services in dollars. More importantly, however, Celsinho also "lusted after" (57) this man, who, presumably, was aware he might well encounter people at the Club Erótica who, for only that night or for a longer period of time and to one degree or another, had chosen to alter their sex, their sexual expression, or their gender, to become, in short, a sexual other. While the text clearly tells us that "the big man appealed to her [Carla]" (57), it tells us nothing about what, if anything, the "big man" felt toward Celsinho/Moleirão (Moleirão being "her" stage name), who was envious of Carla for having attracted the man to her. The need for money and the unfettered expression of desire thus establish themselves as the principal complicating pressures in this closely interwoven tale of libidinal transformation and exchange.

The story ends abruptly after this turning point scene, however, with an angry and jealous Celsinho (the transsexual) screaming, ironically, at Carla, "[Y]ou're not a real woman! . . . You . . . are no woman at all!" (57). This conclusion also returns the reader to the dual issue of gender and being, a topic that, as we have seen, is endemic to Lispector's work. Here, however, it plays a decisive role in the story's overall structuring, which, to a large extent, it can also be said to destabilize. Dealing with the entwined problems of identity as orchestrated by the rules governing our conduct at work, at play, and in our sexuality (the three areas that, for Freud, define human existence), gender, for Clarice Lispector, as for Kristeva and Lacan, emerges as an issue of gynic conflict, of a realization of how words determine and control our multiform identities and our existences. Characters like Luísa/Carla and Celsinho/Moleirão thus embody what Derrida had in mind when he declared that "there is no outside the text"; her characters "live language" as if they themselves were texts speaking endlessly to other texts, which, in many ways, is fundamentally what they are.

What Lispector does throughout her long career, in fact, with the problem of how particular language constructs gender us, not only in the view(s) we hold of ourselves and others but in the very roles and activities we will be permitted (and will permit ourselves) to assume, has a surprisingly close parallel to the argument made by the French Marxist philosopher Louis Althusser, in *Writings on Psychoanalysis: Freud and Lacan* (1997). Althusser utilizes the basic principles of Freudian and Lacanian psychoanalysis (specifically the latter's concepts of "the imaginary" and the "unconscious") to explain the various ways ideology (also a function of language use and understanding in the Marxian sense of the term) shapes and orders society. Because texts like "Plaza Mauá" show us, both implicitly and explicitly, that the rules determining gender are the sociopolitical manifestations of the ways we choose to organize the relationships between the unconscious and human society and between sex, money, and power (Barbosa 1997, 27–28), they can also show, as Lacan seeks to do, that the unconscious is a function of language and desire, both of which are preeminently fluid, shifting forces whose value, or significance, fluctuates constantly.

This is why it is so surprising when, at the conclusion of "Plaza Mauá," we learn that the transsexual Celsinho, who yet in another deviation from orthodox gender roles, has adopted a little girl and who, as "a real mother to her" (PM 56), "naturally" (according to the conventional laws of gender, which, ironically, determine Celsinho's identity as a caregiver but not as a sexually active human being) wants his little girl to marry "a man of fortune" and have lots of children and jewels (56). Calling attention to both the sexual ("a man") and the economic ("of fortune") aspects of what s/he wants for the child, Lispector's text emphasizes the ironic contrast between Celsinho's utterly conventional desires (for his child) as a caregiver and his similarly unconventional desires as an active transsexual.

Also emphasized, however, is the additional irony that marks his relationship with Carla/Luisa, who, in contrast to the human being that Celsinho/Moleirão cares for, has a cat, a creature whose welfare is quite lightly regarded by its master, of whom the text says, "Carla scarcely had time to take care of the creature" (56). So while this comic and poignantly rendered tale of ongoing gender reversal, of identity transformed by desire, and the volatility of relationships presents a world in which reality is realized and expressed as a function of erotically charged psycholinguistic exchange (even at the unconscious level), it leads the reader to ponder the multiple meanings at play in Celsinho's final condemnation of Carla (his erstwhile friend and colleague at the Erótica), where Celsinho screams: "You are no woman at all! You don't even know how to fry an egg! And I do! I do! I do" (57). Thus implying that regardless of biological sex a "real" woman's identity is based solely on such "skills" as frying an egg (that is, on a compliance with conventional gender expectations rather than self-realization, and on servitude, whether familial, domestic, social, economic, or political), this key line transforms Carla back into the repressed Luísa, who, devastated by this unexpected turn of events, immediately leaves the Club: "On foot, in black, on the Plaza Mauá at three in the morning. Like the lowest of whores. Alone. Without recourse" (58). Then, underscoring one final time the unexpected and destabilizing ironies that, as in real life, have given shape to this story, she reflects: "It was true: she didn't know how to fry an egg. And Celsinho was more of a woman than she" (58).

Like so many of Lispector's protagonists, Luísa is thus alone at the end of her tale, silently reflecting on her situation. However, what is not clear here (because there is no explicit textual evidence to guide the reader on this point) is how she herself feels about her predicament. We know only that "she breathed deeply" and that "[s]he looked at the lampposts" (58). Was she at this point—that is, as Luísa and alone again—

still distraught? Or was she more resigned than distraught, taking a kind of ill-defined and vaguely perceived solace (as if from Lacan's "imaginary" or Kristeva's "semiotic") from her isolation and solitude, as so many other Lispector characters do? The ambiguity of the text's final lines would seem to make this interpretation entirely feasible, especially given the pattern of shifting identities, realignments of power, personal agendas, and conflicts (conscious and unconscious) that preceded it. Life goes on, even in the anxiety of the poststructural universe. Reminiscent, in both tone and imagery, of the conclusion of Machado de Assis's *Quincas Borba* (1891), Lispector's story thus winds down with Carla-cum-Luísa standing alone, perplexed and "in the dark," literally and figuratively, outside the Club Erótica, the unrepressed site of psychological and physical free play where, as if giving vent to repressed desires within her unconscious, she, signlike, had earlier been able to transform herself into the sexually and economically empowered being known as Carla, the desired and desiring exotic dancer.

Another of Lispector's most challenging short texts, "Pig Latin," also features sexuality as a powerful force in not only the formation (and deformation) of human identity but in the reader's ability to interpret the story as well. This tale, however, goes a step further to link sexuality with what Lacan describes as the conflicted relationship between our various modes, kinds, and degrees of identity, our different motivations and their relationships to "the imaginary" levels of the ego, which Lacan understands linguistically, as a function of a subject (or subjects) spread out, like the links of a chain, between and among the various discourses that constitute it (*Écrits* 168–70). This accounts for the difference that, for Benveniste, exists between the "I" who is the "subject of the enunciation" and the "I" who is the "subject of the enunciating," the person making the actual statement. In ordinary discourse, these "I's" are felt to be more or less the same, but as Lacan would argue and as Lispector shows time after time, the "I" that tells a story about itself cannot ever quite get the two (or more) "I's" unified; words simply cannot fully, completely *be* a person. A gulf, or gap, always exists between language and its referents, and it is here, both Lacan and Derrida assert, that indeterminacy plays havoc with our desire for semantic perfection and stability. It is also here that Lispector grounds her texts. Words, as symbols, can only substitute for being, stand in for or point to the vague, slippery, evanescent realities I have in mind when I speak of myself, as so many of Lispector's characters do. Perhaps this helps explain why overwhelmingly their composition tends to employ the kind of syntax that calls attention to this very act of enunciating, the process of language's own making and remaking, as the most fecund, most revealing aspect of their "content."[5]

One of Lispector's most controversial stories, "Pig Latin" places this issue in a complex matrix involving human sexuality, multiple and shifting subjects (all of which reflect different psychological aspects of the protagonist), the reliability and perspective of the narrative voice, gender, power, and rape. Having caused considerable consternation among the editorial staff of *Ms.* magazine,[6] which first published the English translation of the story, "Pig Latin" features (typical of Lispector) a story line that, on the surface, is very simple: a young woman (an English teacher) is traveling on a train to Rio de Janeiro, where, after a brief stay, she will depart to New York, a city in which she expects to be able to perfect her English. Just after she boards her train, however, she becomes aware of two men looking at her and talking. She comes to believe that they are talking about her in pig Latin and that they plan to rape her[7] when the train passes into an upcoming tunnel. In order to prevent them from doing so, she decides to act like a whore, which she feels will so discourage them that they will let her alone. She proceeds to do so with the result that (1) the men laugh at (but do not touch) her; (2) she is thrown off the train for engaging in what is judged to be lascivious, "immoral" conduct; (3) she is "scorned" by another young woman (who subsequently boards the same train); (4) she is arrested and interrogated by the police for three days; and (5) she is released and proceeds to Rio. After her release, however, she reads in a newspaper that a girl was raped and killed on the train, the same girl (she believes) who had earlier "scorned" her. She then throws the paper away (not wanting to know the details) and, in her own "Pig Latin," thinks to herself, "Fate is implacable" (PL 62).

Yet if the conclusion of "Pig Latin" is ambiguous (as is the case with virtually all of Lispector's work), then so, too, is what precedes it, for on careful consideration the text undercuts, or decenters, itself on a number of crucial and closely interrelated issues. For example, although an initial reading of this narrative clearly suggests that it constitutes a powerful indictment of the violence and aggression visited on women by men (the rape/murder theme), a second reading reveals that—without denying the validity of the first—it also involves the question of the protagonist's motives and reliability; since we get the story only from her perspective, how can we be sure she is telling the truth, or the whole truth? Indeed, how can we be sure she herself knows the truth, or even that there is a single, perfect, unambiguous "truth" to be known?

A third reading, however, might also lead one to question, as in psychoanalysis, Freud's belief that because language replaces or substitutes for the thing it is supposed to represent (that is, to "re-present"), the subject who speaks cannot be quite the same as the subject referred to. And since in "Pig Latin" most of these self-referential remarks involve material of a sexual nature (and, through this, the integrally related issues of power, gender, and identity), the reader can reasonably wonder about both the perspective (the referent) and the perspicacity of the protagonist's voice.

Yet as a subsequent reading reminds us, the story does end with a rape. But because the reader learns this only through the eyes and mind of the protagonist, the question of the rape's relationship to the protagonist becomes problematic; is "Pig Latin" more a story about male aggression, violence toward women, and rape (as understood in this context), or could it also be read as an insight into the workings of a single, sexually frustrated human mind, as a portrait of a repressed and pathetic young woman whose desire for sexual expression is at odds with her superego-like admonition to remain chaste or asexual, a virgin, all in accordance with a rigidly and restrictively gendered social code that sends contradictory, and therefore damaging, messages to people (among whom women emerge as the most egregiously victimized)? And while from a poststructural perspective one reading does not cancel out another (indeed, it expands it), a reconsideration of "Pig Latin" along these lines reveals an exceptionally complex text, one that functions as a kind of psychic battleground on which conflicting forces at work in the protagonist's unconscious are being played out.

Several points in the story function as virtual markers, or "semiotic" eruptions, of these conflicts. To begin with, the reader learns (through a text that, at critical moments, seems to be flowing from out of Cidinha's anxious mind) that after the two men sit down on the seat in front of her (and before they have either looked at her or talked about her), it is the young woman who first expresses a sexual thought, specifically, that the two men desire her, sexually speaking, and that she is still a virgin: "My God, thought the girl, what could they want from me? There was no answer. And on top of it all she was a virgin. But why, oh why, had she thought of her own virginity?" (59–60). Interpreted from a psychoanalytic perspective, the sexually charged words that filter through Cidinha's mind might be taken as the conscious manifestation of a neurosis stemming from sexual repression. Read in this light, the story's more deeply seated conflict could thus turn not on whether Cidinha will be raped, or on what happened to the other young woman, but on her expression of what she thinks (or imagines) the two men are saying. The reader's reception of the narrative comes from the nuanced interplay between the omniscient voice and the voice within Cidinha's mind, the latter a voice that, in vintage Lispector fashion and recalling Benveniste's theory, oscillates ambiguously between the character's conscious and unconscious mind, the one infiltrating and affecting the other.

Because, according to Cidinha (a language teacher by profession), the men are not only speaking "Pig Latin" but speaking it "to perfection" (60), the reader is totally dependent on Cidinha's explanation of what happened and what it meant, all of which depends on her interpretation of what the two men, speaking in a language (pig Latin) that only Cidinha can understand, were saying. Do we believe her or not? Moreover, given the way the text is structured, are we not being led to question not only what Cidinha says, but our own response to it? Although we are to learn that "to understand would be dangerous for her" (60)—a line that itself suggests the presence of a deeply seated neurosis—we are only told that:

> Iay antway otay crewsay atthay irlgay. Atwhay outabay ouyay?
> Emay ootay. Enwhay eway etgay otay ethay unneltay.
> In other words they were going to rape her in the tunnel. . . . (60)

In terms of the story's structuration, this is the decisive moment, for the reader must act here, must either accept, and thereby collaborate with, Cidinha's interpretation of what the men were saying, or hold it in abeyance, remaining open to other possibilities and interpretations. And, as is characteristically the case in Lispector's fluid, unstable verbal world, it is also possible that, whichever avenue of interpretation we choose, we may end up in the same parlous situation, still not knowing for certain what happened and trapped in the ambiguities of language, sentenced to endlessly pondering realities that become meaningful to us only through a language usage that is deeply rooted in our most primal psychological fears and desires and that dictates our identities and our outlooks from this perspective.

Facing what she suspects, then, is her imminent rape, Cidinha decides on a defensive strategy that, as if effecting a union between the pleasure-seeking urges of the id and the censorship and morality of the superego, ironically allows her to flaunt a sexuality that, presented in a certain socially unacceptable way (that of a prostitute), will save her from being assaulted:

> Then the idea came to her: if I pretend that I am a prostitute, they'll give up, they wouldn't want a whore. (61)

Putting her plan into action, Cidinha then "pulled up her skirt" and "made sensual movements" ("A língua do 'p'" 87; PL 61). The reader, at this critical juncture in the story, is then told, in a statement again seemingly suggestive of Cidinha's sexual repression and neurosis, that (referring to the "sensual movements" she was making), "she didn't even know she knew how, so unknown was she to herself" (61), a point she had just made a moment earlier (60). Immediately after learning this for the second time, then, about Cidinha, the reader is then informed that she "opened the top buttons on her blouse, leaving her breasts half exposed" (61). The men, we discover, are left "suddenly in shock" (61) by her actions and, for whatever reason, do not touch her but, instead, laugh at her.

At this point, the conductor (yet another symbol of patriarchal authority) appears and, having observed Cidinha's actions (but knowing nothing, of course, of her motivations), determines, apparently displeased (superego-like) at what he interprets as her lascivious (and therefore forbidden) conduct, that she must be turned over to the police. What the police do to Cidinha—she is taken to jail, booked, called the "worst names" (62; presumably of a sexual nature) and held "brutally" for three days—can be likened to the role of the repressive control that, in Freudian terms,[8] the ego exerts on the id, the superego being the "conscience," a repository of all society's codes and rules of conduct.

When the id, the ego, and the superego are in harmony with each other, an individual is considered, in traditional Freudian psychotherapy, to be happy and well adjusted. But as we may infer from the case of Cidinha, when the ego allows the id to "break the rules" (in Cidinha's case, to express her sexuality, which, however, she feels she can do only as a prostitute), the superego can cause anxiety, frustration, feelings of guilt, and other manifestations of a tormented conscience. If we consider Cidinha's plight in this more psychoanalytic context, we are not surprised to learn that "[f]inally they [the police] let her go. She took the next train to Rio. She had washed her face, she wasn't a prostitute anymore" (62).[9] But at this moment, in what may be the story's most revealing and yet most psychologically complicating line, we are told:

What was bothering her was the following: when the two had spoken of raping her, she had wanted to be raped. She was shameless. Danay Iay maay aay orewhay. That was what she had discovered. Humiliation. (62)

With this startling and unsettling line, Lispector seems suddenly to be casting (what may be) Cidinha's neurotic behavior in terms of a repressed sexuality and a desire for self-debasement, both of these suggesting the tortured struggle of a deeply troubled psyche.

To further complicate our attempt to come to grips with this story, we recognize that the text generates at least one additional interpretation: that Cidinha correctly interpreted the "Pig Latin" of the two men (in other words, that she discovered that they did intend to rape and murder her), but that, as we sense in the line "so unknown was she to herself" (61), she was still sexually repressed and therefore still susceptible to "humiliation" at the hands of others (the conductor or the police, for example) as well as because of what may be her own also very real neurosis. This particular reading of the story, indeed, gains credibility in the conclusion, when, "desgraçada" (desolate) and walking around the streets of "desgraçada Copacabana" ("A língua do 'p'" 89; PL 62), Cidinha reads, in a newspaper, the following headline:

"GIRL RAPED AND KILLED IN TRAIN.

She trembled all over. It had happened, then. And to the girl who despised her." (62)

But this interpretation is itself undercut, in vintage Lispectorian fashion, when Cidinha, not wanting "to know the details" (and thereby also preventing the reader from knowing the details, which might have revealed that the story dealt with a different girl), throws the paper away and thinks to herself (in a thought that, once again, the reader must either accept or reject): "Atefay siay placableimay. Fate is implacable" (62). The story, one of Lispector's most disturbing, thus ends on a note of near perfectly orchestrated psycholinguistic ambiguity. Replete with the ethos of violence and degradation, and driven by its powerful undertones of sexual desire, repression, and frustration, "Pig Latin" probes the shrouded and painful relations between textuality and the negotiation of sexual desire.

From the perspective of Freudian and, especially, Lacanian, psychoanalysis, then, Lispector's texts—her fiction as well as her "nonfiction"

—embody certain recurring themes, images, and tensions. Prominent among these, as we have seen, are Lispector's anxiety-filled depictions of human sexuality, especially female sexuality. Freud's tripartite structuring of an individual's mental activity (the interplay between the id, the ego, and the superego) is, as Richard Mazzara and Lorri Parris have shown,[10] useful in approaching Lispector's work. Of these three forces, it would seem to be the id and the superego that dominate the characters of her fiction while it is the ego that perhaps manifests itself most forcefully in her nonfiction work, where there is less sexual tension and more reason, more circumspection, and also more self-revelation.

Few, if any, of Lispector's characters, however, illustrate an id driven totally by a blind, unbridled drive toward the gratification of desire, with no consideration of possible consequences or punishments. Although some come closer to this condition than others (Joana, Lóri, the voice in *The Stream of Life*, Maria Angélica de Andrade, from "But It's Going to Rain," and Senhora Jorge B. Xavier, from "In Search of Dignity," come to mind), the great majority of Lispector's characters are marked, in Freudian terms, by the dominance of the regulating ego over the pleasure-seeking id. In psychoanalytic terms, Freud believed that neurosis (as he argues in *Studies in Hysteria*, 1895) has a sexual basis, one stemming from an ongoing conflict between the desires of the id and the curbs imposed on it by the ego, which, in contrast to the "pleasure principle" of the id, operates under the aegis of the so-called reality principle, a force that, often taking the form of phallocentric culture, figures prominently in a number of Lispectorian works.

Seen from this tripartite Freudian perspective and, above all, in the language they speak, Lispector's characters typically reflect the ceaseless struggle between the id, driven by the powerful sexual energy of its libido, and the restraining force of the ego, with its desire to avoid punishment; very few of them develop primarily along the lines of conflict with conventional morality or social convention, although, as we have seen, when we contextualize the latter issue in terms of power structures and sexual mores involving class, race, age, and gender, then several of her characters can be so interpreted, the stories involving the sexuality of older women being the prime example. My point in this regard is that, in the main, Lispector's characters do not develop what we ordinarily understand as a crisis of conscience or morality; while the external restrictions with which they are forced to contend (gender, for example, or propriety) clearly affect their development, their more essential conflicts—as reflected in the language that inscribes them—are ontological and often transgressively sexual in nature.

Sexuality, to put it another way, functions as a much more important aspect of these characters' being or identity, public as well as private, than is immediately apparent in reading their stories. If we interpret these conflicts—so often shrouded (as in a dream) by symbols, metaphors, and semantic (as well as syntactic) ambiguities—as constituting aspects or manifestations of a neurosis, which Freud believed nearly always had a sexual basis, then we are better able to appreciate the extent to which sexuality, both expressed and repressed, plays a role in Lispector's work. Far from serving merely as a salacious fillip to what is often taken to be Lispector's overwhelmingly intellectual universe, sexuality functions as one of the Brazilian writer's most primary aspects of being, one that, as Lacan and Kristeva argue, is inextricably bound up not only in our use of language but, as we see depicted in such fluid and interpenetrating narrations "from within" as "Plaza Mauá" and "Pig Latin," in language's constituency of the mind itself.

The critical question, however, for a writer like Clarice Lispector, whose work, from beginning to end, brims with sexual tension and sexually charged characters, is the following: Why is there so little actual sex in her work? A corollary question might then be: Of the sexuality that is present in her novels, stories, and *crônicas*, why is it so obliquely depicted? Only in *An Apprenticeship, or The Book of Delights* (1969) [11] and *The Stations of the Body* (1974), a work published late in Lispector's life (only three years before her death from cancer) and one that she felt compelled to explain and defend in a self-reflective preface to the work (her "Explanation"), [12] did she finally approach even a slightly more explicit representation of human (read female) sexuality. [13] Yet even here, in the only one of her many works to deal openly with such themes as masturbation, lesbianism, and transvestism, the author mutes what could naturally be explicitly sexual. It is entirely possible, as Marta Peixoto suggests (*Passionate Fictions* 72–81), that in *The Stations of the Body* Lispector is deliberately cultivating a "parodic version . . . of a commercialized popular culture," one that "in most cases" signals "the victory of women over patriarchal law," but such an explanation might not explain everything at work in these texts. Representations of the female body, both young and old, abound in this underappreciated collection, as Vieira and Urbaitel-Solares note, [14] to the point of constituting a thematic base of the collection. Yet at the same time other images that might, by a different author, be developed as sexually arousing or explicit are here cast, often to ironic effect, as simple, unadorned statements intimating that a sexual act merely occurred. Focusing on two female characters, one example of this rather singular representation of sexuality comes from the story "The Body":

> Às vezes as duas se deitavam na cama. . . . E, apesar de não serem homossexuais, se excitavam uma à outra e faziam amor. Amor triste. ("O corpo" 30)

> Sometimes the two women would stretch out on the bed. . . . And, although they were not homosexuals, they excited each other and made love. Sad love. ("Body" 18)

What strikes the reader here, even in translation, is the curious tone that the text establishes. On the one hand, we are clearly told that Lispector's two women (neither of whom, in the conventional terms of patriarchal society, is depicted as a "beauty") "excited each other" sexually; yet at the same time, their clearly implied state of mutually desired sexual arousal[15] is undercut, or decentered, by the declaration that their liaison was not an entirely felicitous one, that, indeed, they were doomed to having to make "amor triste," or "sad love."

Several questions arise here: although the question of love, its protean nature (including the question of its mercurial relationship to hate) and the pressure it exerts in shaping human identities and relationships (in particular the issue of love as possession), ranks among the most fundamental of the many ontologically oriented issues that inform Lispector's work,[16] in this scene it is imbued with an ambiguity that, though almost totally unexplained, appears to rest on an issue of sexual identity. Generated initially by the hopeful prospect of a mutually satisfying sexual encounter between two women (both of whom are cast as victims, or losers,[17] in the male-dominated power structure, symbolized by Xavier and his "bull-like strength," which envelops them) who might reasonably become lovers (and thereby help each other gain at least a modicum of happiness and satisfaction in a culture that does not make it easy for people like them), the scene ends unhappily, with the potentially saving force of love undercut by the author's use of the adjective "sad." Why? Why does Lispector write it this way? And why are we told, categorically, that the two women were "not homosexuals"? If Carmen and Beatrice were at first depicted as having "excited each other" sexually (and, one feels, emotionally and perhaps intellectually as well), why were they then forced to make only "sad love"? Why not "joyous" love, "affirming" love, or "passionate" love? Or, simply, "love"? Why would Clarice Lispector, a woman some fifty-four years old when this story was published and a writer already renowned for the power and imagination of her probing explorations of human (especially female) existence and being, have introduced the role a nonstandard sexuality plays in the lives of these two female characters and then seem to back away from, or curtail, it? Is it possible that, at this point in her life, Lispector herself felt the power of sexuality as an underrepresented or misunderstood aspect of her own identity as well as of her characters?

An orthodox Freudian critic, for example, might well answer these questions in the affirmative, that one most certainly could read a text like "The Body" (or *The Apple in the Dark*) as an example of an author who, in very guarded fashion, is expressing her own fantasies or desires, while at the same time discussing an issue of intense and very real social significance. This interpretation gains credence when we recall that, as the story draws to an end, the two women (now apprehended by the police and facing the prospect of life imprisonment) ask if they could be placed in the same cell. It requires no great stretch of either the text or one's imagination to think of these two women as "cell/soul mates," that is, as two female lovers imprisoned, literally in a jail but figuratively in a cruel and unforgiving society, condemned to live out their lives as pariahs, as being in violation of patriarchal law. This condition, in theory and in actual life, is indeed sad, and so for these women (and women like them) there is perhaps no other kind of love except "sad" love. There are no alternatives.

Interpreted from a Freudian perspective, then, the basic conflict in "The Body" does not derive from the ego's efforts to regulate the id's drives into non-self-destructive behavior patterns, but from the conflict that exists between one's deepest feelings about identity and being (the sexually driven and gender-blind id) and the censorial weight of social convention and moral rectitude (the superego) replete with its punitive arm, the law, represented in the story by the policeman who comes to arrest the two women. The irony of their story, arising in the final scene and functioning as if a symbol of the illegitimacy of the repressive androcentric code, is that the two women are allowed to go free, to "go and live in Montevideo," for to have prosecuted them would have produced "lots of noise, lots of paperwork, lots of gossip" (*Soulstorm* 24). In psychoanalytic terms, the two women "lovers" have destroyed the man who oppresses them and, by being allowed by the police to go free, have symbolically proven not only the legitimacy but even the superiority of their relationship.

Although this reading is plausible, there is another that, developing in a more sequentially structured fashion, suggests that the love between Beatrice and Carmen not only overcomes the obstacles that would inhibit its development but achieves a psychosexual fruition, one that, in the end, implies the enduring strength of love (in this case lesbian love) and female solidarity in the face of a violent (Xavier) and capricious (the police) patriarchal world. Like the earlier interpretation, this one begins at the point where the two women "excited each other and made love. Sad love" (18). The verbal signs of the text indicate that we are not permitted to call them "homosexuals" because, given the context of Lispector's poststructural outlook, to do so would be to label them, to force on them a kind of linguistically prepackaged and restrictive identity, one generated not by their own words (their own psyches) and actions but imposed on them by society's rigid conventions, mores, and stereotypes, all of which, as we see in works like "Flight" and "The Burned Sinner," are presented in Lispector's world as being not only damaging but lethal as well. The love that exists between Carmen and Beatrice, in contrast, is an unstable but eventually unifying site of conflicting tensions and attractions, an initially inchoate force that is subject to transformation and ambiguous as to its meaning(s) but also ultimately life affirming in its potency.

Beatrice and Carmen, then, enter into a love affair that is simultaneously both "sad" and "exciting," with each of these modifiers tending (as if exemplifying Derrida's "dissemination") to enrich, rather than simplify, the signifying potency of the other. The result is the presentation of a relationship that the reader cannot be sure about, one that generates a number of interpretations, all of which seem plausible. When, for example, Carmen and Beatrice one day tell Xavier about their relationship, he also becomes "excited," apparently by the prospect of witnessing an act of lesbian lovemaking, for, we are told, he "trembled" and "wanted the two of them to make love in front of him that night" ("O corpo" 30; *Soulstorm* 18). Immediately after this point, however, the reader is induced to consider the nature of the patriarchal power structure at work here, for, as we read, "ordered up like this"—a clear expression of Xavier's power over the two women—their lovemaking "all ended in nothing. The two women cried, and Xavier became furious" (18). This latter reaction functions as yet another sign of his capacity for violence.[18]

The crucial turn in this reading occurs next, however, when we learn that while Xavier, in his anger at the women for having failed to do his bidding, refused even to speak to them "For three days," we are then told that "during this period, and without any request, the two women went to bed together and succeeded" ("O corpo" 30; TB 18). This sentence contains two elements that catch the reader's attention: first, the fact that Carmen and Beatrice are now going to bed together of their own volition, and not at the behest of Xavier, strongly suggests that their sexual involvement has grown to the point that they are now beginning to free themselves from his domination and to establish their own relationship, which, until this moment, had been "sad," a modifier that, now absent, has been replaced with a more positive field of reference.

The second decisive element relates to their development as a couple, an issue that the reader, dealing here with yet another example of Lispector's deliberate cultivation of semantically open-ended and ambiguous referents, will interpret according to the following question: With what did the women "succeed"? Certainly not only with the carrying out of the sexual act itself, since, by this point, they have attained this type of involvement for some time; and, seemingly, not only with "love," since, in one fashion or another, they have achieved this as well. Rather more than these isolated things, one feels that what Carmen and Beatrice have finally "succeeded" at here is the attaining of what is no longer "sad love" but joyous love, true, complete love, the kind of love that, as a life-affirming force, throws into sharp relief the selfishness, perversity, and exploitativeness of Xavier's understanding and practice of love. After this point, the reader feels, Carmen and Beatrice no longer merely make love, they are in love, and so the power dynamic of the triangular relationship of the three characters begins to change, with the two women drawing closer and closer together while Xavier, the formerly domineering male, is cast as an increasingly pathetic character, a man more and more marginal to the emergence of the two women, who now form a couple.

Emanating from out of the metaphoric use of food (and eating) as sex that helps sustain not only the visceral appeal of this elaborate story but its not inconsiderable comic dimension as well, Beatrice, apropos of this interpretation, drolly proceeds to make a potato salad not for the three of them, as she had done earlier, but "for the two of them" (19), that is, for herself and Carmen; the original threesome has become a twosome, a transformation that, in reverse fashion, recalls similarly erotic structurations in *Near to the Wild Heart* and *The Apple in the Dark*, among others. After this decisive alteration of the relationship, we learn that "[t]hat afternoon, *they* went to the movies. *They* ate out and didn't come home until midnight. *They* found Xavier beaten, sad, and hungry" (19; emphasis mine), the three latter adjectives ("beaten," "sad," and "hungry") supplying textual evidence of how dramatically the tables have now been turned in the women's relationship, how, in symbolic terms, patriarchy has been subsumed by both female "jouissance" and "puissance" and by female unity in the face of oppression.

Yet because Carmen and Beatrice, slowly awakening to the strength of their growing love (or, one feels, their sexually based power), "felt heartbroken" (19), that is, pity, for Xavier's now pathetic plight (caused by his abuse of them and his subsequent loss of power), they now freely decide to do for him what he had earlier demanded that they do (with negative result): "That night the two women made love in front of him, and he ate out his heart with envy" (19). What Xavier, now shorn of his power over the two women, saw this night was therefore not merely the act of physical "love" that is sex, but the act of love, freely given and freely received, and expressed in all its myriad forms, emotional, intellectual, political, and sexual. Xavier is envious, of course, because he can neither control nor attain this kind of love, and he knows it. In a telling reversal of roles, the women now permit him to watch their lovemaking (for reasons that the text never makes explicitly clear), but he will not be able to enter into it without their consent.

It is significant then, that, when Carmen invites the "beaten, sad, and hungry" Xavier (who says that he sometimes wants to "do it" during the day) to "come home" and, presumably have sex with either herself, Beatrice, or, conceivably, with both of them (as, within a very different power relationship, they had done earlier), she is not necessarily wielding her newly attained female "power" as an exclusionary force; indeed, it would seem that the women's now unfettered, unrepressed sexuality, whether regarded as experimentally heterosexual, homosexual, or bisexual in expression, is both sufficiently strong and capacious to absorb, overcome, or perhaps even heal someone like Xavier.

The possible redemption of Xavier (and, by extension, the symbolic redemption of patriarchal society) by women's love comes to naught, however, because Xavier, perhaps hopelessly consumed by his lust for power and control (an attitude represented by his inability or refusal to stop procuring the services of prostitutes, and an action that infuriated Beatrice and Carmen), seeks out a prostitute even after Carmen has generously offered him entrée into the ever stronger relationship she now enjoys with Beatrice. The abuse heaped on the two women in their original relationship with Xavier, coupled now with what amounts to his final betrayal of them (to traffic once again in the buying and selling of sex and "love"), thus leads, at this point in the story, to the women's decision to murder Xavier, an act that serves to undercut the reader's ability to see Xavier as the text's most violent presence. Archly posing the decisive question, the text openly asks, "How did the desire for revenge begin?" (20), and the reader is left to ponder the psychological and sociopolitical significance of this utterance.

This highly charged if opaque question, however, is then followed immediately by a declaration that implies an answer already known to the careful reader: "The two women drew closer all the time and began to despise him" (20). As the bond between the women continues to grow, Xavier—and his deeds—seem increasingly pathetic, to the point that (given his rejection of their offer of love) their sympathy for his situation has now led them "to despise him"—and to wish him dead, a state unto which, by means of two butcher knives, they subsequently render him. The violence of their homicide vividly underscores, as Marta Peixoto has shown,[19] the degree to which violence permeates Lispector's world generally as well as the role it plays in the evolution of the complex and shifting relationship between these three characters.

Having dispatched him, the two women then proceed to bury Xavier in the garden, whereupon Beatrice, "great romantic that she was" (22), decides to plant a rose in the fertile soil over his grave. Although this rose stalk, which might be understood either phallically or as a symbol of the flowering love between the two women, initially prospers, its growth is interrupted when the police, come to investigate Xavier's disappearance, discover and disinter his body, an action that, riven with symbolic complexity, destroys the roses, "which," we are coyly told, "suffered this human brutality for no reason at all" (23). Yet in spite of what happens to the roses, the love between the two women is not destroyed, for, as they await arrest and imprisonment for Xavier's murder, Carmen says to one of the policemen, "[L]et us be in the same cell" (23). But as we know, the two women do not go to prison; instead, and in order to avoid the "paper work" and "gossip," the police order Carmen and Beatrice to pack their bags and go live in Montevideo, which, saying thank you very much, they do, the story thus closing on yet another surprising and destabilizing turn of events.

The problem of living/existing with a repressed male homosexuality, or with a desire for gender experimentation, also appears in Lispector's work, including *Discovering the World*, where, in keeping with the generally discursive tone of the *crônica*, its treatment (as in "The Lucidity of the Absurd," 28 April 1973; "Good Friends," 10 March 1973; "Hateful Charity," 6 December 1969; or "Discovering the World," 6 July 1968) is that of a sympathetic analyst, a person trying rationally to figure things out, to understand (as G. H. does). In more deliberately fictional works like "Plaza Mauá," "He Soaked Me Up," and "A Sincere Friendship," however, Lispector takes up the theme of male homosexuality in ways closely analogous to those that, stylistically and structurally, define her representations in the stories involving female homosexuality. And in comparing Lispector's various depictions of homosexuality (if that, indeed, is what they are) it seems clear that for her the question of "morality" is secondary to the more fundamental issue of love as a problem of being, of human existence. And of all love's myriad and diverse representations, none is more destabilizing than sexuality, a pervasive if muted force in Lispector's fictive world yet one that exemplifies the author's sense of being and identity as a volatile, evolving process, one that in the end seems more psycholinguistic than biological.

And because Lispector weaves the psychosexual impulse into her texts as a powerful and visceral yet often ambivalent and ambiguous part of human identity, she does not limit herself to portraits of female sexuality. Although such portraits outnumber the male ones, Lispector did, as we have seen, produce a few texts that deal with male sexuality. The stories of Martim and Ulisses are of this type, as are, in more explicit terms, those of such later (1974) characters as Celsinho (of "Plaza Mauá"), a "successful transvestite"; Serjoca (of "He Soaked Me Up"), who "liked men"; and the two male "friends" of "A Sincere Friendship," whose mysterious but overwhelming attraction to each other exudes powerful sexual undercurrents.

Of all Lispector's depictions of male (homo)sexuality, however, "A Sincere Friendship" is unique for several reasons: it is one of the very few narratives Clarice Lispector ever wrote that features only male characters (indeed, a self-conscious first-person male "I" enigmatically tells the story about his male "friend" and their special relationship); it is the only narrative written by Lispector that deals almost totally with a relationship (the exact nature of which is never made clear) between two males; and it ranks among the most complex, the most artfully structured, and the most thoroughly ambiguous of all the author's narratives that deal with this subject. Indeed, the entire tale, which, intriguingly, also has an overt—if unexplained—political dimension to it, turns on what we, as readers, make of certain key words: friend/friendship, adultery, suffering, loneliness, relief, and sacrifice. The poststructural concern with how texts generate meaning(s) thus quickly establishes itself as this text's prime dynamic. If, for example, we read the word "friendship" (which, in the text, possesses a leitmotif-like quality) as "love" (and "friend" as "lover"), the story immediately becomes very different; suddenly less oblique about what happens and why, it turns into a poignant (and finally ill-fated) tale about two young men who, responding to their mutually perceived attraction to each other, find their "sincere friendship" transformed into love. At the same time, however, the reader discovers that theirs is a love that, because it could not be countenanced by society, was destined to end in, first, repression and unhappiness and, finally, separation, the denial of love, the kind of "death in life" that we associate with the neurosis-producing repression of desire, and a theme endemic to Lispector's work.

Unquestionably the most "dreamlike" of all Lispector's narratives, "Where You Were at Night" (1974) is also the one that most exemplifies Freud's concept of the "dream-work," the process by which a dream evolves through the mechanisms of condensation, displacement, and finally, symbolization (Freud, *A General Introduction of Psycho-Analysis*, 178–92). Because, as these key terms themselves suggest, the language of psychoanalysis has so much in common with the language of poetry, it is tempting to read a text like "Where You Were at Night" as a lyrically rendered attempt at self-analysis on Lispector's part, one structured, moreover, around the fundamental technique of psychoanalytic treatment: free association. The mysterious and polymorphous "I" that thinks, speaks, and writes in this most singular short narrative also resembles the "enunciating I" that Kristeva describes in *Revolution in Poetic Language*. Developing, seemingly, in abeyance of rational, moral, or ethical control, the gender-evolving "I" of "Where You Were at Night" generates a welter of personae, all of which may, however, be thought of as masks, or "displacements," for the mysterious and protean being whose libido animates the text. One can speculate, in this sense, whether the multiple "characters," presences, and voices that give shape to this nightmarish narrative are really various manifestations, or "condensations," of Lispector's own psyche.[20]

Indeed, in terms of its macrostructures and its imagery, the text can be said to replicate a journey through the unconscious. Beginning in the sleeplike "darkest night" of a "scalding summer," the reader is swept along in a dizzying "climb up the mountain" (*Soulstorm* 114), a dream image that, for Freud, is always associated with sexuality (Freud, *A General Introduction*, 165). Building on recurring and interlocking images of sensually half-opened orifices (*Écrits* 314–15), mixing (of gendered being and undifferentiated desire, for example) and the Eros-versus-Thanatos dynamic, the text depicts the men and women involved in it as being "free" to "[l]atency that was throbbing, light, rhythmic, uninterrupted," as being able to live "freely" because "there was no repression" ("Night" 116–17). Wanting to "savor the forbidden" (118), they were "orgiastic" (119) at finding themselves finally "cast loose" in "the harem of He-she" (121), the deliberately androgynous being whose presence dominates the story.

When the "failed female writer" (122), however, declares, drolly, that her life is "a true romance" (122), the reader suddenly feels drawn into the presence of a seemingly autobiographical reference to Lispector herself, one that is immediately "condensed" into a larger image devoted to an "exaltation of the body" (122), to "the pleasure of Evil" (122), and to "waves of orgasm" (122). And as if to remind the reader of the vital nexus between the unconscious and language, the text, expanding on the metaphor of the life of the "failed female writer" as a novel/romance, then drives this poststructural orientation home by focusing on the word "cacography" (124), a complex sign that is "the most difficult word in the language" (124) not because it is obscure but, ironically, because it symbolizes both the indecipherability of language use and our utter dependence on it.

At this juncture, with everything awash in "[s]ex. Pure sex" (124), the dreamlike quality of the text gives way to a dawning that, as in the action of waking up from a very deep sleep, seems analogous to the conscious mind's reassertion of control over its unconscious urges. Indeed, we are told, of the now "satisfied" characters, that "[t]hey woke up, then, a bit tired, satisfied with their deep, deep night of sleep" (126). The specter of the text's possibly autobiographical basis then suddenly reappears, again drolly, as the voice of the "failed female writer" declares: "I rebel! But I cannot manage to diet: I'm dying of hunger" (127). Although the text ostensibly speaks of her failure to curb her "appetite" (an image that recalls Xavier's "hunger"), the reader is left wondering whether, at this point in a narrative so drenched in sexual references and imagery, our "failed writer's" "hunger," which she says is killing her, might not be an issue of sex rather than of food. Following one final reference to the (male) "morning masturbator" (139), the text draws to a close with the "enunciating I"—seemingly the voice of Lispector herself—offering up an enigmatic "Epilogue": "All that I have written is true—it exists. . . . Where were you at night? No one knows" (130).

Although there are other quite viable psychological approaches to Lispector's work, including different female variations on the Oedipal/ Electra complex, dreams, repression and desire (as in "Where You Were at Night"), religion (including both the sacred and the phallogocentric presence of God in her work), and the interplay of Eros and Thanatos, the most distinctive quality of her work is surely the close and vital nexus between the psychic battlegrounds of her characters and language that, like a pulsing vein (a key image in *The Stream of Life* and *A Breath of Life*), so steadily animates it. In terms of current theoretical methodologies, it is, not surprisingly, the work of Jacques Lacan that, as we shall now see, lends itself to Lispector's narratives.

Widely recognized as having been the first to apply, or superimpose, the linguistically based theories of structuralism and poststructuralism to the practice of psychoanalysis, Lacan, who favors Freud's original topographic model of the mind (and not Freud's later, revised model, with its overlapping divisions into the id, the ego, and the superego), believes in approaching psychoanalysis from the perspective of the tension between the conscious and unconscious mind, which he feels Freud's earlier model best describes. Because Lacan has argued that the most accurate representation of mental activity is Freud's early topographic one (a position that explains Lacan's disdain for what he felt was the synthesizing role Freud would later ascribe to his concept of the superego), he upholds a decidedly dialectical (and Hegelian) view of the mind's functioning, paramount among which are the following conflicts or tensions: the conscious and unconscious (with the latter, for Lacan, largely controlling and determining the former); the Subject (which, for Lacan, is split between the conscious and unconscious mind)[21] and object; and desire and satisfaction.[22] Desire,[23] literally and figuratively, nearly always "unsatisfied" (and therefore another aspect of the quest motif that so characterizes her work), must be said to constitute a primary force in Lispector's work, one that, as with Lacan (*Écrits* 256–58), exemplifies the Subject (personified in most of her protagonists) as being irrevocably fragmented and at odds with itself, forever in a futile but irresistible quest of what it feels is "missing," a lack, or absence, that, in turn, generates an increased but ever unfulfilled desire. This keenly felt but ill-defined desire for wholeness or union comes to identify a sentient Subject like Joana, G. H., or Martim as a consciousness anxiously aware that it is lacking something, a vague but psychologically tormented condition that the conflicted Subject is driven to attempt to eliminate. As if in reference to the tumultuous and kaleidoscopic world of Lispector's protagonists, Lacan's theory holds that the Subject (the polychromatic voice of *The Stream of Life*, for example)—characterized to one degree or another by a "lack" or "absence" that is acutely felt but only partially understood (both functions being themselves structurations of language)—is driven, questlike, to seek satisfaction, to replace the disturbing tension or anxiety that stems from frustration with "stasis," which Lacan understands as pleasure attained and which, once attained, would mean the absence of desire. Lacan's insistence that it is desire—which he sees as a psycholinguistic function—that separates humans from other animals (who possess biological "need," not psycholinguistically based "desires") also resonates in Lispector's texts where (as in "The Buffalo," "Monkeys," *The Besieged City*, or "Dry Point of Horses") erotically shrouded images of animals abound. Cast nearly always in terms of the primitive, often sexual "presence" they command in the (un)consciousness of Lispector's human characters,[24] who, as if embodying Lacan's linguistically grounded theory, struggle to fill the lacuna, gap, or "lack" they (like Lacan's Subjects) feel is missing from their identities and their existences, these animal images are basic to Lispector's narratives.

Because Lacan saw the verbalization of the Subject's desires (and of the tensions that define them) as a function issue of language, it is easier to understand the nexus that his work as a psychoanalyst shares with poststructural theory. Both are heavily indebted to linguistics (Lacan, for example, owes a great deal to both Saussure and Jakobson), and both argue for a close and interactive relationship between language and the unconscious. Famous for having declared (*Écrits* 59) that the unconscious is, indeed, structured like a language, Lacan transforms Freud's topographic model of the mind's operations into linguistic terms. In doing this, Lacan makes the unconscious a psychological analogue of the interplay between Saussure's "signifying chain" of signifiers and signifieds and between Jakobson's two fundamental poles of language: metaphor (where, as in semantics, one thing substitutes for another) and metonymy (where, as in syntax, a contiguous chain of relationships is created). Based primarily on Saussurean linguistics, this system allows Lacan to privilege the role played by the signifier, and, in particular, the different (or "other") meanings it generates as it is positioned (and repositioned) in a sentence, a paragraph, or a larger (or smaller) unit of text. When we add to this theory about the relationship between language and human existence the fact that, for Lacan, metonymy is the chief signifier of desire (because what is desired is always displaced or deferred), we begin to understand how crucial these rhetorical, linguistic figures are to Lacan in his attempt to explain how the languagelike unconscious generates meaning(s), how it "signifies."

These theoretical pronouncements about how Lacan believes the mind works bear numerous resemblances to the stylistic, structural, and semantic descriptions already posited concerning Lispector's work. For Lacan, as for Lispector, what matters semantically are the meanings disseminated ("birthed," as Lispector might say) not by the ordinary denotative meanings associated with a particular word but by its position relative to the other words and structures that surround it. Stylistically, we can take this as also being pertinent to the question of syntax (which, for Jakobson, relates to metonymy rather than to metaphor and which, for Julia Kristeva, is the medium through which a Subject presents itself as being "in process"), an aspect of Lispector's unmistakable style that has been noted by a number of commentators, prominent among whom is Gregory Rabassa, one of her translators. Of the importance and singularity of Lispector's syntax, Rabassa has written:

> Most of the elements that go to make up the current trend in Brazilian fiction can be seen in her work. The invention is not as obvious as in Guimarães Rosa because it is less a matter of neologisms and recreation than of certain radical departures in the use of syntactical structure . . . Lispector marshaling the syntax in a new way that is closer perhaps to original thought patterns than the language had ever managed to approach before.[25]

The issue of her unusual syntactical complexity was, apparently, of sufficient interest to Lispector herself that, referring to Rabassa directly, she responded to his observation by saying, in a 12 June 1971 crônica: "One thing, however, did puzzle me. . . . Rabassa claims I am more difficult to translate than Guimarães Rosa, because of my syntax. I am not aware that there is anything very unusual about my syntax. I am prepared to believe him. Gregory Rabassa must know what he is talking about" (DW 463).

Another of Lispector's major translators, Giovanni Pontiero, has also noted her "unorthodox use of syntax and punctuation" and how these, working in concert with "her bold rhythms and syncopated phrasing contribute to the overall impression of tense, haunting lyricism" (Heart 191). Assuming that Lispector is not being disingenuous here, pretending not to be aware of how complex and probing her lyrically wrought writing is, it is quite possible to accept both these responses to her syntax; although her style is "natural," and not unorthodox for her because it reflects and embodies what I have argued is her essentially poststructural perception of reality, for the reader (the most complete of whom, as Rabassa has often observed, is always the translator) who does not share her sense of the symbiotic, mutually creative relationship between reality and language, her style can seem opaque and mysterious, inimical to concise, critical pronouncements. Like good poetry, as we have seen, Lispector's narratives, her "chains of signifiers," resist easy generic categorization and interpretational reduction.

Structurally, then, as well as stylistically and semantically, Lispector's texts, from *Near to the Wild Heart* (1944) to the posthumous *Breath of Life: Pulsations* (1979), present the reader with the endlessly shifting play of signifiers that Lacan understands to be the psycholinguistic source of desire, a lack never wholly eradicated but frustratingly endured. Because language, too, works by such lack, difference, or absence, Lacan concludes that to enter the world of language, which he believes we do at the moment the unconscious comes into being, is to feel desire. The tension that results from a desire both sensed and unfulfilled is precisely the force, manifesting itself in surges of erotically charged yet nonexplicit language, that animates Lispector's best work.

In *Near to the Wild Heart*, for example, the scene in which Joana— responding to Lídia's probing question, "Are you unhappy?" (136)— reveals to the reader the full extent of her hitherto nascent awareness of her own non-gender-specific "desire" (136), which, in a startling suggestion of same-sex eroticism, she connects directly, if amorphously, with Lídia, in many ways her carnal "other" or alter ego: "I should like to spend at least a day watching Lídia . . . until it was time for her bath" (136–37). Then, as if using her narrative to psychoanalyze herself in Lacanian terms, Joana (whom we might think of as Lispector) silently asks herself, "Was this perhaps what had always been missing in my life? Why is she [Lídia] so powerful?" (137). The psychologically revealing and deeply sexual pulse of this scene quickly comes to a climax when, as we have seen, Joana/Lispector finally thinks, openly, to herself about wanting a woman with large breasts to bathe her, dress her in a nightgown, and put her to bed (137).

If we think of this enigmatic line as expressing the unresolved desire of the unconscious to merge with her same-sex origins surging up into the conscious (yet remaining, as a function of language, private, unspoken, and silent inside Joana's/Lispector's mind), we are led to interpret it as a confluence, or, in Freudian terms, a "condensation," of the maternal and the sexual, of Joana's/Lispector's unfulfilled need for both a mother's gentle nurturing and a woman's sexual aggressiveness. In psychoanalytic terms, this interpretation could be said to be rooted in Lispector's childhood and in her early relationships with her father, mother, and siblings, relationships that may well have been reproduced in the early chapters of Lispector's markedly autobiographical first novel, *Near to the Wild Heart*.[26]

Cut off from a sense of mastery of Lispector's narratives in the same way that we are cut off from what Lacan calls "the Real," a realm outside the symbolic order and that "lies beyond the insistence of signs" (*Four Fundamental Concepts of Psycho-Analysis*, 53–54) and their significations, the reader enters the Brazilian writer's deeply textualized world by entering into a state of endless yearning, of sexual desire manifesting itself in metaphysical anxiety, a world brilliantly depicted as early as *Near to the Wild Heart* and later elaborated in such extraordinary achievements as *The Passion according to G. H.* (1964), *The Stream of Life* (1973), "Where You Were at Night," and *A Breath of Life: Pulsations* (1977). These latter works, but, to a lesser degree, most of Lispector's other narratives as well, give free rein to an unconscious that, functioning as Lacan believes the unconscious functions (that is, as a language), expresses itself—by speaking and writing (with the latter mode of expression, as evidenced in *The Stream of Life*, Lispector's predominant mode)—less in terms of stable signs and meaning than in terms of the endlessly shifting signifiers that form the "interferences and pulsations . . . of language" (*Écrits* 68) that constitute "desire" (68) and whose signifieds (or meanings) "are often inaccessible to us because they are 'repressed'" (Eagleton 168). To sum up, then: consistent with Lacan's theories, Lispector's narratives underscore for us the organic and symbiotic relationship between language and being by showing her anguished speaking and writing protagonists, or Lacanian Subjects, as transforming (or seeking to transform) not only themselves and their unconsciousness but their desires as well. Because the unconscious is, for Lacan, linguistic in nature, it cannot be other than a pulsating, destabilizing, and endlessly creative force within its own fields of structuration and reception by the reader, a description that accurately describes Lispector's endlessly probing *écriture*. "For a Lacanian psychoanalytic criticism," declares Elizabeth Wright, in fact, as if describing Lispector's narratives, "a text will be first and foremost a discourse of desire, with the result that the emphasis will be not on an appropriation of the author's meaning but on an expropriation by the reader," whose creative participation in the ebb and flow of texts like *The Stream of Life* or "Where You Were at Night" converts the act of reading into an interpretive process that parallels Lacan's famous analysis of the play of the decentered (and decentering) subject ("Modern Psychoanalytic Criticism," *Modern Literary Theory*, 2d ed., 161).

As suggested earlier, however, another psychoanalyst whose theories concerning language and psychoanalysis are also useful for interpreting Lispector's texts is Julia Kristeva. Profoundly influenced by Lacan (whose patriarchal "symbolic order" clearly poses a problem for feminist critics), Kristeva, in *Revolution in Poetic Language* (1974), challenges Lacan's notion of the "symbolic" with her concept of the "semiotic," "a pattern or play of forces which we can detect inside language" and that can "be discerned as a kind of pulsional pressure within language itself, in tone, rhythm, the bodily and material qualities of language, but also in contradiction, meaninglessness, disruption, silence and absence" (Eagleton 188). In effect, as many critics have pointed out, Kristeva transforms Lacan's distinction between the imaginary and the "symbolic order" into a distinction between the semiotic and the "symbolic." As we have seen, a number of these latter terms, which characterize Kristeva's "semiotic," are also basic motifs of Lispector's work; images of and references to such issues as "pulsional pressure," body imagery (particularly that relating to the female body, and especially involving female breasts, the womb, ovaries, and the placenta), unsettling sexual urges, water, paradox, silence, darkness, the "moment," and absence abound in Lispector's work. These recurrent images, when taken together with the fluid and often paradoxical process of signification that defines her writing, confirm the degree to which Lispector's poetically driven and philosophically sustained world of *écriture* embodies Kristeva's notion of the "semiotic," especially in its subversive approach to all forms of patriarchy and androcentric cultural codes of conduct.

But the "semiotic" is not the only aspect of Kristeva's thought that finds literary expression in Lispector's work. Like Kristeva's "subject-in-process," Lispector's main characters—Joana, G. H., and Martim, for example—do not exemplify traditional notions about what the "I" of epistemology is like; rather, like G. H. or Joana, Lispector's characters tend, especially after 1961 and *The Apple in the Dark*, to exemplify what Kristeva calls a "subject of enunciation," a "phenomenological conception of the speaking subject" awakened by the potentialities of "poetic language."[27] Kristeva's subject, which she understands as a multivoiced speaking subject, thus emerges as a distinctly verbal being whose identity is open to interpretation and who "comes to life" only through the enunciation of self that constitutes the "signifying act" (this process reaching its fullest expression in *The Stream of Life*, though it typifies what transpires in Lispector's other texts as well), which views language as a continuous and potentially contradictory discourse rather than the logically progressive argument of a single epistemological system. Moreover, it is the self-reflective, poetic, and philosophical dimension of Lispector's work that, as with Kristeva's "poetic language," leads characters like Joana, Martim, or G. H. to simultaneously construct and deconstruct themselves (and, by extension, their cultures) through language. The literary reality of such characters is thus fundamentally poststructural in nature, forcing the reader, because of the semantic fecundity of poetic language, to deal at every step with a protean construct who is, as Kristeva puts it, "a questionable subject-in-process" ("From One Identity to Another" 1163).

Kristeva's theory, as we know, is based on a concept of "poetic language" that functions in a text (*The Apple in the Dark*, *The Passion according to G. H.*, *The Stream of Life*, and *A Breath of Life*, for example) as an "unsettling process—when not an outright destruction—of the identity of meaning and speaking subject," what, in French, Kristeva terms the "mise en procès" and which is like the "sujet en procès" in that it refers to "a constantly changing subject whose identity is open to question" (1163). Stylistically and structurally, then, Lispector's diverse texts give literary expression to several of the theories propounded by Kristeva, though most especially her concept of the relation between the disruptive nature of "poetic language" and the "speaking" (or, more appropriate to the case for Lispector, writing) "subject-in-process." Authorially self-expressive characters like Joana, G. H., the voice in *The Stream of Life*, or Rodrigo S. M. all exemplify the kinds of verbally inscribed existences that stem from language's status as an "unsettling process . . . of meaning and . . . subject" (1163)—rather than a rigid coherence of identity existing outside of language and that could be understood as its stable, reliable referent—and, in so doing, demonstrate their relevance to Kristeva's socially and politically pertinent arguments.

With its emphasis on how texts—and especially literary texts—express the relationship between language and the operation of the mind and how meaning is generated and received or processed, modern psychoanalytic criticism has moved beyond its traditional function of analyzing the symbols and tensions in a literary work. And in this particular case, it seems likely, as a number of commentators have suggested, that, given the psychologically revealing nature of her work, the texts of Clarice Lispector suggest a great deal about the author herself at the same time that they respond well to the application of theories proposed by such language-conscious psychoanalysts as Jacques Lacan and Julia Kristeva. Moreover, within the context of the general applicability of psychoanalytic criticism to Lispector's narratives, it is also clear that the throb of transgressive sexuality, expressed via her own unique version of "desire in language"[28] and closely linked to both the angst-ridden condition of her characters and to their conflicted senses of self and being, emerges as one of the most powerful and destabilizing forces at work in her entire fictive universe.

CONCLUSION

In the preceding pages, I have tried to show that the defining characteristics of Lispector's work not only embody but humanize the language-
based issues that inform poststructural thought.

It has not, however, been my intention to either praise or delimit
Clarice Lispector as a specifically poststructural writer. Rather, I have
sought to demonstrate that the basic intellectual concerns of poststructuralism go a long way toward explaining the nature of her work, its
characterizations and style as well as its thematic concerns. While I do
not argue that every line of every text she ever wrote exemplifies the
poststructural outlook, the majority, I believe, do, and it is this postula-
tion that provides the basis for the current study. The result, as I have
tried to show, is that poststructuralism provides not an ultimate explanation of every Lispectorian novel, story, or *crônica* but an overall intellectual framework in which to consider her work.

Moreover, I do not claim either that poststructuralism is the only
correct way to read Lispector or that it should replace other interpretations of her texts, which, virtually without exception, demonstrate a lifelong concern with the entwined problems of language, meaning, and
identity, and which admit a variety of interpretive strategies. In Lispector's fictional world, however, these sorts of concerns tend to develop themselves in the contexts of relationships, relationships, however,
that reveal themselves preeminently to be functions of both language
and identity (public as well as private). It is at this critical juncture of
language, consciousness, and being that Lispector's work demonstrates
why it must be considered in terms of its larger political context, that
is, in terms of how people see themselves and their relationships with
other people. From beginning to end, Lispector's narratives emphasize
the ways in which our value systems, our political structures, and our
ideas about the "correct," "proper," or "most desirable" relationships
between things are, at bottom, psycholinguistic constructs, and, as such,
subject to both continual interrogation and change. This, as Lispec-

tor's texts show us, is basically what human existence is, a day-to-day, moment-to-moment negotiation with life, a negotiation that takes place in and through the medium of language. Certain physical realities of life—death, for example, or hunger—of course exist independently of language, but what these mean to us, and how we deal with them, return us to the unstable realm of language.

I have also attempted to demonstrate how a powerful, if muted, sexuality pervades Lispector's texts, animating them with an intensity and eroticism not immediately associated with a writer widely regarded as being very esoteric and cerebral in nature. For Lispector, as for Shoshana Felman, sexuality is a function of "rhetoric" (Felman 112), or language, whose "divisions, contradictions, and ambivalences" mark "the disruptions of sexuality" (Leitch 293) that so destabilize human existence. Expressed in a poetic language that exudes a pansexual energy and tension, this sense of undifferentiated and typically unfulfilled desire tends, in presences as diverse as Joana, Laura, G. H., Martim, the voice of *The Stream of Life*, and Macabéa, to develop characters as frustrated, anxiety-filled sites of psychic conflict rather than as stable, coherent subjects. And because this visceral connection between language and being emerges as Lispector's primary thematic ground, the mercurial site to which all her narrative paths eventually lead, she and her characters (many of whom can easily be read as extensions or expressions of herself) seem always to be in quest of something else, something very akin to Lacan's Other (*Écrits* 292–325), that part of a person's linguistically structured unconsciousness that, paradoxically, is felt to be present precisely because it is absent, or lacking, a vague, undefinable need that has to be met but that cannot be met. Prototypically expressed in *The Passion according to G. H.* (1964), one of the most powerful Latin American novels of the 1960s, this amorphous but urgent need reveals itself to be, in essence, a problem of Lacanian "méconnaissance," or "misrecognition," a futile quest for the "raw material" of existence, for the "center," the "transcendental signified" that would somehow stand outside the system that gives it meaning and that guarantees its intelligibility. Similarly, if less overtly, sought out in nearly everything else she wrote, this most basic "raw material" of life reveals itself everywhere in Lispector's universe to be language, the semiotic system that most determines who and what we are and how we interpret our unstable, ephemeral condition.

For Clarice Lispector, the world truly is poststructural *texte*, and all our attempts to understand or decipher it are inescapably "intertextual," a struggle not merely to establish some meaning for a particular word or phrase but to divine how it is possible for language to generate meaning at all, and how we might understand the fluid, unstable process that is meaning. This explains why G. H., in many ways the definitive Lispectorian character, opens her narrative with the declaration that she is simply "trying to understand," to gain some degree of control over the confrontation with the dizzyingly infinite play of language that she has experienced and with which, in her all too human frustration and anxiety, she is attempting to come to grips. Transformed from the abstract to the human, G. H.'s struggle, her thwarted desire "to understand," thus reflects the drama of poststructural thought as it applies to the human condition: for however much we may desire to step outside it and grasp the "transcendental signified," we cannot, for, trapped in the world of words as we are, we have no recourse but to think about language in language. Often deeply eroticized in nature, as in *Near to the Wild Heart, The Apple in the Dark, The Stream of Life,* or *The Stations of the Body,* this desire felt but never fulfilled is also a defining characteristic of Lispector's human landscape.

Yet for however much these quests for Self, for Other, and for the fulfillment of desire mark the development of Lispector's characters, they are always carried out in terms of language, which, everywhere in her world, calls attention to itself as a particular kind of self-conscious writing, one best understood as *écriture* and which constantly leads back to itself as a ceaselessly protean and differentially related sign system. Exemplifying, stylistically and structurally, what Derrida means with the term "différance" (*Positions* 8–10, 24–29), and very close to what Kristeva outlines in *Desire in Language* (18), Lispector's constant preoccupation with words, with language, and with writing also embodies what Barthes describes in "Theory of the Text" as "a differentiated signifying system, dependent on a typology of significations (and not on a universal matrix of the sign)," one in which the process of signification occurs through "a labour in which both the debate of the subject and the Other, and the social context, are invested in the same movement" (*Untying the Text: A Post-Structuralist Reader,* ed. Young, 36).

Through her intense cultivation of writing as ontological act, Lispector struggles with language and being in her work in a way that both concretizes and humanizes Derrida's "grammatology" and that shows its vital, often erotic embodiment of Lacan's assertion that "the law of language" is "the law" of the human experience (*Écrits* 61). Employing a style that, because it is profoundly poetic and metaphoric, is also semantically indeterminate, Lispector's poststructural "textes," which, as I have tried to show, exemplify the free play of signifiers and signifieds that Derrida stresses as the true nature of language, elude the reader's efforts to impose on them a single, unified system of meaning or even to limit them to a single range of meanings. Constantly undercutting or decentering themselves, and thereby constantly disseminating new semantic possibilities and frames of reference (including, as in her critique of gender and sexuality, sociopolitical ones), Lispector's "textes" convincingly demonstrate how the inherent rhetoricity and self-referentiality of language resist our logocentrically driven desire to extract from them a single, stable meaning.

Although Lispector's narratives typically demonstrate a surface structural unity (often, as in *The Apple in the Dark*, a type of circularity), it is, paradoxically, a "unity" that, under the pressure of a close reading, actually reveals itself to be a manifestation of radical disunity, a "unity," in other words, that is constantly being undone at the level of language itself, where the ceaseless slide of signifiers and the endless dispersal of meaning that derives from it, generate a variety of often conflictive meanings, all of which, however, stem from the very language that structures her works as well as from the language that each reader uses to interpret them.

With her insistent probing of the fluid and eroticizing interplay between language and being, whether private or public, and with her sense of writing as the ultimate act of self-affirmation, Clarice Lispector is a writer whose tangled, intense, and always language-based vision of human existence exemplifies the defining philosophical and literary issues of late-twentieth-century thought. Never a great storyteller, Lispector and her meditatively self-conscious and often autobiographical narratives plunge us into the anxiety and uncertainty that is life understood as language. And it is precisely from this preoccupation with the concept of language-as-being, from her feeling that life and writing are a "searching for the word in the darkness" (*Hour* 70), and from her belief that "each thing became the cipher of something else" and that "everything was symbolic" ("The Obedient Ones," *DW,* 583), that Lispector emerges from her narratives as a writer driven by a fundamentally poststructural outlook.

Exemplifying that play of "différance" and desire that Derrida, Lacan, and Kristeva (*Positions* 14; *Écrits* 256–80) see as the source of all true meaning, Lispector's poetically and politically charged "textes" transform what are all too often the disembodied abstractions of poststructural thought into the simultaneously transgressive and conformist urges that define the complex inner reality of the human experience. The relationship between life, or "reality," and language does not permit an either/or choice; the words "life" and "reality" themselves have meaning only insofar as they exist within a language system. They have no special relationship to entities outside of themselves and the other words that provide them with a signifying context. This is what would appear to be the unassailable truth of Saussurean linguistics, which, as we saw in the introduction, provides the conceptual basis of poststructural thought. Hence, the issues raised by poststructuralism, and cultivated literarily by Clarice Lispector, are never extraneous to human existence; they are, Lispector shows us, part and parcel of it.

I. NOVELS

Perto do coração selvagem [Near to the Wild Heart]
O lustre [The Chandelier]
A cidade sitiada [The Besieged City]
A paixão segundo G. H. [The Passion according to G. H.]
A maçã no escuro [The Apple in the Dark]
Água viva [The Stream of Life]
A hora da estrela [The Hour of the Star]
Um sopro de vida [The Breath of Life]
*Uma aprendizagem ou o livro dos prazeres [An Apprenticeship, or The Book
    of Delights]*

II. SHORT STORIES

A legião estrangeira [The Foreign Legion]
  "A pecadora queimada e os anjos harmoniosos" ["The Burned Sinner
    and the Harmonious Angels"]
  "O ôvo e a galinha" ["The Egg and the Chicken"]
  "A quinta história" ["The Fifth Story"]
  "Mas já que se há de escrever" ["Since One Feels Obliged to Write"]
  "A pesca milagrosa" ["Miraculous Fishing"]
  "Escrever, humildade, técnica" ["Writing, Humility, Technique"]
  "Aventura" ["Adventure"]
  "Escrevendo" ["Writing"]
  "A solução" ["The Solution"]
  "Viagem a Petrópolis" ["Journey to Petrópolis"]
  "Macacos" ["Monkeys"]

Felicidade clandestina [Clandestine Happiness]
  "Duas histórias a meu modo" ["Two Stories My Way"]
  "A mensagem" ["The Message"]
  "Os obedientes" ["The Obedient Ones"]
  "Felicidade clandestina" ["Clandestine Happiness"]
  "Restos do Carnaval" ["The Remains of Carnival"]

"Cem anos de perdão" ["One Hundred Years of Pardon"]
"O primeiro beijo" ["The First Kiss"]
"Uma história de tanto amor" ["A Story of Such Love"]
"Uma amizade sincera" ["A Sincere Friendship"]

A via crucis do corpo [Soulstorm: The Stations of the Body]
"A procura de uma dignidade" ["In Search of Dignity"]
"É para lá que eu vou" ["That's Where I'm Going"]
"Praça Mauá" ["Plaza Mauá"]
"Um caso complicado" ["A Complicated Case"]
"Ele me bebeu" ["He Soaked Me Up"]
"Ruído de passos" ["Footsteps"]
"A língua do 'p'" ["Pig Latin"]
"O corpo" ["The Body"]
"Melhor do que arder" ["Better Than to Burn"]
"Mas vai chover" ["But It's Going to Rain"]
"Dia após dia" ["Day by Day"]

Onde estiveste de noite [Soulstorm: Where You Were at Night]
"Onde estivestes de noite" ["Where You Were at Night"]
"O relatório da coisa" ["A Report on a Thing"]
"Silêncio" ["Silence"]
"Tempestade de almas" ["Soulstorm"]
"Vida ao natural" ["Life au Naturel"]
"A partida do trem" ["The Departure of the Train"]
"Seco estudo de cavalos" ["Dry Point of Horses"]

Laços de família [Family Ties]
"Amor" ["Love"]
Laços de família ["Family Ties"]
"A imitação da rosa" ["The Imitation of the Rose"]
"Feliz aniversário" ["Happy Birthday"]
"Uma galinha" ["The Chicken"]
"O crime do professor de matemática"
["The Crime of the Mathematics Professor"]
"O búfalo" ["The Buffalo"]

A bela e a fera [Beauty and the Beast]
"A bela e a fera, ou a ferida grande demais" ["Beauty and the Beast, or
The Wound Too Great"]
"História interrompida" ["Interrupted Story"]

III. *Crônicas* [CHRONICLES]

A descoberta do mundo [Discovering the World]
"Perdoando Deus" ["Forgiving God"]

"Dois modos" ["Two Ways"]
"Forma e conteúdo" ["Form and Content"]

IV. CHILDREN'S BOOKS

Quase de verdade [Almost True]
A vida íntima de Laura [Laura's Intimate Life]
O mistério do coelho pensante [The Mystery of the Thinking Rabbit]

NOVELS

Near to the Wild Heart (Heart; NWH)
The Chandelier (Chandelier; C)
The Besieged City (City; BC)
The Passion according to G. H. (Passion; PAGH)
The Apple in the Dark (Apple; AD)
The Stream of Life (Stream; SL)
The Hour of the Star (Hour; HS)
The Breath of Life (Breath; BL)
An Apprenticeship, or The Book of Delights (Apprenticeship; ABD)

SHORT STORIES

The Foreign Legion (FL)

"The Burned Sinner and the Harmonious Angels" ("Sinner"; BSHA)
"The Egg and the Chicken" ("Egg"; EC)
"The Fifth Story" ("Fifth"; FS)
"Since One Feels Obliged to Write" ("Obliged"; SOFOW)
"Miraculous Fishing" ("Fishing"; MF)
"Writing, Humility, Technique" ("Technique"; WHT)
"Adventure" ("Adventure"; A)
"Writing" ("Writing"; W)
"The Solution" ("Solution"; S)
"Journey to Petrópolis" ("Journey"; JP)
"Monkeys" ("Monkeys"; M)
"The Foreign Legion" ("Legion"; FL)
"The Message" ("Message"; M)

Clandestine Happiness

"Two Stories My Way" ("Stories"; TSMW)
"The Obedient Ones" ("Obedient"; OO)

"Clandestine Happiness" ("Clandestine"; CH)
"The Remains of Carnival" ("Remains"; RC)
"One Hundred Years of Pardon" ("Pardon"; OHYP)
"The First Kiss" ("Kiss"; FK)
"A Story of Such Love" ("Story"; ASSL)
"A Sincere Friendship" ("Friendship"; ASF)

Soulstorm (INCLUDES BOTH THE STORIES FROM *The Stations of the Body* AND *Where You Were at Night*)

The Stations of the Body

"In Search of Dignity" ("Search"; SD)
"That's Where I'm Going" ("Going"; TWIG)
"Plaza Mauá" ("Plaza"; PM)
"A Complicated Case" ("Complicated"; CC)
"He Soaked Me Up" ("Soaked"; HSMU)
"Footsteps" ("Footsteps"; F)
"Pig Latin" ("Pig"; PL)
"The Body" ("Body"; B)
"Better Than to Burn" ("Better"; BTB)
"But It's Going to Rain" ("Rain"; BIGR)
"Day by Day" ("Day"; DD)

Where You Were at Night

"Where You Were at Night" ("Night"; WYWN)
"A Report on a Thing" ("Report"; ART)
"Silence" ("Silence"; S)
"Soulstorm" ("Soulstorm"; S)
"Life *au Naturel*" ("Life"; LN)
"The Departure of the Train" ("Departure"; DT)
"Dry Point of Horses" ("Horses"; DPH)

Family Ties

"Love" ("Love"; L)
"Family Ties" ("Family"; FT)
"The Imitation of the Rose" ("Imitation"; IR)
"Happy Birthday" ("Birthday"; HB)
"The Chicken" ("Chicken"; C)
"The Crime of the Mathematics Professor" ("Crime"; CMP)
"The Buffalo" ("Buffalo"; B)

Beauty and the Beast

"Beauty and the Beast, or The Wound Too Great" ("Beauty"; BB)
"Interrupted Story" ("Interrupted"; IS)

CHRONICLES

Discovering the World

"Forgiving God" ("Forgiving"; FG)
"Two Ways" ("Ways"; TW)
"Form and Content" ("Form"; FC)
"A Pleasant Interview" ("Interview"; API)
"The Perilous Adventure of Writing" ("Perilous"; PAW)
"Good Friends" ("Friends"; GF)
"The Lucidity of the Absurd" ("Lucidity"; LA)
"The Unreality of Realism" ("Unreality"; UR)
"Writing" ("Writing"; W)
"Style" ("Style"; S)
"How Does One Write?" ("How"; HDOW)
"Passing Themes" ("Passing"; PT)
"Adventure" ("Adventure"; A)
"About Writing" ("About"; AW)
"Hateful Charity" ("Hateful"; HC)
"Too Good to Be True" ("Good"; TGT)
"Dialogue" ("Dialogue"; D)

CHILDREN'S BOOKS

Almost True (True; AT)
Laura's Intimate Life (Life; LIL)
The Mystery of the Thinking Rabbit (Mystery; MTR)

INTRODUCTION

1. Barbara Mathie has noted the connection between existentialism, feminism, and poststructuralism that exists in Lispector's work; see Mathie, "Feminism, Language, or Existentialism: The Search for the Self in the Works of Clarice Lispector," in *Subjectivity and Literature from the Romantics to the Present Day*, ed. Philip Shaw and Peter Stockwell (London: Printer Publishers, 1991), 121–34. Mathie focuses her comments especially on *Laços de família* and *A via crucis do corpo*. Ivaldo Bittencourt also considers a poststructural approach to Lispector (in addition to structuralism and reception theory); see his "As matrizes textuais em *Perto do coração selvagem*" and "Determinação das matrizes," in *Neo-análise da produção literária em Clarice Lispector* (Recife: Editôra Universitária de Pernambuco, 1987), 77–86. Finally, Maria José Somerlate Barbosa's *Clarice Lispector: Spinning the Webs of Passion* (New Orleans: University Press of the South, 1997) also notes the applicability of poststructuralism to Lispector's work (11–12, passim).

2. Other critics and readers who, directly or indirectly, have at least considered this approach to Lispector's work include the following: Hélène Cixous, "*Água viva*: How to Follow a Trinket of Water," in *Reading with Clarice Lispector*, ed., trans., and introduced by Verena Andermatt Conley (Minneapolis: University of Minnesota Press, 1990), 11–59; Nelson Vieira, *Ser Judeu e escritor: Três casos brasileiros: Samuel Rawet, Clarice Lispector, Moacyr Scliar*, Papéis Avulsos, no. 25 (Rio de Janeiro: Centro Interdisciplinar de Estudos Contemporâneos, Escola de Comunicação, Universidade Federal de Rio de Janeiro, 1990); Clarissa Fukelman, "A palavra em exílio: Uma leitura de Clarice Lispector," in *A mulher na literatura, no terceiro encontro nacional da ANPOLL (Rio de Janeiro)*, 3 vols. (Belo Horizonte: Imprensa da Universidade Federal de Minas Gerais, 1990), vol. 2 ed. Nádia Battella Gotlib, 2 : 161–67; Ivaldo Bittencourt, *Analyse de la production textuelle d'après certains notions sémiologiques, et psycho-phénoménologiques (suivi de l'analyses du texte Água viva, Clarice Lispector)* (Ph.D. diss., Université de Paris III, 1977); Miriam Chnaiderman, "Passeando entre a literatura e a psicanálise," *Minas Gerais, Suplemento Literário* (hereafter cited as *MGSL*), 19 December 1987, 5; and most directly, Mathie, "Feminism, Language, or Existentialism," 121–34. My purpose, then, in writing this book is to go further in terms of applying a

poststructural optic to Lispector's work, to evaluate it more systematically in order to determine how the basic tenets of poststructural thought manifest themselves in it.

3. For a more complete statement of this, see Julia Kristeva's 1968 interview of Derrida, *Positions*, 17–36.

4. *Diacritics* 12 (spring 1982): 2–24.

5. For however much Derrida does "textualize" the world (that is, see existence as "text"), he has stated clearly that he still maintains a belief in the referent: "When it is said about the deconstructive perspective that there is nothing outside the text, then I say to myself: If deconstruction *really* consisted in saying that everything happens in books, it wouldn't deserve *five* minutes of anybody's attention . . . never have I said that there is no referent" ("Deconstruction in America: An Interview with Jacques Derrida," trans. J. Creech, in *Critical Exchange*, no. 17 [winter 1985]: 15, 19).

6. *Concepts of Criticism*, 2d ed. (Mountain View, Calif.: Mayfield Publishing Co., 1994), 335–46.

7. See Earl Fitz, "The Passion of Logo(centrism), or The Deconstructionist Universe of Clarice Lispector," *Luso-Brazilian Review* 25, no. 2 (winter 1988): 33–44. See also David William Foster, *Cultural Diversity in Latin American Literature* (Albuquerque: University of New Mexico Press, 1994), 16, and Barbosa, *Clarice Lispector: Spinning the Webs of Passion*, 12.

8. See Ann Banfield, "Écriture, Narration, and the Grammar of French," in *Narrative: From Malory to Motion Pictures*, ed. Jeremy Hawthorn (London: Arnold, 1985). The poststructural significance of the term *écriture* dates, of course, from Roland Barthes's *Degré Zéro de l'écriture* (1953). For a useful study of the various narrative modes utilized by Lispector, see Maria Luisa Nunes, "Narrative Modes in Clarice Lispector's *Laços de família*: The Rendering of Consciousness," *Luso-Brazilian Review* 14, no. 2 (winter 1977): 174–84.

9. "For Derrida," as Jeffrey T. Nealson writes (as if in reference to Lispector's *escritura*, or "writing"), "it is the nature or structure of the field—of systematicity or metaphoricity—rather than some sort of inherent ambiguity in the use of tropes or figural language that is the ground of undecidability" ("The Discipline of Deconstruction," *PMLA* 107, no. 5 [October 1992]: 1266–79). In the sense that Derrida uses the term, then, undecidability is not solely an issue of figurative language's ability to generate an infinite number of plausible meanings; rather, as he writes in *Dissemination*, "'Undecidability' is not caused here [he is discussing the word "hymen" in Mallarmé] by some enigmatic equivocality, some inexhaustible ambivalence of a word in a 'natural' language" (220). While Derrida is certainly interested in the metaphoricity of language, for him undecidability is more profoundly an issue of the nature of the signifying "field" itself and of our desire for closure. As he says, "If totalization no longer has any meaning, it is not because the infiniteness of a field cannot be covered by a finite

glance or a finite discourse, but because the nature of the field . . . excludes totalization" (*Writing and Difference* 289).

10. In a *crônica* entitled "Humility and Technique" (4 October 1969), Lispector refers to her own style of writing as "a humble quest" (*Discovering the World* [hereafter cited as *DW*] 309), while Ellen Douglass has, in "Myth and Gender in Clarice Lispector: Quest as a Feminist Statement in 'A imitação da rosa'" (*Luso-Brazilian Review* 25, no. 2 [winter 1988]: 15–31), identified the quest motif as central to Lispector's best work.

CHAPTER I

1. Although "deconstruction" is closely related to poststructuralism, it should not be regarded as a synonym. While the former refers to a particular reading strategy, the latter, a more comprehensive way of thinking about the relationship between language, meaning, and reality, refers to the critique of certain of structuralism's basic principles that began to take place after the appearance of Barthes's *S/Z* in 1970. "Deconstruction" is thus best understood as the application of a particular aspect of poststructural thought (that, as a function of language, texts cannot avoid "deconstructing," or contradicting, themselves rather than generating a single stable and identifiable meaning) to the process of reading and writing.

Deconstruction is also the form grammatology takes "when it turns its attention to specific texts" (Ann Jefferson, "Structuralism and Post-Structuralism," in *Modern Literary Theory: A Comparative Introduction*, ed. Jefferson and David Robey [Totowa, N.J.: Barnes and Noble, 1982 ed.], 110). "It will tease out the text's implied presuppositions and point out the (inevitable) contradictions in them" (110). "A deconstructive reading . . . will take the metaphysical, logocentric oppositions at work in a text, reverse them, and then question them in such a way as to 'neutralize' them" (110). And, as Lispector's texts repeatedly show, since we can never escape logocentrism, the most we can do, once having come to recognize its power, is to struggle against its limits, to resist the siren call of its inauthenticity. "Deconstruction" is thus both (1) the critical process by which a text's (binary) oppositions can be shown to be falsely or unjustifiably based and (2) the process by which a text shows these oppositions to be undercutting or subverting themselves. Both these cases accurately describe the texts written by Clarice Lispector, the "fictional" ones as well as the "nonfictional" ones.

Yet we should regard Lispector's texts as essentially "poststructuralist," rather than "deconstructive," because (1) they deal with historical, sociological, and political issues and (2) they also seem to call for psychoanalytic interpretations, particularly those associated with the language-based theories of Lacan, Kristeva, and Derrida.

2. See Ivaldo Bittencourt, "*Água Viva*: Unificação que instiga a ciência do texto," *Neo-análise da produção literária em Clarice Lispector* (Recife: Universidade

Federal de Pernambuco, 1987). Bittencourt has applied this approach to other of Lispector's texts as well.

3. Eduardo Portella, writing about *A hora da estrela*, comes to a similar conclusion. See "O grito do silêncio," introduction to *A hora da estrela* (Rio de Janeiro: José Olympio Editôra, 1977), 9–12.

4. See "That's Where I'm Going" (*Soulstorm*).

5. While there is a wealth of books and articles that deal tangentially with poststructuralism, the following works are particularly useful in defining it: *Untying the Text: A Post-Structuralist Reader*, ed. Robert Young (London: Routledge and Kegan Paul, 1981); Chris Weedon, *Feminist Practice and Poststructuralist Theory* (Oxford: Basil Blackwell, 1987); Luce Irigaray, "La Mystérique," in *Speculum of the Other Woman*, trans. Gilliam C. Gill (Ithaca: Cornell University Press, 1985), 191–202; Terry Eagleton, "Post-Structuralism," *Literary Theory: An Introduction* (Minneapolis: University of Minnesota Press, 1983), 127–50; Madan Sarup, *An Introductory Guide to Post-Structuralism and Postmodernism* (Athens: University of Georgia Press, 1989); Jefferson, "Structuralism and Post-Structuralism," in *Modern Literary Theory*, 2d ed., 92–121; Roland Barthes, *S/Z* (Paris, 1970); Jacques Derrida, *De la grammatologie* (Paris, 1967) and *Positions* (Paris, 1972); Raman Selden, "Poststructuralist Theories," *A Reader's Guide to Contemporary Literary Theory*, 2d ed. (Lexington: University Press of Kentucky, 1985), 70–113; and Robert C. Holub, *Crossing Borders: Reception Theory, Poststructuralism, Deconstruction* (Madison: University of Wisconsin Press, 1992). Finally, in *Beyond Poststructuralism: The Speculations of Theory and the Experience of Reading*, ed. Wendell V. Harris (University Park: Pennsylvania State University Press, 1996), Harris argues, quite correctly, I think, that the "problems" often ascribed to poststructuralist theory are "largely based on confusion about Saussure's views of language" (xi). While these critical misinterpretations are made manifest in them, the essays in this book do not refute either Saussure's or Derrida's basic theories, however; indeed, they throw into sharp relief the unique kind of writing practiced by Clarice Lispector.

6. Although 1966 is the year most frequently given as marking the beginning of poststructuralism in the United States (where its dissemination was largely and problematically a function of certain key texts being translated and the sequence in which these texts, translated in whole or in part, appeared), it was already, by this date, in decline in Europe, where it had long been recognized as a viable intellectual mode of thought, one germane not only to philosophy and literature but also to issues of politics, history, and social discourse.

7. This is so because since at least part of any sign's meaning is a function of what that sign is not—"cat," for example, means whatever it means because it is not "hat," "fat," "bat," "sat," etc.—its meaning is also partly absent.

8. This little-known work, a subtle though effective form of what we might term an allegorical protest play, was written around 1949, although it did not appear in print until 1964, when it was included in *The Foreign Legion*, a collec-

tion of stories, *crônicas*, and sundry narrative fragments. (References to *The Foreign Legion* will be made parenthetically in the text, as *FL*.) See Earl Fitz, "The Burned Sinner and the Harmonious Angels: Clarice Lispector as Dramatist," *Luso-Brazilian Review* 34, no. 2 (winter 1997): 25–39.

9. Ellen Douglass, for example, speaking for a number of other critics, notes that Lispector's first novel, *Near to the Wild Heart*, was "at least partially autobiographical" ("*Near to the Wild Heart*," in *Clarice Lispector: A Bio-Bibliography*, ed. Diane E. Marting, [Westport, Conn.: Greenwood Press, 1993], 133). Another critic, José Américo Motta Pessanha, has noted something similar in the posthumously published novel, *A Breath of Life*. See Pessanha, "Os acordes do ser," *Veja*, 7 February 1979, 69–70. See also Maria Helena Werneck, "Indisfarçados tesouros," the preface to *Clandestine Happiness*, 7th ed. Lispector herself discusses the autobiographical dimension of her work (she denies that she writes autobiographical novels but acknowledges that others feel that she reveals herself through them) in "Another Letter" (24 February 1968, *DW* 106–7). Lispector also notes here how closely entwined the reader and writer are.

10. This quest by Lispector's characters can be interpreted in terms of what Saussure understood as language's inherent "logocentrism," the semantic stability of any linguistic sign as "fully" recognized by the rational, self-conscious speaking subject, an assumption that Derrida and others have challenged. In a *crônica* entitled "Humility and Technique" (4 October 1969) Lispector refers to her own style of writing as "a humble quest" (*DW* 309), while Ellen Douglass has, in "Myth and Gender in Clarice Lispector: Quest as a Feminist Statement in 'A imitação da rosa,'" *Luso-Brazilian Review* 25, no. 2 (winter 1988): 15–31, identified the quest motif as central to some of Lispector's best work.

11. Although the issues that define the term "feminism" are all present in Lispector's work, she herself did not like to be referred to as a "feminist" or a "feminist writer." See Maria Luisa Nunes, "Clarice Lispector: Artista andrógina ou escritora?," *Revista Iberoamericana* 50, no. 126 (January–March 1984): 281–89. One possible explanation for their seeming incongruity (one that would be consistent with the rest of her work and its handling of the relationship between language and being, between words and our sense of identity) is that Lispector was loath to be "labeled," for to allow oneself to be "labeled" (a socialist, a "feminist," a "democrat," etc.) was tantamount to allocating oneself to be limited, or restricted, in terms of what we can say, do, or be. And given Lispector's views about the fluid relationship between language and being, such limitations or restrictions would have been anathema to her, completely inconsistent with the overall thrust of her work, which was to disavow borders and to promote both the possibilities and the dangers inherent in fluidity. We can conclude, then, that while Lispector's work most definitely reflects and embodies feminist issues, she herself did not accept being "labeled" a feminist, for to do so would mean accepting the restrictive "either/or," "correct/incorrect," "acceptable/unacceptable" kind of thinking required of categories and their definitions. In

this same context, it should also be noted that Lispector would most likely have objected to being termed a "poststructuralist writer." My use of this term is as a description of her writing; it is not meant to limit or restrict her in any way.

12. See Hélène Cixous, in *Reading with Clarice Lispector*. The pertinent quote (by Verena Conley) is as follows: "Paradoxically, Cixous begins her reading of Lispector with one of the Brazilian writer's later texts, *Água Viva* (*The Stream of Life*). Cixous claims to have been overwhelmed by her encounter with *Água Viva*. In it she finds the finest practice of 'écriture féminine'" (vii). As recent studies by Marta Peixoto (*Passionate Fictions* [Minneapolis: University of Minnesota Press, 1994]) and Anna Klobucka ("Hélène Cixous and the Hour of Clarice Lispector," *SubStance* 73 [1994]: 41–62) show, however, Cixous's appropriation of Lispector is highly problematic.

13. See "Post-Feminist Discourse in Clarice Lispector's *A hora da estrela* [*The Hour of the Star*]," in *Splintering Darkness: Latin American Women Writers in Search of Themselves*, ed. Lucía Guerra Cunningham (Pittsburgh: Latin American Literary Review Press, 1990), 63–78.

14. For discussions of the issue of gender as it pertains to *The Apple in the Dark*, see Hélène Cixous, "*The Apple in the Dark:* The Temptation of Understanding," in *Reading with Clarice Lispector*, 60–97; and especially, Mara Negrón, "A gênese de um pensar-sentir-mulher em *A maçã no escuro*," *Clarice e o feminino*, a special issue of *Tempo Brasileiro* 104 (January–March 1991): 73–81. For other gender-related studies in regard to Lispector's work, see Lúcia Helena, "Genre and Gender in Clarice Lispector's 'The Imitation of the Rose,'" *Style* 24, no. 2 (1990): 215–27; and Rita Terezinha Schmidt, "Pelos caminhos do coração selvagem, sob o signo do desejo," *Clarice e o feminino*, 83–100.

15. For a brief discussion of this issue, see K. David Jackson, "Onde estivestes de noite," in *Clarice Lispector: A Bio-Bibliography*, 105–8.

16. Another representative example is that of Martim (of *The Apple in the Dark*), whose triangular story involves two women while also epitomizing the five "codes" (the hermeneutic, the semic, the symbolic, the proairetic, and the cultural) that Roland Barthes discusses in *S/Z* (1970), as does the voice of *The Stream of Life*.

17. See Benedito Nunes, *Leitura de Clarice Lispector* (São Paulo: Edição Quirón, 1973). Nunes reads *O lustre* in conjunction with *Near to the Wild Heart* and argues that both works illustrate Lispector's efforts to experiment with new modes of third-person narration, focus, and voice.

18. For Barthes, these "codes" are "the hermeneutic code through which an enigma is posed and eventually solved in a text; the semic code which determines themes; the symbolic code which is the sphere where meanings become multivalent and reversible; the proairetic code which determines action and behavior; and finally the cultural code which provides social and 'scientific' information" (Jefferson, "Structuralism and Post-Structuralism," 101).

19. See Benedito Nunes, *O mundo de Clarice Lispector* (Manaus: Edições do

Governo do Estado de Amazonas, 1996); *Leitura de Clarice Lispector*; and "Dos narradores brasileiros," *Revista de cultura* 9, no. 29 (December 1969): 187–204. For other critics who have discussed Heidegger's relevance to Lispector, see Cixous, "*Água viva*," 11–59; Hélène Cixous, "L'approche de Clarice Lispector: Se laisser lire (par) Clarice Lispector—*A paixão segundo G. H.*," *Poétique* 40 (November 1979): 408–19; and Ronald W. Sousa, "At the Site of Language: Reading Lispector's G. H.," *Chasqui* 18, no. 2 (November 1989): 43–48. For another important discussion of the philosophical base of Lispector's work, see Massaud Moisés, "Clarice Lispector: Ficção e cosmovisão," *Estado de São Paulo, Suplemento Literário* (hereafter cited as *ESPSL*), 26 September 1970, 1.

20. I do not wish to imply that a text like *The Stream of Life* is in any way identical to works like *Near to the Wild Heart* and *The Chandelier*; my point is only that their other "differences" notwithstanding, Lispector's early novels share with the later, post-1961 texts an awareness of language and its relationship to human cognition and the fluid, nonlinear process of forming an identity that we now recognize as being decidedly poststructural in nature. Given the generally positive reception French critical thought has long had in Brazil (structuralism being a case in point), it is entirely possible that Lispector, whose circle of friends and acquaintances included some of Brazil's most prominent writers, critics, and artists, would have read or heard about poststructuralism and its concepts. But it is also likely, given her disdain of intellectual theorizing (see, for example, the *crônica* "An Intellectual? Certainly Not!," 2 November 1968, *DW* 198–99), that Lispector would have ignored it, even though, after seeing through its jargon, she would have instinctively understood its basic concerns and seen their affinity with her own work. For another expression of this sentiment, see "De uma conferência no Texas" (20 July 1968, *DW*), where Lispector discusses her "lack of intellectual pursuits" (157) and of an "intellectual life" (157) in terms of her own career as a writer.

21. Less concerned, perhaps, with Lévi-Strauss's anthropological structuralism than with Western metaphysics (specifically its "logocentrism") and the nature of language, Derrida shows, in "Structure, Sign, and Play in the Discourse of the Human Sciences" (cf. *The Structuralist Controversy*, 1970), that the language of structuralism, which requires, by definition, that a "structure" be "structured," also requires a "center" of the structure even when this cannot be, since, because of Saussure's process of "signification," the ceaseless deferral of meaning between signifiers (*différance*) prohibits it. Texts like *The Stream of Life* are, effectively speaking, the literary analogues of Derrida's philosophical theorizing, which constitutes, of course, a critique of structuralism and its adherence to rigidly maintained oppositions.

22. Jonathan Culler, *On Deconstruction: Theory and Criticism after Structuralism* (Ithaca: Cornell University Press, 1982), 92.

23. Given his interest in this range of issues, it is no surprise that Derrida and his thought have inspired a great deal of interest in literary communities;

indeed, it may be said that Derrida has had a greater impact in the field of literary study (where his work has generated passionate debate) than in philosophy. In certain crucial ways, Derrida's arguments rest so heavily upon Saussure's linguistics that to refute Derrida necessitates a refutation of Saussure's theory, and this has not yet occurred. Until it does, we, in literature, like our colleagues in philosophy, will have to accord Derrida the possibility that he is right, and we will have to reevaluate the host of questions that stem from his conclusions about the relationship between language, reality, and human existence.

24. Lispector herself described *The Stream of Life* as a "fiction," while she subtitled *A Breath of Life* "Pulsations." (All further references to *The Stream of Life* will be made parenthetically in the text, as *SL*.) For Lispector's discussion of how her "novels" compare with what we understand as the "traditional novel," see "The 'True' Novel" (*DW* 400–401). It is interesting to note how aware Lispector was of how "different" her novels were from the established norm and how comfortable she was with what she was writing and why. See also "About Writing" and "Form and Content" (20 December 1969, *DW* 331).

25. For discussions of the role this "it" plays in *The Stream of Life*, see Ana Maria de Almeida, "O it/id da escritura," *MGSL*, 1 June 1985, 6–8; and Gina Michelle Collins, "Translating a Feminine Discourse: Clarice Lispector's *Água viva*," in *Translation Perspectives: Selected Papers, 1982–1983*, ed. Marilyn Gaddis Rose (Binghamton: State University of New York–Binghamton Translation Research and Instruction Program, 1984), 119–24.

26. Lispector discussed in several different *crônicas* how closely she identified writing with her own existence. As Pontiero observes, for example, "In a television interview in February 1977, she confessed: 'When I am not writing, I am dead'" (*DW* 30). For more of Lispector's discussions of this key issue, see "Como é que se escreve?" (30 November 1968), "Escrever" (14 September 1968), "As três experiências" (11 May 1968), "Temas que morrem" (24 May 1969), "Aventura" (4 October 1969), and "Um degrau acima: O silêncio" (22 April 1972). In "Passing Themes," for example, she writes, "Sometimes it is the fear of touching upon a word which might release thousands of other words and all of them undesirable. Yet I feel this urge to write. Pure impulse—even when I have no theme. . . . Sometimes my silence makes me seek out people who might unwittingly provide me with the key word. But who? Who obliges me to write? That is the mystery: no one. Nonetheless, I still feel this compulsion to write" (*DW* 258).

27. For a discussion of this issue, see Nelson Vieira, "A expressão Judaica na obra de Clarice Lispector," *Remate de males* (Campinas) 9 (1989): 207–9, and "A 'linguagem espiritual' de Clarice Lispector," *Travessia* 14 (June 1987): 81–95. See also Sônia Régis, "O pensamento Judaico em Clarice Lispector," *ESPSL*, 14 May 1988, 8–9. This latter article argues that Lispector's basic attitude toward language, writing, and reality compare favorably with these same issues as they appear in Jewish philosophy.

28. One of Lispector's most definitive works, *The Passion according to G. H.*, is prototypical of this tendency.

CHAPTER 2

1. Earl Fitz, "Clarice Lispector and the Lyrical Novel: A Re-examination of *A Maçã no Escuro*," *Luso-Brazilian Review* 14, no. 2 (winter 1977): 153–60; for other discussions of this issue, see Sérgio Milliet, "Agosto, 27," *Diário Crítico*, 8 vols. (São Paulo: Brasiliense, 1945–55), 7 (1953): 33–44; and Antônio Olinto, "*A Maçã no Escuro*," *A verdade da ficção: Crítica do romance* (Rio de Janeiro: Companhia Brasileira de Artes Gráficas, 1966), 213–16.

2. This is the conclusion also reached by Alexis Levitan, another of Lispector's translators (cf. *Soulstorm*). In Levitan's opinion, "Clarice Lispector is fundamentally a poet" (173). A similar point is made by Gilda de Mello e Sousa (in reference to *The Chandelier*) in "*O Lustre*," *Remate de Males* (Campinas) 9 (1989): 171–75; and (also in reference to *The Chandelier*) by Marie Pierre Gueutier in "'Sunday, before Falling Asleep': A Primal Scene," *Art Press* (Paris) 151 (October 1990): 64. Finally, Emir Rodríguez Monegal has noted that her novels "are written like poems" ("The Contemporary Brazilian Novel," in *Fiction in Several Languages*, ed. Henri Peyre [Boston: Beacon Press, 1968], 16).

3. Monegal, "The Contemporary Brazilian Novel," 15–16.

4. Mark Strand, ed., *The Best American Poetry: 1991*, David Lehman, series ed. (New York: Macmillan, 1991).

5. For one of Lispector's most revealing comments on this issue (which links the function of the reader to that of the writer in a seamless web of words), see "Escrever as entrelinhas" (*Descubrimento do mundo*, 6 November 1971 and 20 December 1969); see also "A perigosa aventura de escrever" (*DW*, 5 April 1969).

6. Intensifying what is, at this point, an already extant poststructural anxiety, the opening of *The Passion according to G. H.* reads as follows: "I keep looking, looking. Trying to understand. Trying to give what I have gone through to someone else, and I don't know who, but I don't want to be alone with that experience. I don't know what to do with it, I'm terrified of that profound disorganization" (*Passion* 3).

7. See Fredric Jameson, *The Prison-House of Language* (Princeton: Princeton University Press, 1972).

8. George Steiner, *After Babel: Aspects of Language and Translation* (New York: Oxford University Press, 1975).

9. See, for example, Michelle Collins, "Translating Feminine Discourse: Mediating the Immediate," *Translation Review* 17 (1985): 21–24. For a critique of Cixous's appropriation of Lispector, see Marta Peixoto, *Passionate Fictions* (Minneapolis: University of Minnesota Press, 1994), and Anna Klobucka, "Hélène Cixous and the Hour of Clarice Lispector," *SubStance* 73 (1994): 41–62.

10. Hélène Cixous, her foreword to *The Stream of Life*, Clarice Lispector, trans. Elizabeth Lowe and Earl Fitz (Minneapolis: University of Minnesota Press, 1989), ix–xxxv. All further references to this work will be made parenthetically in the text (as *SL*); see also Hélène Cixous, "*Água Viva:* How to Follow a Trickle of Water," in *Reading with Clarice Lispector*, ed., trans., and with an introduction by Verena Andermatt Conley (Minneapolis: University of Minnesota Press, 1990), 3–10 and 11–59, respectively, and Cristina Peri Rossi's introduction to her Spanish translation of *Where You Were At Night*, entitled *Silencio* (Barcelona: Grijalbo, 1988).

11. G. H. is a woman known, except for the inferences we can draw from the text about her race and class, to the reader only by the initials of her name— G. H.—that are embossed on a suitcase.

12. For a further discussion of the narratee in Lispector's work, see Keith Brower, "The Narratee in Clarice Lispector's *Água viva*," *Romance Notes* 32, no. 2 (winter 1991): 111–18.

13. Gregory Rabassa's introduction to his English translation of *A maçã no escuro, The Apple in the Dark* (New York: Knopf, 1967), xii.

14. Terry Eagleton, *Literary Theory: An Introduction* (Minneapolis: University of Minnesota Press, 1983), 134.

15. See Affonso Romano de Sant'Anna, "Clarice Lispector: Linguagem," in *Por um novo conceito da literatura brasileira* (Rio de Janeiro: Eldorado, 1977), 198– 210; see also Sant'Anna, "Clarice Lispector: A Linguagem," I–III, *Estado de São Paulo, Suplemento Literário*, 2 June 1962, 2; 9 June 1962, 2; 16 June 1962, 2.

16. In Derrida's terminology, a "negative" is associated with a belief in the existence of fixed, extralinguistic points of reference or determination, referents that somehow lie beyond the semiotic systems in which these "transcendental signifiers" are said to exist. For a further discussion of this issue, see *Positions*.

17. Nihilism is not a necessary consequence of poststructural thought, which may, indeed, actually be empowering to those individuals who, like many of Lispector's characters, wish to remake themselves and their world by confronting language's inherent arbitrariness and by taking personal responsibility for its use, its power to determine who and what we are. One might say, in fact, that far from being "nihilistic," this is precisely how we humans have always dealt with language, for "change" is not necessarily "nihilistic"; indeed, it may be beneficial.

18. Neutrality, a Lispectorian variation on both androgyny and being, constitutes a major thematic presence in both *The Passion according to G. H.* and *The Stream of Life* as well as in numerous other works.

19. The word "palavra" (word) is so omnipresent in Lispector's work that it must be considered one of her most basic motifs.

20. We have already seen how profoundly the paradox figures into Lispector's writing, to the point that it, too, becomes one of her most basic motifs.

21. For Derrida, the concept of a "center" implies the presence of an unassailable, immovable sect of all knowledge and authority and the point of origin, position, or premise upon which all other structures or systems of belief were securely built, or centered. See his "Structure, Sign, and Play in the Discourse of the Human Sciences," in *Modern Criticism and Theory*, ed. David Lodge (London: Longman, 1988), 108–23.

22. Lispector has disavowed the existence of this type of knowledge in her work; see, for example, "Not to Understand," a *crônica* published 1 February 1969, and *The Passion according to G. H.*, where the goal of attaining perfect, definitive knowledge and understanding lies beyond G. H.'s reach. This same quality also accounts for the sense of "transcendence," "becoming," and "imminence" that permeates Lispector's work.

23. There is a strong affinity between Derrida's infamous pronouncement "There is no outside the text" and the way Lispector's characters develop almost exclusively within language. This condition does not, of course, prevent them from being read in a more sociopolitical context.

24. In contrast to the kinds of ambiguity discussed by William Empson, for example, in *The Seven Types of Ambiguity*, Lispector's ambiguities are always functions of the nature of language itself. Her ambiguity thus stems from her syntax and from what appears to have been her innate faith in what we take to be the unique ability of poetry, or poetic formulations, to express what certain other critics describe as the inherently poststructural nature of language.

25. For a discussion of Lispector's "it" in *The Stream of Life*, see Gina Michelle Collins, "Translating a Feminine Discourse: Clarice Lispector's *Água Viva*," in *Translation Perspectives: Selected Papers, 1982–1983*, ed. Marilyn Gaddis Rose (Binghamton: State University of New York–Binghamton Translation Research and Instruction Program, 1984), 119–24.

26. In a 3 July 1971, *crônica* entitled "In Amicable Conversation with Tom Jobim (I)," Lispector writes of her own work that "my books are not overloaded with events, but rather the repercussions of those events on the characters" (*DW* 473).

27. Other motiflike images cultivated by Lispector include images of half-open eyes and, more frequently, half-open lips (an image which, alluding, perhaps, to female genitalia, also underscores the powerful female sexuality inherent in Lispector's texts), flowers, animals, semen, silence, words, female breasts, wombs, ovaries, fire, sex, God, and death.

28. See, for example, Robert Scholes, *Structuralism in Literature: An Introduction* (New Haven: Yale University Press, 1974).

29. Marta Peixoto, "Rape and Textual Violence in Clarice Lispector," in *Rape and Representation*, ed. Lynn A. Higgins and Brenda R. Silver (New York: Columbia University Press, 1991); see also Marta Peixoto, "Rape and Textual Violence," *Passionate Fictions*, 82–99.

30. Before them, Nietzsche, who greatly influenced Derrida, Heidegger (whose importance for Lispector has often been noted), and Saussure, upon whose revolutionary linguistics both structuralism and poststructuralism rest.

31. Cixous, *Reading with Clarice Lispector*, x, xvii, 63, 68, 72.

32. See, for example, Earl Fitz, "A Discourse of Silence: The Postmodernism of Clarice Lispector," *Contemporary Literature* 28, no. 4 (winter 1987): 420–32.

33. Of her own work, Lispector has written, in "Humility and Technique," a *crônica* dated 4 October 1969: "This inability to perceive, to understand, makes me instinctively . . . do what? Makes me seek a way of expressing myself which might help me to understand more readily"—a way that she goes on to describe as a "quest" (*DW* 308–9).

34. Discussing *The Besieged City*, for example, Lispector writes, "The struggle to achieve reality . . . that way of seeing or point of view—can change reality even while creating. . . . Our way of looking at a man also creates that man. Our way of seeing determines our perception of reality" ("Reply Overdue," 21 February 1970, *DW* 354–55).

35. Christiane Makward, in conversation, Pennsylvania State University, fall 1991.

36. Peixoto, *Passionate Fictions*, 39–59.

37. In the chapter of *Speculum of the Other Woman* entitled "La Mystérique" (The Mystic/Hysterical Woman), Irigaray examines female mysticism, especially in the context of what she regards as the liberating ecstasy of the orgasmically mystical state, a psychosexual condition that pertains to a number of Lispector's texts, but most notably to *The Stream of Life*.

38. References to female breasts appear throughout Lispector's work, and while these are most often positive in nature, they are not always so. As Joana (of *Near to the Wild Heart*) the child learns about her aunt, for example, female breasts can be oppressive and smothering. Other common female body–based images for Lispector include placentas, wombs, ovaries and hips, and of course, perhaps the most common of all, birthing in general.

39. See *Writing and Difference*, *Of Grammatology*, and *Speech and Phenomena*.

CHAPTER 3

1. See *Literature and Psychoanalysis: The Question of Reading, Otherwise*, ed. S. Felman (Baltimore: Johns Hopkins University Press, 1982).

2. Vincent B. Leitch, *American Literary Criticism from the Thirties to the Eighties* (New York: Columbia University Press, 1988), 293.

3. Giovanni Pontiero, his afterword to *The Foreign Legion* (Manchester: Carcanet, 1986), 218.

4. For a more detailed discussion of this play and its relation to the remainder of Lispector's work, see Earl Fitz, "'A pecadora queimada e os anjos har-

moniosos': Clarice as Dramatist," *Luso-Brazilian Review* 34, no. 2 (winter 1977): 25–39.

5. Although they are open to other interpretations, certain scenes in *Near to the Wild Heart* do seem to imply that Joana engages in masturbation.

6. A number of my female students through the years have observed that the ebb and flow of *The Stream of Life*, the force of its style and structuring, seem to embody the act of masturbation.

7. See Nelson Vieira, "The Stations of the Body: Clarice Lispector's *Abertura* and Renewal," *Studies in Short Fiction* 25, no. 1 (winter 1988): 55–69; see also Earl Fitz, "A Writer in Transition: Clarice Lispector and *A via crucis do corpo*," *Latin American Literary Review* 16, no. 32 (July–December 1988): 41–52; and Celso Arnaldo Araújo, "Clarice Lispector: Uma escritora no escuro," *Manchete* 1202 (3 May 1975): 48–49.

8. Nancy Gray Diaz, "*A maçã no escuro*," in *Clarice Lispector: A Bio-Bibliography*, ed. Diane E. Marting (Westport, Conn.: Greenwood Press, 1993), 96.

9. For an excellent discussion of the presence language has in this novel, see Affonso Romano de Sant'Anna, "Clarice Lispector: Linguagem," a review of *The Apple in the Dark* in *Por um novo conceito de literatura brasileira* (Rio de Janeiro: Eldorado, 1977), 198–210; the author argues, in fact, that language is the novel's primary concern. See also Sant'Anna, "Clarice Lispector: A Linguagem, I–III," *ESPSL*, 2 June 1962, 2; 9 June 1962, 2; and 16 June 1962, 2.

10. Mara Negrón-Marrero, "Au-delà du savoir," from Savoir féminin, Deux exemples: George Sand, Folklore-Feminité/Clarice Lispector, au-delà du savoir" (Ph.D. diss., Université de Paris VIII [St. Denis], 1990), 221–507.

11. Mara Negrón, "A gênese de um pensar-sentir-mulher em *A maçã no escuro*," *Clarice e o Femenino*, special issue of *Tempo Brasileiro* 104 (January–March 1991): 73–81.

12. From *The Foreign Legion* (1964).

13. Christine Froula, "Rewriting Genesis: Gender and Culture of Twentieth-Century Texts," *Tulsa Studies in Women's Literature* 7, no. 2 (fall 1988): 197–220.

14. This seems true, even though after their structurally climactic sexual encounter we are told that Ulisses had lost his professional tone (169). The question is: Does he ever really lose it? Does he drop his logocentric perspective?

15. For a brief discussion of this aspect of the novel, see Maria Luisa Nunes, *Becoming True to Ourselves* (Westport, Conn.: Greenwood Press, 1987), 46–48.

16. Luciene Samor, "O anticonto por excelência," *MGSL*, 5 December 1981, 14; see also Pavla Liomilová, "*Felicidade Clandestina*," in *Clarice Lispector: A Bio-Bibliography*, ed. Diane E. Marting (Westport, Conn.: Greenwood Press, 1993), 33–34.

17. Although it appears here as a short story, this same text appears, with only minor alterations, as a chapter in *An Apprenticeship, or The Book of Delights*.

Although it was common for Lispector to incorporate images, lines, or whole sections of earlier works into later ones, this particular text, given the changes that were made, seems to have been of special significance for her, perhaps because of the strongly mythic quality that is evoked by the female presence. This same scene also echoes part of a chapter ("The Aunt") in *Near to the Wild Heart* while also underscoring the importance water imagery has generally in Lispector's work.

18. This interpretation rather closely parallels the argument made by Luce Irigaray in *An Ethics of Sexual Difference*, trans. Carolyn Burke and Gillian C. Gill (Ithaca: Cornell University Press, 1994).

19. See n. 27, XXX.

20. Rolmes Barbosa, "Mapa dos caminhos sem saída," *ESPSL*, 30 June 1974, 2. Noting the touches of surrealism and grotesque humor that Lispector employs in this collection, Barbosa also argues that, in seeking an original language, these texts "deconstruct" themselves in the process of showing the absurdity of life.

21. See Cristina Sáenz de Tejada, "The Eternal Non-Difference: Clarice Lispector's Concept of Androgyny," *Luso-Brazilian Review* 31, no. 1 (summer 1994): 39–56. For other useful articles on this important topic, see Maria Luisa Nunes, "Clarice Lispector: Artista andrógina ou escritora?" *Revista Iberoamericana* 50, no. 126 (January–March 1984): 281–89; Rita Terezinha Schmidt, "A modernidade e o feminino na pulsação do discurso," *Brasil/Brazil* 2 (1989): 59–67; and Ana Luiza Andrade, "In the Inter(t)sex(t) of Clarice Lispector and Nelson Rodrigues: From Drama to Language," in *Tropical Paths: Essays on Modern Brazilian Literature*, ed. Randall Johnson (New York: Garland, 1993), 133–152. For a study that provides a wider context in which to evaluate this issue, see Caroline Heilbrun, *Toward a Recognition of Androgyny* (New York: Knopf, 1973).

22. David Forgacs, "Marxist Literary Theories," in *Modern Literary Theory*, 2d ed., ed. Ann Jefferson and David Robey (Totowa, N.J.: Barnes and Noble, 1986), 198. The connection between Lispector and Kristeva rests on the issue of "poetic language" and on how language analysis can become a valid basis for larger social, political, and economic inquiries into the nature of a particular text or writer and (as in the case of Lispector) of their relationships to society.

CHAPTER 4

1. See Daphne Patai, "Clarice Lispector and the Clamor of the Ineffable," *Kentucky Romance Quarterly* 27 (1980): 133–49; and Carol Armbruster, "Hélène–Clarice: Nouvelle Voix," *Contemporary Literature* 24, no. 2 (1983): 145–57. For two more-positive approaches to the question of Lispector's "mysticism," see Marco Antonio Coutinho Jorge, "L'initiée sans secte" (trans. into French by Claire Varin), *Clarice Lispector, 1920–1977*, a special issue of *Parole Métèque*

(Montreal) 2 (autumn 1989): 11–13; and Richard A. Mazzara and Lorri A. Parris, "The Practical Mysticism of Clarice Lispector's *Uma aprendizagem ou o livro dos prazeres*," the afterword to the English translation (by Mazzara and Parris) of *Uma aprendizagem ou o livro dos prazeres* (Austin: University of Texas Press, 1986), 117–26.

2. See Diane E. Marting, "*Family Ties* and *Alguns contos*," in *Clarice Lispector: A Bio-Bibliography*, ed. Diane E. Marting (Westport, Conn.: Greenwood Press, 1994), 57–60.

3. Giovanni Pontiero, in his introduction to *Family Ties* (Austin: University of Texas Press, 1972), 19.

4. Lispector wrote often (especially in her *crônicas*) about being a mother and the "maternal" instinct. See, for example, "A Pleasant Interview" (30 December 1970), "Tiresome Children" (19 August 1967), "A Loving Mother" (12 October 1968), and "Mummy's Escapades" (15 December 1973). And, of course, many of Lispector's fictional characters (like Ana of "Love" and Catarina of *Family Ties*) are mothers as well, though the problem of the absent mother versus the present father is also omnipresent in Lispector's world.

5. The entire line, in Portuguese, is as follows: "No instante seguinte desviou os olhos com vergonha pelo despudor de sua mulher, que, desabrochada e serena, ali estava" ("Laços de família" 58).

6. In this novel the marriage (an issue that is brought up by the man involved, not the woman) would, ostensibly, be one in which both parties, if not entirely "identical," at least make the effort to simultaneously both support and liberate the other, a situation that reflects the curiously paradoxical force of love: one is simultaneously "liberated" and "imprisoned." In this sense, the problem of being in love is similar to the problem experienced in *Family Ties*. For a comment on the novel's treatment of this issue, see also Maria Luisa Nunes, *Becoming True to Ourselves* (Westport, Conn.: Greenwood Press, 1987), 46–48.

7. It is, for example, the clearest exposition we have in all Lispector's work of an attempt to build a satisfying love relationship, one based in large part on both sexual and psychological satisfaction. See Earl Fitz, *Clarice Lispector* (Boston: G. K. Hall, 1985), 81–84.

8. Maria Luisa Nunes, "Clarice Lispector: Artista Andrógina ou Escritora?" *Revista Iberoamericana* 50, no. 126 (January–March 1984): 218–89.

9. It is also interesting to note that, of these two professionally trained men, it is Otávio, the lawyer, who comes closer to understanding how profoundly our world is shaped and structured by language. For however much the law, the legal code, rests on the making of "clear" and "unambiguous" distinctions, definitions, and hierarchies, its practitioners know that it is inevitably in flux, involved always in the process of interpretation and change. As a character, Otávio's flaw is that he has been seduced by power, and while part of him understands this, the greater part of his conscious being leads him, eventually, to "reject" Joana (who has already rejected him) and seek the comfort, affection, and security he

believes is "rightfully" his—given his gender and class—in the willing arms of Lídia, a young woman who, pregnant with his child, embodies all the stereotypes of the "perfect woman" as determined by the phallogocentric society that Otávio both represents and upholds.

10. For other examples of Joana's sexuality and power, see pp. 134 and 140 of *Near to the Wild Heart.*

11. In Lispector's world, and as exemplified in the early novel *Near to the Wild Heart,* fathers (plus other male authority figures, like teachers)—and not mothers—tend to predominate. In a later work (*A via crucis do corpo,* 1974), however, the nature of motherhood and of the mother's social, political, economic, and sexual place in androcentric society are more intensely examined.

12. See Earl Fitz, "Clarice Lispector and the Lyrical Novel: A Re-examination of *A maçã no escuro,*" *Luso-Brazilian Review* 14, no. 2 (winter 1977): 153–60.

13. For a more detailed examination of humor in Lispector's writing, see Valerie C. Lastinger, "Humor in a New Reading of Clarice Lispector," *Hispania* 72, no. 1 (March 1989): 130–37.

14. In *The Stream of Life,* for example, we read, "Hallelujah, I shout, an hallelujah that fuses with the darkest human howl of the pain of separation but is a shout of diabolical happiness" (*SL* 3).

15. The fact that, in both the original Portuguese and in the English translation, the word "others" is written in italics suggests that Lispector intended that the reader think about not only the identity of the "others" but the implications their opinions possess as well. Overall, the "others" would seem to be a reference to the weight of orthodoxy and social convention, to the power of conformity, which is clearly being interrogated here.

16. In one of her *crônicas* for the *Jornal do Brasil,* Lispector actually responds, a bit acerbically, to certain things said (in an early book review of *The Besieged City*) concerning the character Lucrécia Neves; see "Reply Overdue," 21 February 1970.

17. A distinctly autobiographical note is sounded by Rodrigo when, for example, he declares (in a way that sounds very much like Lispector herself): "I am forced to seek a truth that transcends me. Why should I write about a young girl whose poverty is so evident? Perhaps because within her there is seclusion. Also because in her poverty of body and soul one touches sanctity and I long to feel the breath of life hereafter. In order to become greater than I am, for I am so little. I write because I have nothing better to do in this world: I am superfluous and last in the world of men. I write because I am desperate and weary. I can no longer bear the routine of my existence and, were it not for the constant novelty of writing, I should die symbolically each day" (*Hour* 20–21).

18. For additional commentary by Lispector on the issue of "meaning," see, from *Discovering the World:* "Without Human Significance," 28 June 1969; "Words Purely Physical," 12 December 1970; "About Writing," 20 December

1969; "Making Conversation: 1972," 8 January 1972; "The Stranger's Dialogue," 6 May 1972; and "Without Any Warning," 20 May 1972.

19. In "Writing," a Lispector *crônica* dated 18 November 1972, for example, she writes, "One does not *make* a sentence. A sentence is born."

20. For comments on reading and on her readers, see, from *Discovering the World:* "Another Letter," 24 February 1968; "The Columnist," 22 June 1968; "One Final Clarification," 14 November 1970; and "In Amicable Conversation with Tom Jobim (I)," 3 July 1971. In "Another Letter" Lispector writes, "[T]he reader is so closely involved with the writer that the two actually become one and the same person" (107).

21. In one of her most beguiling and sexually charged *crônicas*, Lispector, in response to an interviewer's query about whether her female characters were better defined than her male characters, said that she did not entirely agree, that (thinking, perhaps, of Martim, of *The Apple in the Dark*) she had created a male character who dominated an entire book and who could hardly have been more masculine. See "A Pleasant Interview," *DW,* 30 December 1967.

22. Published posthumously in 1977, *A Breath of Life* also purports to have a male author (the "autor"), though one whose authorial presence continues in much the same vein as that of the previous work.

23. See "The Unreality of Realism," *DW,* 20 January 1968.

24. See p. 18 of *The Hour of the Star* for Rodrigo's own recognition of this condition.

25. In a television interview (TV Cultura) on 1 February 1977 ("Panorama Especial," with Júlia Lerner), Lispector confessed, "When I am not writing, I am dead" (my translation). See Giovanni Pontiero's introduction to *Discovering the World*, trans. G. Pontiero (Manchester: Carcanet, 1992), 30. In this same interview, Lispector declares that she was not a "professional" writer (which is precisely what Rodrigo, of *The Hour of the Star*, says of himself on p. 17), that she was an "amateur" who wrote when she felt compelled to do so. A similar point is made, however, in an early *crônica*, "A Perfect Encounter" (18 November 1967), and in "An Intellectual, Certainly Not!" (2 November 1968).

26. This same thought, one with which Derrida and Barthes would certainly agree, is expressed almost verbatim in the 1 February 1977 TV Cultura interview (1977 being the same year *The Hour of the Star* appeared).

27. Interestingly, however, Lóri and Ulisses are portrayed to a great degree as androgynous characters, particularly in regard to their gendering, an implicit challenging of which emerges as the novel's hidden theme.

28. Rodrigo can be understood as a male version of G. H. as well as of Lispector herself, and perhaps even as her "male" alter ego.

29. For Barthes, "writing degree zero" is a "colourless writing, freed from all bondage to a pre-ordained state of language" (*Writing Degree Zero* [New York: Hill and Wang, 1967], 82).

30. This, too, is an issue (often in relation to the larger issue of gender) dealt with in a number of her *crônicas*. See, for example, from *Discovering the World*: "Hateful Charity," 6 December 1969; "Love, Raccoon, Dog, Feminine and Masculine," 9 October 1971; "Too Good to Be True," 15 April 1972; "The Sloth," 21 October 1972; "The Morning Sea," 7 April 1973; "The Lucidity of the Absurd," 28 April 1973; "An Adolescent: C. J.," 19 May 1973; and "Mummy's Escapades," 15 December 1973.

31. See the 1 February 1977 TV Cultura interview with Júlia Lerner (n. 25).

32. Though she may well have had very different feelings about the subject of God at other times, in a *crônica* dated 21 December 1968 ("My Christmas"), Lispector describes herself as "not religious" (*DW*, 212); the complete sentence, in both Portuguese and English, is as follows: "Mas houve um Natal em que minha amiga quebrou a combinação e, sabendo-me não religiosa, deu-me um missal" (*Dm* 234); [But one Christmas my friend had to cancel our arrangement and, though knowing I was not religious, she gave me a Holy Missal (*DW* 212)]. Perhaps the issue of Lispector's religiousness is best approached as a conflict between faith and orthodoxy or between freedom and constraint.

33. Overall, Lispector's utilization of God in her narratives reflects much of what Jack Miles writes about God in *God: A Biography* (New York: Knopf, 1995), a work that reads the Hebrew God as a literary character, a male with multiple—and conflicting—personalities who can envision Himself as a woman and whose development moves between speech and silence. Cixous discusses Lispector's work in the context, interestingly, of Heidegger's essays on poetry; see "L'approche de Clarice Lispector," *Poétique* 40 (October 1979): 408–19. See also Debra A. Castillo, *Talking Back: Toward a Latin American Feminist Literary Criticism* (Ithaca: Cornell University Press, 1992); Castillo links Lispector to both Heidegger and Derrida: "Jacques Derrida could as easily be writing about Lispector as Heidegger, in these comments from 'How to Avoid Speaking: Denials'" (196).

34. In the 1 February 1977 TV Cultura interview, Lispector says that she "didn't understand" this story.

35. Lispector comments on what animals mean to her in her interview with Elizabeth Lowe, "The Passion according to C. L.," *Review* 24 (June 1979): 34–37. See also Roy Rosenstein's summary of this issue in *Clarice Lispector: A Bio-Bibliography*, where he writes (of *Como nasceram as estrelas*), "[T]hese animal stories are not to be read as fables. The animal world is seen as fundamentally different from ours, though often contiguous or overlapping. Lispector refuses to anthropomorphize animals. Rather, she points to the mark of the beast in each of us: '. . . it is I who animalize myself,' she said in 'Animals' ("Bichos—I," *Jornal do Brasil* 13 March 1971 [*Descoberta do mundo* 520])" (162–63); *DW* 436–42; and "Eu me arranjaria" ("Making Adjustments"), 5 February 1972 (*DW* 533).

36. For Lispector's discussion of this relationship, see "Reply Overdue," *DW*, 21 February 1970.

37. For further discussions of this story, see Clarice Lispector, "Clarice Lispector, a explicação que não explica," *Jornal do Brasil*, 11 October 1969, 2 (reprinted in *A descoberta do mundo*, 363–66); Judith Rosenberg, "Taking Her Measurements: Clarice Lispector and 'The Smallest Woman in the World,'" *Critique: Studies in Modern Fiction* 30, no. 2 (winter 1989): 71–76; and A. M. Wheeler, "Animal Imagery as Reflection of Gender Roles in Clarice Lispector's *Family Ties*," *Critique: Studies in Modern Fiction* 28, no. 3 (spring 1987): 125–34.

CHAPTER 5

1. Daphne Patai, "Clarice Lispector and the Clamor of the Ineffable," *Kentucky Romance Quarterly* 27 (1980): 130–49.

2. Carol Armbruster, "Hélène–Clarice: Nouvelle Voix," *Contemporary Literature* 24, no. 2 (1983): 145–57.

3. An example of this tendency to "desacralize" things would be Lispector's frequently challenging, or contentious, references to God; another would be her use of semantically ambiguous, and even contradictory, religious imagery.

4. For a discussion of this story's other political dimensions, see Roy Rosenstein, "Lispector's Children's Literature," in *Clarice Lispector: A Bio-Bibliography*, ed. Diane E. Marting (Westport, Conn.: Greenwood Press, 1994), 159–63. For *crônicas* that deal with this story, see "Hermetic?" (24 February 1968, *DW* 107) and "A Live Experience" (15 August 1970, *DW* 398–99).

5. As Hubert Juin suggests, Lispector's approach to writing is uniquely present in this story as an urgent and essential expression of existence; see "Clarice Lispector et la vie nue," a review of *Où Étais-tu pendant la nuit? Monde*, 10 January 1986).

6. That is, the semantic difference cannot be heard; it must be read, as a function of written language.

7. Sexual repression may, indeed, constitute one of the great and as yet unexamined themes of Lispector's work.

8. Nelson Vieira, "The Stations of the Body: Clarice Lispector's *Abertura* and Renewal," *Studies in Short Fiction* 25, no. 1 (winter 1988): 55–69.

9. For an excellent, if concise, discussion of this story, see Marta Peixoto, *Passionate Fictions* (Minneapolis: University of Minnesota Press, 1994), 87–89.

10. Lispector, who described herself as being politically conscious and even "engaged," writes, in this 1967 *crônica*, "Frankly, I see myself as being committed. Everything I write relates, at least deep down inside me, to the reality around us. Perhaps this aspect of my writing will become more forceful one day" (*DW*, 30 December 1967, 84). Lispector, clearly, was very much aware of Brazil's urgent sociopolitical problems. Hunger, for one, was an issue she often wrote about, especially in her *crônicas*; see, for example, from *Discovering the World*: "Twenty-Five Years Hence," 16 September 1967; "Excess and Privation," 14 September 1968; "Divine Wisdom," 13 December 1969; and "Ques-

tions and Answers for a School Notebook," 29 August 1970; see also Pontiero's comment on this issue (*DW* 29).

11. Read in this context, Lispector's political potentialities (and limitations) also parallel those inherent in Julia Kristeva's concept of the "semiotic," a "pattern or play of forces which we can detect inside language and which represents a sort of residue of the pre-Oedipal phase," a "kind of pulsational pressure within language itself, in tone, rhythm, the bodily and material qualities of language, but also in contradiction, meaninglessness, disruption, silence and absence" (Terry Eagleton, *Literary Theory: An Introduction* [Minneapolis: University of Minnesota Press, 1983], 188). All these qualities are inherent in Clarice's texts, but they are especially prominent in *The Passion according to G. H.*, *The Stream of Life*, and *A Breath of Life: Pulsations*.

12. Lispector did not care to have this label applied to her work, even though it is clear that the condition of women was a constant feature of her work. For a discussion of this issue, and its crucial relationship both to artistic creativity in general and to the specific issue of androgyny, see Maria Luisa Nunes, "Clarice Lispector: Artista andrógina ou escritora?" *Revista Iberoamericana* 50, no. 126 (January–March 1984): 281–89. See also the *crônica* "One Woman Too Many" (8 June 1968, *DW* 146). See also Elizabeth Lowe's interview with Clarice Lispector, "The Passion according to C. L.," *Review* 24 (June 1979): 34–37.

13. Maria José Somerlate Barbosa, "*A Hora da Estrela* and *Um Sopro de Vida*: Parodies of Narrative Power," *Chasqui* 20, no. 2 (November 1991): 116–21.

14. Ângela Pralini of *A Breath of Life* is possibly the same character who appears in the story "The Departure of the Train," from *Where You Were At Night*.

15. Earl Fitz, "Caracterizção o e a visão fenomenológica nos romances de Clarice Lispector e Djuna Barnes," *Travessia* (Florianópolis) 14 (1st semester 1987): 135–47.

16. See, for example, Vilma Areas, "Que mistérios tem Clarice?" Illustrada, *Folha de São Paulo*, 29 November 1977, 33.

17. See Lowe, "The Passion according to C. L."

18. Mara Gálvez-Breton, "Post-Feminist Discourse in Clarice Lispector's *The Hour of the Star*," in *Splintering Darkness: Latin American Women Writers in Search of Themselves*, ed. Lucía Guerra Cunningham (Pittsburgh: Latin American Literary Review Press, 1990), 63. For a further discussion of Lispector's politicized "feminine discourse," see Rita Terezinha Schmidt, "A modernidade e o femenino na pulsão do discurso," *Brasil/Brazil* 2 (1989): 59–67.

19. Based openly on a theory of sexuality that calls for the giving and receiving of pleasure and on a sharing of power, the text, which relies on dialogue far more than any of Lispector's other works, also suggests that (as symbolized in Lóri and Ulisses) while very real social and political inequalities do exist, they can—and should—be overcome. The doing of this, however, begins, as always in Lispector's world, with one character coming to grips with her or his own sense of being and then, having resolved that issue (of self-identity), attempting

to make contact or communication with another human being, yet seeking to do so without either possessing the other person or being possessed, both issues reflecting the ontological dilemma of "love," which is one of Lispector's most decisive thematic motifs. See, for example, *Near to the Wild Heart* (1944). The key line of *An Apprenticeship* is as follows: "You seduced me. She smiled again" (113).

20. Elizabeth Lowe, "Liberating the Rose: Clarice Lispector's *Água viva* [*The Stream of Life*] as a Political Statement," in *Splintering Darkness*, ed. Cunningham, 82.

21. Earl Fitz, "A Discourse of Silence: The Postmodernism of Clarice Lispector," *Contemporary Literature* 28, no. 4 (winter 1987): 420–36. Although "silence," as a term and a motif, occurs throughout Lispector's fiction, it is also an issue that she discussed in many of her *crônicas*, particularly with respect to what it meant to her as a writer; see, for example, the following *crônicas*, from *Discovering the World:* "Fear of the Unknown," 7 October 1967; "Pep Pills," 9 December 1967; "Anonymity," 10 February 1968; "Persona," 2 March 1968; "The Death of a Whale," 17 August 1968; "True and False Solitude," 14 June 1969; "Words from the Typewriter," 29 May 1971; and "Love," 11 September 1971.

22. The issue addressed here, the problem of knowing, is also taken up in the *crônica* "Not to Understand" (1 February 1969), in which Lispector writes that she feels herself "more complete" when she does "not understand" (*DW* 227). She goes on to say that although the phrase "I do not understand" is so overwhelming that it transcends any "understanding," "The desirable thing is to be intelligent and not to understand," for to attain this state of being "is a strange blessing, like experiencing madness without being insane" (227). Sounding like G. H., Lispector then wryly concludes this epistemological meditation by writing, "I should like to understand a little. Not too much: but at least to understand that I do not understand" (227).

23. In the *crônica* "Without Human Significance" Lispector wrote about her own need to impose meaning on the world: "How must things and people have been before we imposed some meaning with our human hope and vision? It must have been dreadful. . . . How frightened I become unless I can impose some human meaning on the world" (*DW* 269, 28 June 1969).

CHAPTER 6

1. The self-conscious narrator of one of Lispector's most famous and respected novels, *The Passion according to G. H.*, in fact opens her narrative by declaring, "I'm trying to understand" (my translation).

2. Important studies that deal with or touch on Lacanian psychoanalysis in regard to Lispector's work include Gina Michelle Collins, "Translating Feminine Discourse: Mediating the Immediate," *Translation Review* 17 (1985): 21–24; Rita Terezinha Schmidt, "Clarice Lispector: The Poetics of Transgression,"

Luso-Brazilian Review 26, no. 2 (winter 1989): 103–15; Miriam Chnaiderman, "Passeando entre a literatura e a psicanálise," *MGSL*, 19 December 1987, 5; María Clark, "Facing the Other in Clarice Lispector's Short Story 'Amor,'" *Letras femininas* 16, no. 1–2 (spring–fall 1990): 13–20; and Nehy de Aguiar Peixoto, "A linguagem articulada pelo paradoxo," in *Discurso literário: Seu espaço, teoria e prática de leitura*, ed. Diva Vasconcelos da Rocha (Rio de Janeiro: Francisco Alves, 1975), 93–101.

3. Emile Benveniste, *Problems in General Linguistics* (Coral Gables: University of Miami Press, 1971). Benveniste's theory is important to poststructural thought because it permits one to discuss, thinking of Lispector's *escritura*, the "personal" or "subjective" elements of a particular language utterance (whether spoken or written) without having to refer to correlatives outside the language system itself. For Benveniste, these "personal" aspects of language use relate to the inherent reflexivity, or self-referentiality, of language itself, rather than to any "real" referents outside of language, a distinction Barthes employs to discuss narration as a self-contained system operating with its own internally generated rules.

4. Giovanni Pontiero, one of Lispector's most important translators, was researching a biography of the Brazilian author at the time of his death.

5. Indeed, so all-consuming was Lispector's preoccupation with the dynamic between language and being that virtually everything she wrote was informed by this characteristic, including her ostensibly nonfiction and often autobiographical *crônicas*, published collectively in *Discovering the World* (1984).

6. I learned this in conversation with the story's translator, Alexis Levitan, who explained that the editors were concerned that the story made it appear that the protagonist actually wanted to be raped.

7. For a discussion of this issue in a larger Lispectorian context, see Marta Peixoto, "Rape and Textual Violence in Clarice Lispector," in *Rape and Representation*, ed. Lynn A. Higgins and Brenda R. Silver (New York: Columbia University Press, 1991), 182–203.

8. For studies taking a Freudian approach to Lispector's work, see Avanilda Torres, "O onirismo em Clarice Lispector," *Momentos de crítica literária: Actas dos congresos brasileiros de teoria e crítica literária e seminário internacional de literatura* (Campina Grande) 7 (September 1990): 71–75; Ana Maria de Almeida, "O it/id da escritura," *MGSL*, 1 June 1985, 6–8; and especially, Richard A. Mazzara and Lorri A. Parris, "Clarice Lispector's Psychological Approach toward a Philosophy of Existence in *A maçã no escuro*," *Journal of Evolutionary Psychology* 5, no. 3–4 (August 1984): 263–68.

9. The act of changing one's identity, or being, by the washing of one's face is a motif that Lispector used more than once in her work. See, for example, "The Remnants of Carnival," from *Clandestine Happiness*, and "He Soaked Me Up," from *The Stations of the Body*.

10. Mazzara and Parris, "Clarice Lispector's Psychological Approach," 263–68.

11. Interestingly, this novel is said to be the one that Lispector "liked least"; see Diane E. Marting, ed., *Clarice Lispector: A Bio-Bibliography*, xxix.

12. Nelson Vieira, "A Via Crucis do Corpo," in *Clarice Lispector: A Bio-Bibliography*, 150.

13. For further discussions of this collection of narratives, see Nelson Vieira, "The Stations of the Body: Clarice Lispector's *Abertura* and Renewal," *Studies in Short Fiction* 25, no. 1 (winter 1988): 55–69; Earl Fitz, "A Writer in Transition: Clarice Lispector and *A Via Crucis do Corpo*," *Latin American Literary Review* 16, no. 32 (July–December 1988): 41–52; and Ana Luiza Andrade, "Do Edipo à esfinge: No inter(t)sex(t)o de Clarice Lispector e Nelson Rodrigues," in *A mulher na literatura, no segundo encontro da ANPOLL (Rio de Janeiro)*, 3 vols. (Belo Horizonte: Imprensa da Universidade Federal de Minas Gerais, 1990), vol. 3 ed. Nádia Battella Gotlib, 3:185–93.

14. See Vieira, "Stations of the Body," 55–69; and Miryan Natalia Urbaitel-Solares, "O código do corpo em *A via crucis do corpo*" (master's thesis, University of Texas at Austin, 1986).

15. For a different, perhaps less reserved or repressed author, this scene might well have resulted in an artfully detailed, if not necessarily graphic, representation of an erotic encounter. One thinks, in this regard, of Anaïs Nin's contention that the truly erotic can only be achieved by means of poetic language.

16. Implicitly and explicitly, the theme of love permeates Lispector's writing, including many of the "nonfiction" newspaper columns collected in *Discovering the World*; see, for example: "A Pleasant Interview," 30 December 1967; "Pointless Scandal," 27 April 1968; and "Love," 11 September 1971, which also deals with the themes of words, writing, and silence.

17. Of Carmen, for example, the text says, "poor nothing that she was" (TB 18). Vieira's essay, "The Stations of the Body: Clarice Lispector's *Abertura* and Renewal," offers an especially cogent discussion of Lispector's class consciousness and repression as represented in this unusual collection of texts.

18. Ironically, his capacity for violence is itself undercut by the violence done to him by the two women, who, as we know, stab him to death.

19. Peixoto, "Rape and Textual Violence," 182–203.

20. In the "Explanation" that opens the *Stations of the Body* section of *Soulstorm* ("Onde estivestes de noite" ["Where You Were at Night"] appears in the book called *Estivestes de noite*, also published in 1974, and also appears in English in *Soulstorm*), Lispector feigns, or truly feels, "shame" and "amazement" at the violence and sexuality of her stories. As she enigmatically puts it, "All the stories in this book are bruising stories. And the one who suffered most was me myself. I was shocked by reality. If there are indecencies in these stories, the fault is not mine" (*Soulstorm* 3).

21. *Écrits* 256–59 et al. Analogous to Freud's topographic model, Lacan's Subject is split between the conscious mind and the unconscious mind, the latter

dominating the former and understood as a matrix of powerful drives and urges and lending itself to the concept—crucial for an application of Lacanian psychoanalysis to the writing of Clarice Lispector—of "otherness," that which, though ardently desired or yearned for, remains forever unattainable, missing, or absent thereby producing anxiety as well as increased desire.

22. The fulfillment of desire and the at least potential attainment of satisfaction are two key features of *An Apprenticeship, or The Book of Delights* (1969) that make it one of Lispector's most singular works.

23. For Lacan, the signifier of desire is metonymy, for what is "desired" is eternally being displaced or deferred, endlessly appearing and reappearing in another form and relationship (*Écrits*, 156, 164, et al.). Metaphor, by way of contrast, involves, for Lacan, not displacement but substitution (*Écrits*, 53, 156–57, 199–200, 303–4). For the linguist Roman Jakobson, whose work, along with that of Saussure, greatly influenced Lacan, metonymy is thus "syntactic" while metaphor is "semantic" in nature.

24. Of the importance of animals in her work, Lispector has said, "Animals are a force of nature. They are our brothers. They confront our own animality in the urbanized world we live in" ("The Passion According to C. L." [Elizabeth Lowe interviews Clarice Lispector], *Review* 24 [June 1979]: 34–36).

25. Gregory Rabassa, from his introduction to his English translation (*The Apple in the Dark*) of *A maçã no escuro* (New York: Knopf, 1967), xii.

26. Lispector's mother was an invalid and, as such, could be said to have been "absent" during her formative and adolescent years. This might well have intensified Lispector's relationship with her father, perhaps even along Oedipal/Electra lines and perhaps even gaining expression in the conflicted relationship of child (Joana), father, and mother outlined in Chapters 1 and 3 of the novel. Entering into the stream of consciousness of Joana the child (that is, as Joana enters into the realm of language), the reader learns, for example, that "she was frightened of Elza [the mother]. But one cannot be frightened of one's own mother. A mother was like a father" (*Heart* 26).

27. Julia Kristeva, "From One Identity to Another," in *Critical Theory since Plato*, rev. ed., ed. Hazard Adams (New York: Harcourt Brace Jovanovich, 1992), 1162–73. See also Earl Fitz, "Caracterização e a visão fenomenológica nos romances de Clarice Lispector e Djuna Barnes," *Travessia* 14 (1st semester 1987): 135–47.

28. See Julia Kristeva, *Desire in Language: A Semiotic Approach to Literature and Art* (New York: Columbia University Press, 1980).

BIBLIOGRAPHY

Almeida, Sandra. "The Imitation of the Rose": Lispector's Portrayal of an 'Unburdened and Serene' Woman.'" *Aleph* 7 (1995): 4–11.

Andrade, Ana Luiza. "A escritura feita iniciação feminina: Clarice Lispector e Virginia Woolf." *Língua e Literatura* 15 (1986): 9–21.

———. "In the Inter(t)sex(t) of Clarice Lispector and Nelson Rodrigues: From Drama to Language." In *Tropical Paths: Essays on Modern Brazilian Literature*, edited by Randal Johnson, 133–52. New York: Garland, 1993.

———. "*O livro dos prazeres*: A escritura e o travesti." *Colóquio/Letras* 101 (January–February 1988): 47–54.

Aneja, Anu. "The Mystic Aspect of L'Ecriture Féminine: Hélène Cixous' Vivre l'Orange." *Qui Parle* 3, no. 1 (spring 1989): 189–201.

Armbruster, Carol. "Hélène–Clarice: Nouvelle voix." *Contemporary Literature* 24, no. 2 (1983): 145–57.

Atkins, G. Douglas, and Michael Johnson, eds. *Writing and Reading Differently: Deconstruction and the Teaching of Composition and Literature*. Introduction by G. Douglas Atkins and Michael Johnson. Lawrence: University Press of Kansas, 1985.

Banfield, Ann. "Écriture, Narration, and the Grammar of French," In *Narrative: From Malory to Motion Pictures*, edited by Jeremy Hawthorn. London: Arnold, 1985.

Barbosa, Maria José Somerlate. "Brás's Delirium and G. H.'s Reverie: The Quest for the Origin of Time." *Luso-Brazilian Review* 29, no. 1 (summer 1992): 19–27.

———. *Clarice Lispector: Spinning the Webs of Passion*. New Orleans: University Press of the South, 1997.

———. "*A hora da estrela* and *Um sopro de vida*: Parodies of Narrative Power." *Chasqui* 20, no. 2 (November 1991): 116–21.

Barthes, Roland. *A Barthes Reader*. Edited by Susan Sontag. New York: Hill and Wang, 1982.

———. "From Work to Text." In *Textual Strategies: Perspectives in Post-Structuralist Criticism*, edited and with an introduction by Josué V. Harari, 73–81. Ithaca: Cornell University Press, 1979.

———. *The Pleasure of the Text*. Translated by Richard Miller. New York: Hill and Wang, 1975.

———. *S/Z*. Translated by Richard Miller. London: Cape, 1970.

———. *Writing Degree Zero*. Translated by Annette Lavers and Colin Smith. New York: Hill and Wang, 1967.

Barzilai, Shuli. "Borders of Language: Kristeva's Critique of Lacan." *PMLA* 106, no. 2 (March 1991): 294–305.

Bell, Shannon. *Reading, Writing, and Rewriting the Prostitute Body*. Bloomington: Indiana University Press, 1994.

Belsey, Catherine. *Critical Practice*. London and New York: Methuen, 1980.

Bergman, Emilie L., and Paul Julian Smith, eds. *Entiendes? Queer Readings, Hispanic Writings*. Durham: Duke University Press, 1995.

Bittencourt, Ivaldo. "As matrizes textuais em *Perto do coração selvagem*" and "Determinação das matrizes." In *Neo-análise da produção literária em Clarice Lispector*, 77–86. Recife: Editôra Universitária de Pernambuco, 1987.

Borelli, Olga. *Clarice Lispector: Esboço para um possível retrato*. Rio de Janeiro: Nova Fronteira, 1981.

Brower, Keith H. "The Narratee in Clarice Lispector's *Água viva*." *Romance Notes* 32, no. 2 (winter 1991): 111–18.

Butler, Judith. *Gender Trouble: Feminism and the Subversion of Identity*. London: Routledge, 1990.

Callinicos, Alex. *Against Postmodernism*. London: Polity Press, 1989.

Castillo, Debra A. "Negation: Clarice Lispector." In *Talking Back: Toward a Latin American Feminist Literary Criticism*, 185–215. Ithaca: Cornell University Press, 1992.

Castro-Klarén, Sara. Introduction to *Women's Writing in Latin America*, edited by Sara Castro-Klarén, Sylvia Molloy, and Beatriz Sarlo, 3–26. Boulder, Colo.: Westview Press, 1991.

Cixous, Hélène. "L'approche de Clarice Lispector." *Poétique* 40 (November 1979): 408–19.

———. "From the Scene of the Unconscious to the Scene of History." In *The Future of Literary Theory*, edited by Ralph Cohen. New York: Routledge, 1990.

———. *L'heure de Clarice Lispector*. Paris: Des Femmes, 1989.

———. "The Laugh of the Medusa." Translated by Keith Cohen and Paula Cohen. *Signs: Journal of Women in Culture and Society* 1, no. 4 (summer 1976): 875–93.

———. "Reaching the Point of Wheat, or A Portrait of the Artist as a Maturing Woman." *New Literary History* 19, no. 1 (autumn 1987): 1–21.

———. *Readings: The Poetics of Blanchot, Joyce, Kafka, Kleist, Lispector, and Tsvetayeva*. Edited, translated, and with an introduction by Verena Andermatt Conley. Minneapolis: University of Minnesota Press, 1991.

———. *Reading with Clarice Lispector*. Edited, translated, and with an introduction by Verena Andermatt Conley. Minneapolis: University of Minnesota Press, 1990.

———. *Three Steps on the Ladder of Writing*. Translated by Sarah Cornell and Susan Sellers. New York: Columbia University Press, 1993.

———, and Catherine Clément. *The Newly Born Woman*. Translated by Betsy Wing, with a foreword by Sandra M. Gilbert. Minneapolis: University of Minnesota Press, 1986.

Collins, Gina Michelle. "Translating a Feminine Discourse: Clarice Lispector's *Água viva*." In *Translation Perspectives: Selected Papers, 1982–1983*, 119–24. Binghamton: State University of New York–Binghamton Translation Research and Instruction Program, 1984.

Crowley, Sharon. "Writing and Writing." In *Writing and Reading Differently*, edited by G. Douglas Atkins and Michael L. Johnson, 93–100. Lawrence: University Press of Kansas, 1985.

Culler, Jonathan. *Framing the Sign: Criticism and Its Institutions*. Norman: University of Oklahoma Press, 1988.

———. *On Deconstruction: Theory and Criticism after Structuralism*. Ithaca: Cornell University Press, 1982.

———. *The Pursuit of Signs: Semiotics, Literature, Deconstruction*. Ithaca: Cornell University Press, 1981.

———. *Structuralist Poetics*. Ithaca: Cornell University Press, 1975.

Cunningham, Lucía Guerra, ed. *Splintering Darkness: Latin American Women Writers in Search of Themselves*. Pittsburgh: Latin American Literary Review Press (Yvette E. Miller, general ed.), 1990.

Davis, Robert Con, and Ronald Schleifer, eds. *Criticism and Culture: The Role of Critique in Modern Literary Theory*. Essex, England: Longman, 1991.

Derrida, Jacques. *Acts of Literature*. Edited by Derek Attridge. New York: Routledge, 1992.

———. *Dissemination*. Translated by Barbara Johnson. Chicago: University of Chicago Press, 1981.

———. *Glas*. Translated by John P. Leavey Jr. and Richard Rand. Lincoln: University of Nebraska Press, 1986.

———. *Margins of Philosophy*. Translated by Alan Bass. Chicago: University of Chicago Press, 1982.

———. *Of Grammatology*. Translated by Gayatri Spivak. Baltimore: Johns Hopkins University Press, 1976.

———. *Positions*. Translated by Alan Bass. Chicago: University of Chicago Press, 1981.

———. "Signature Event Context." *Glyph* 1 (1977): 172–97.

———. "Structure, Sign, and Play in the Discourse of the Human Sciences." In *Modern Criticism and Theory*, edited by David Lodge, 108–23. London: Longman, 1988.

————. *Writing and Difference*. Translated by Alan Bass. Chicago: University of Chicago Press, 1978.

Douglass, Ellen H. "Female Quest toward 'Água Pura' in Clarice Lispector's *Perto do coração selvagem*." *Brasil/Brazil* 3 (1990): 45–61.

————. "Myth and Gender in Clarice Lispector: Quest as a Feminist Statement in 'A imitação da rosa.'" *Luso-Brazilian Review* 25, no. 2 (winter 1988): 15–31.

Eagleton, Terry. "Post-Structuralism." In *Literary Theory: An Introduction*, 127–50. Minneapolis: University of Minnesota Press, 1983.

Felman, Shoshana, ed. *Literature and Psychoanalysis: The Question of Reading, Otherwise*. Baltimore: Johns Hopkins University Press, 1982.

————. "Turning the Screw of Interpretation." *Yale French Studies* 55–56 (1977): 94–207.

Felski, Rita. *Beyond Feminist Aesthetics: Feminist Literature and Social Change*. Cambridge: Harvard University Press, 1989.

Fish, Stanley. *Is There a Text in This Class?* Cambridge: Harvard University Press, 1980.

Fisher, Claudine. "Hélène Cixous's Window of Daring through Clarice Lispector's Voice." In *Continental, Latin American, and Francophone Women Writers*, edited by Eunice Myers and Ginette Adamson. Lanham, Md.: University Press of America, 1987.

Fitz, Earl E. "Clarice Lispector." *Dictionary of Literary Biography*. Modern Latin-American Fiction Writers, 1st ser., edited by William Luis, 113 : 197–204. Detroit: Bruccoli Clark Layman Books, Gale Research, Inc., 1992.

————. "Clarice Lispector and the Lyrical Novel: A Re-examination of *A maçã no escuro*." *Luso-Brazilian Review* 14, no. 2 (winter 1977): 153–60.

————. "A Discourse of Silence: The Postmodernism of Clarice Lispector." *Contemporary Literature* 28, no. 4 (winter 1987): 420–36.

————. "The Leitmotif of Darkness in Seven Novels by Clarice Lispector." *Chasqui* 7, no. 2 (February 1978): 18–27.

————. "The Passion of Logo(centrism), or The Deconstructionist Universe of Clarice Lispector." *Luso-Brazilian Review* 25, no. 2 (winter 1988): 33–44.

Forgacs, David. "Marxist Literary Criticism." In *Modern Literary Theory: A Comparative Introduction*, 2d ed., edited by Ann Jefferson and David Robey, 166–203. Totowa, N.J.: Barnes and Noble, 1986.

Foster, David William. *Cultural Diversity in Latin American Literature*. Albuquerque: University of New Mexico Press, 1994.

Freedman, Ralph. *The Lyrical Novel*. Princeton: Princeton University Press, 1963.

Frizzi, Adria. "The Thread of Return: Notes on the Genesis of Literary Discourse in Clarice Lispector's *A paixão segundo G. H.*" *Luso-Brazilian Review* 26, no. 2 (winter 1989): 24–32.

Froula, Christine. "Rewriting Genesis: Gender and Culture in Twentieth-

Century Texts." *Tulsa Studies in Women's Literature* 7, no. 2 (fall 1988): 197–220.

Fukelman, Clarissa. "A palavra em exílo: Uma leitura de Clarice Lispector." In *A mulher na literatura, o terceiro encontro nacional da ANPOLL*, Rio de Janeiro, May 1988. 3 vols. Vol. 2, edited by Nádia Gotlib, 161–80. Belo Horizonte: Universidade Federal de Minas Gerais, 1990.

Gadamer, Hans-Georg. "The Expressive Power of Language: On the Function of Rhetoric for Knowledge." Translated by Richard Heinemann and Bruce Krajewski. *PMLA* 107, no. 2 (March 1992): 345–52.

Gálvez-Breton, Mara. "Post-Feminist Discourse in Clarice Lispector's *A hora da estrela*." In *Splintering Darkness: Latin American Women Writers in Search of Themselves*, edited and with an introduction by Lucía Guerra Cunningham, 63–78. Pittsburgh: Latin American Literary Review Press (Yvette E. Miller, general ed.), 1990.

Gasché, Rodolphe. "Deconstruction as Criticism." *Glyph* 6 (1979): 177–215.

Gilio, María Ester. "Tristes trópicos" (interview with Clarice Lispector). *Crisis* 4, no. 39 (1976): 43–45.

Goodheart, Eugene. *The Skeptic Disposition in Contemporary Criticism*. Princeton: Princeton University Press, 1984.

Gotlib, Nádia Battella. "Un apprentissage des *sens*." Translated to French by Consuelo Forte Santiago, revised by Nicolas Tabiteau. In *Clarice Lispector: Le souffle du sens*, a special issue of *Études Françaises* 25, no. 1 (2d trimester 1989): 69–80.

Grant, Linda. *Sexing the Millennium: Women and the Sexual Revolution*. New York: Grove, 1994.

Habermas, Jürgen. *The Philosophical Discourse of Modernity*. Translated by Frederick G. Lawrence. Cambridge: MIT Press, 1990.

Harari, Josué V., ed. *Textual Strategies: Perspectives in Post-Structuralist Criticism*. London: Methuen, 1980.

Harland, Richard. *Superstructuralism: The Philosophy of Structuralism and Post-Structuralism*. London: Methuen, 1987.

Harvey, Irene. "The Différance between Derrida and de Man." In *The Textual Sublime: Deconstruction and Its Differences*, edited by Hugh Silverman and Gary Aylesworth, 73–86. Albany: State University of New York Press, 1990.

Hécker, Paulo Filho. "Uma mística em tempo de Deus morto." *Estado de São Paulo, Suplemento Literário*, 4 October 1969, 6.

Heilbrun, Carolyn G. *Toward a Recognition of Androgyny*. New York: Knopf, 1973.

Herrero, Alejandro. "The Filming of a Novel: An Analysis of Lispector's *The Hour of the Star* and Amaral's Adaptation." *Aleph* 5 (1990): 4–11.

Hertz, Neil. "Recognizing Causabon." In *The End of the Line: Essays on Psychoanalysis and the Sublime*. New York: Columbia University Press, 1985.

Higgins, Lynn A., and Brenda R. Silver, eds. *Rape and Representation*. New York: Columbia University Press, 1991.

Hill, Amariles G. "A experiência de existir narrando." In *Seleta de Clarice Lispector*, edited by Renato C. Gomes and Amariles G. Hill. Rio de Janeiro: José Olympio Editôra, 1976.

Holman, C. Hugh, and William Harmon, eds. *A Handbook to Literature*, 6th ed. New York: Macmillan, 1992.

Holub, Robert C. *Crossing Borders: Reception Theory, Poststructuralism, Deconstruction*. Madison: University of Wisconsin Press, 1992.

Irigaray, Luce. *Ce sexe qui n'en est pas un*. Paris: Éditions de Minuit, 1977.

Jackson, K. David. "Onde estivestes de noite." In *Clarice Lispector: A Bio-Bibliography*, edited by Diane E. Marting, 105–8. Westport, Conn.: Greenwood Press, 1993.

Jameson, Fredric. *The Political Unconscious: Narrative as a Social Symbolic Act*. Ithaca: Cornell University Press, 1981.

———. *The Prison-House of Language: A Critical Account of Structuralism and Russian Formalism*. Princeton: Princeton University Press, 1972.

Jefferson, Ann. "Structuralism and Post-Structuralism." In *Modern Literary Theory: A Comparative Introduction*, 2d ed., edited by Ann Jefferson and David Robey, 92–121. Totowa, N.J.: Barnes and Noble, 1986.

Johnson, Barbara. "Writing." In *Critical Terms for Literary Study*, edited by Frank Lentricchia and Thomas McLaughlin, 39–49. Chicago: University of Chicago Press, 1990.

Jozef, Bella. "Chronology: Clarice Lispector." Translated by Elizabeth Lowe. *Review* 24 (1979): 24–27.

Kauffman, Linda, ed. *Gender and Theory*. Oxford, England: Basil Blackwell, 1989.

Keesey, Donald. "Poststructural Criticism: Language as Context." In *Contexts for Criticism*, 2d ed., 335–46. Mountain View, Calif.: Mayfield Publishing Company, 1994.

Klobucka, Anna. "Hélène Cixous and the Hour of Clarice Lispector." In *SubStance: A Review of Theory and Literary Criticism* 73 (1994): 41–62.

———. "A intercomunicação homem/animal como meio de transformação do Eu em 'Axolotl' de Julio Cortázar e 'O Búfalo' de Clarice Lispector." *Travessia* 14 (1987): 161–76.

Krabbenhoft, Kenneth. "From Mysticism to Sacrament in *A paixão segundo G. H.*" *Luso-Brazilian Review* 32, no. 1 (summer 1995): 51–60.

Krieger, Murray. *Words about Words about Words: Theory, Criticism, and the Literary Text*. Baltimore: Johns Hopkins University Press, 1988.

Kristeva, Julia. *Desire in Language: A Semiotic Approach to Literature and Art*. Translated by Thomas Gora, Alice Jardine, and Leon Roudiez. New York: Columbia University Press, 1980.

———. "From One Identity to Another." In *Critical Theory since Plato*, rev. ed., edited by Hazard Adams, 1161–73. New York: Harcourt Brace Jovanovich, 1992.

————. *Revolution in Poetic Language.* Translated by Margaret Waller. New York: Columbia University Press, 1974.

————. "Semiotics: A Critical Science and/or a Critique of Science." Translated by Sean Hand. In *The Kristeva Reader*, edited by Toril Moi, 74–88. New York: Columbia University Press, 1986.

Lacan, Jacques. *Écrits: A Selection.* Translated by Alan Sheridan. New York: Norton, 1977.

————. *Feminine Sexuality.* Edited by Juliet Mitchell and Jacqueline Rose and translated by Jacqueline Rose. New York: Norton, 1983.

————. *The Four Fundamental Concepts of Psycho-Analysis.* Translated by Alan Sheridan. New York: Norton, 1978.

————. *The Language of the Self.* Translated, with notes and commentary, by Anthony Wilden. Baltimore: Johns Hopkins University Press, 1968.

Laplanche, J., and J. B. Pontalis. *The Language of Psychoanalysis.* Translated by Donald Nicholson-Smith. New York: Norton, 1973.

Lapouge, Maryvonne, and Clelia Pisa, eds. *Brasileiras: Voix, écrits du Brásil.* Paris: Des Femmes, 1977.

Lastinger, Valerie C. "Humor in a New Reading of Clarice Lispector." *Hispania* 72, no. 1 (March 1989): 130–37.

Latimer, Dan, ed. *Contemporary Critical Theory.* New York: Harcourt Brace Jovanovich, 1989.

Laurentis, Teresa de. "Desire in Narrative." In *Alice Doesn't: Feminism, Semiotics, Cinema.* Bloomington: Indiana University Press, 1984.

————. *Technologies of Gender: Essays on Theory, Film, and Fiction.* Bloomington: Indiana University Press, 1987.

Leitch, Vincent B. *American Literary Criticism from the Thirties to the Eighties.* New York: Columbia University Press, 1988.

Lentricchia, Frank, and Thomas McLaughlin, eds. *Critical Terms for Literary Study.* Chicago: University of Chicago Press, 1990.

Lewis, Philip. "The Post-Structuralist Condition." *Diacritics* 12 (spring 1982): 2–24.

Lindstrom, Naomi. "A Discourse Analysis of 'Preciosidade' by Clarice Lispector." *Luso-Brazilian Review* 19, no. 2 (winter 1982): 187–94.

————. "A Feminist Discourse Analysis of Clarice Lispector's 'Daydreams of a Drunken Housewife.'" *Latin American Literary Review* 9, no. 19 (fall–winter 1981): 7–16.

Lins, Álvaro. "A experiência incompleta: Clarice Lispector." In *Os mortos de sobrecasaca,* 186–93. Rio de Janeiro: Civilização Brasileira, 1963.

Lispector, Clarice. *Água viva.* 3d ed. Rio de Janeiro: Editôra Nova Fronteira, 1978.

————. *An Apprenticeship, or The Book of Delights.* Translated and with an afterword by Richard A. Mazzara and Lorri A. Parris. Austin: University of Texas Press, 1986.

————. *The Apple in the Dark*. Translated and with an introduction by Gregory Rabassa. New York: Knopf, 1967.

————. *Uma aprendizagem ou o livro dos prazeres*. 3d ed. Rio de Janeiro: Edições Sabiá, 1969.

————. "Beauty and the Beast, or The Wound Too Great." Translated by Earl E. Fitz. In *Scents of Wood and Silence: Short Stories by Latin American Women Writers*, a special issue of the *Latin American Literary Review* (Kathleen Ross and Yvette E. Miller, eds.) 19, no. 37 (January–June 1991): 113–20.

————. *A bela e a fera*. Rio de Janeiro: Editora Nova Fronteira, 1979.

————. *A descoberta do mundo*. Rio de Janeiro: Editora Nova Fronteira, 1984.

————. *Discovering the World*. Translated and with a preface by Giovanni Pontiero. Manchester: Carcanet, 1992.

————. *Family Ties*. Translated and with an introduction by Giovanni Pontiero. Austin: University of Texas Press, 1972.

————. *Felicidade clandestina*. 2d ed. Rio de Janeiro: José Olympio Editôra, 1975.

————. *The Foreign Legion*. Translated and with an afterword by Giovanni Pontiero. Manchester: Carcanet, 1986.

————. "Flight." In *One Hundred Years after Tomorrow*, translated and with an introduction by Darlene J. Sadlier. Bloomington: Indiana University Press, 1992.

————. *A hora da estrela*. 3d ed. Rio de Janeiro: Livraria José Olympio Editôra, 1977.

————. *The Hour of the Star*. Translated and with an afterword by Giovanni Pontiero. New York: New Directions, 1992.

————. *Laços de família*. 10th ed. Rio de Janeiro: Livraria José Olympio Editôra, 1978.

————. *A legião estrangeira*. Rio de Janeiro: Editôra do Autor, 1964.

————. *A maçã no escuro*. 3d ed. Rio de Janeiro: José Álvaro, 1970.

————. *Near to the Wild Heart*. Translated and with an afterword by Giovanni Pontiero. New York: New Directions, 1990.

————. *Onde estivestes de noite*. Rio de Janeiro: Editôra Artenova, 1974.

————. *A paixão segundo G. H.* 3d ed. Rio de Janeiro: Editôra Sabiá, 1964.

————. *The Passion according to G. H.* Translated and with an introduction by Ronald W. Sousa. Minneapolis: University of Minnesota Press, 1988.

————. *Perto do coração selvagem*. 4th ed. Rio de Janeiro: Editôra Sabiá Limitada, 1944.

————. *Um sopro de vida: Pulsações*. 3d ed. Rio de Janeiro: Editôra Nova Fronteira, 1978.

————. *Soulstorm*. Translated and with an afterword by Alexis Levitin and with an introduction by Grace Paley. New York: New Directions, 1989.

————. *The Stream of Life*. Translated by Elizabeth Lowe and Earl Fitz and with a foreword by Hélène Cixous. Minneapolis: University of Minnesota Press, 1989.

———. *A via crucis do corpo*. Rio de Janeiro: Editôra Artenova, 1974.

———. "The Woman Who Killed the Fish." Translated by Earl Fitz. *Latin American Literary Review* 11, no. 21 (fall–winter 1982): 89–101.

Lodge, David, ed. *Modern Criticism and Theory: A Reader*. London: Longman, 1988.

Lopes, Maria Angélica. "*A legião estrangeira* and *Para não esquecer*." In *Clarice Lispector: A Bio-Bibliography*, edited by Diane E. Marting, 77–79. Westport, Conn.: Greenwood Press, 1993.

Lowe, Elizabeth. "Liberating the Rose: Clarice Lispector's *Água viva* as a Political Statement." In *Splintering Darkness: Latin American Women Writers in Search of Themselves*, edited and with an introduction by Lucía Guerra Cunningham, 79–84. Pittsburgh: Latin American Literary Review Press (Yvette E. Miller, general ed.), 1990.

———. "The Passion according to C. L." (Elizabeth Lowe interviews Clarice Lispector). *Review* 24 (1979): 34–37.

Lyotard, Jean-François. *Libidinal Economy*. Translated by Iain Hamilton Grant. Bloomington: Indiana University Press, 1993.

MacAdam, Alfred, and Flora Shiminovich. "Latin American Literature." In *The Postmodern Movement*, edited by Stanley Trachtenberg, 251–62. Westport, Conn.: Greenwood Press, 1985.

Marting, Diane E. "The Brazilian Writer Clarice Lispector: 'I Never Set Foot in the Ukraine.'" *Journal of Interdisciplinary Studies* 6, no. 1 (1994): 87–101.

———, ed. *Clarice Lispector: A Bio-Bibliography*. Westport, Conn.: Greenwood Press, 1993.

Mathie, Barbara. "Feminism, Language, or Existentialism: The Search for the Self in the Works of Clarice Lispector." In *Subjectivity and Literature from the Romantics to the Present Day*, edited by Philip Shaw and Peter Stockwell, 121–34. London: Pinter, 1991.

Mazzara, Richard A., and Lorri A. Parris. Afterword to *An Apprenticeship, or The Book of Delights*, translated by Richard A. Mazzara and Lorri A. Parris.

Miller, J. Hillis. "The Search for Grounds in Literary Study." In *Rhetoric and Form: Deconstruction at Yale*, edited by Robert Con Davis and Ronald Schleifer, 19–36. Norman: University of Oklahoma Press, 1985.

Mitchell, Juliet, and Jacqueline Rose, eds. *Feminine Sexuality: Jacques Lacan and the École Freudienne*. Translated by Jacqueline Rose. New York: Pantheon Books, 1982.

Moi, Toril. *Sexual/Textual Politics: Feminist Literary Theory*. London: Methuen, 1985.

Monegal, Emir Rodríguez. "The Contemporary Brazilian Novel." In *Fiction in Several Languages*, edited and with an introduction by Henri Peyre, 1–18. Boston: Beacon Press, 1968.

Nealon, Jeffrey T. "The Discipline of Deconstruction." *PMLA* 107, no. 5 (October 1992): 1266–79.

Neel, Jasper. *Plato, Derrida, and Writing.* Carbondale: Southern Illinois University Press, 1988.

Nunes, Benedito, ed. *Clarice Lispector: A paixão segundo G. H.* Critical ed. Coleção Arquivos, 1988.

———. "Clarice Lispector ou o naufrágio da introspecção." *Colóquio/Letras* 70 (November 1982): 13–22.

———. *O drama da linguagem: Uma leitura de Clarice Lispector.* Série Îemas, vol. 12, Estudos Literários. São Paulo: Ática, 1989.

———. "Introdução do coordenador; nota filológica." In *Clarice Lispector: A paixão segundo G. H.*, edited by Benedito Nunes, xxiv–xxxiii; xxxiv–xxxviii. Coleção Arquivos, 13. Florianópolis: Editôra da Universidade Federal de Santa Catarina, 1988.

———. *Leitura de Clarice Lispector.* São Paulo: Edições Quirón, 1973.

———. *O mundo de Clarice Lispector.* Manaus: Edições do Governo do Estado de Amazonas, 1966.

Nunes, Maria Luisa. *Becoming True to Ourselves.* Westport, Conn.: Greenwood Press, 1987.

———. "Clarice Lispector: Artista andrógina ou escritora?" *Revista Iberoamericana* 50, no. 126 (January–March 1984): 281–89.

———. "Narrative Modes in Clarice Lispector's *Laços de Família*: The Rendering of Consciousness." *Luso-Brazilian Review* 14, no. 2 (winter 1977): 177–84.

Patai, Daphne. "Clarice Lispector and the Clamor of the Ineffable." *Kentucky Romance Quarterly* 27 (1980): 133–49.

Peixoto, Marta. "*The Hour of the Star.*" In *Clarice Lispector: A Bio-Bibliography*, edited by Diane E. Marting, 39–41. Westport, Conn.: Greenwood Press, 1993.

———. *Passionate Fictions: Gender, Narrative, and Violence in Clarice Lispector.* Minneapolis: University of Minnesota Press, 1994.

———. "Rape and Textual Violence in Clarice Lispector." In *Rape and Representation*, edited by Lynn A. Higgins and Brenda R. Silver. New York: Columbia University Press, 1991.

———. "Writing the Victim in the Fiction of Clarice Lispector." In *Transformations of Literary Language from Machado de Assis to the Vanguards*, edited by David K. Jackson. Austin: Dept. of Spanish and Portuguese/Abaporu Press, 1987.

Pereira, Teresinha Alves. "Coincidencia de la técnica narrativa de Julio Cortázar y Clarice Lispector." *Nueva Narrativa Hispanoamericana* 3, no. 1 (January 1973): 103–11.

Pinto, Cristina Ferreira. "A luta pela auto-expressão em Clarice Lispector: O caso de *A hora de estrela.*" *Mester* 16, no. 2 (fall 1987): 18–24.

———. "*Perto do coração selvagem*: Romance de formação, romance de transformação." In *O bildungsroman feminino: Quatro exemplos brasileiros*, 77–109. São Paulo: Perspectiva, 1990.

Pontiero, Giovanni. "Excerpts from the Chronicles of *The Foreign Legion* (by Clarice Lispector)." *Review* 24 (1979): 37–43.

Poster, Mark. *Critical Theory and Poststructuralism: In Search of a Context.* Ithaca: Cornell University Press, 1989.

Quinlan, Susan Canty. *The Female Voice in Contemporary Brazilian Women.* New York: Peter Lang, 1991.

Régis, Sônia. "O pensamento judaico em Clarice Lispector," *Estado de São Paulo, Suplemento Literário,* 14 May 1988, 8–9.

Rorty, Richard. *The Consequences of Pragmatism: Essays, 1972–1980.* Minneapolis: University of Minnesota Press, 1982.

Rosenstein, Roy. "Lispector's Children's Literature." In *Clarice Lispector: A Bio-Bibliography,* edited by Diane E. Marting, 159–63. Westport, Conn.: Greenwood Press, 1994.

Roudinesco, Elisabeth. *Jacques Lacan.* Translated by Barbara Bray. New York: Columbia University Press, 1997.

Sá, Olga de. *A escritura de Clarice Lispector.* Petrópolis: Vozes, 1979.

Sadlier, Darlene J. "The Text and the Palimpsest: Clarice Lispector's 'A bela e a fera/ou a ferida grande demais.'" *Hispanófila* 104 (1992): 77–88.

———, ed. and trans. *One Hundred Years after Tomorrow: Brazilian Women's Fiction in the 20th Century.* Bloomington: Indiana University Press, 1992.

Sant'Anna, Affonso Romano. "*Laços de família* e *Legião estrangeira.*" In *Análise estrutural de romances brasileiros.* Petrópolis: Vozes, 1973.

Santos, Roberto Corrêa dos. *Clarice Lispector.* São Paulo: Atual, 1986.

Sarup, Madan. *Post-Structuralism and Postmodernism.* Athens: University of Georgia Press, 1989.

Saussure, Ferdinand de. *Course in General Linguistics.* Translated by Wade Baskin. New York: McGraw-Hill, 1966.

Schmidt, Rita Terezinha. "A modernidade e o feminino na pulsafão do discurso." *Brasil/Brazil* 2 (1989): 59–67.

Scholes, Robert. *Semiotics and Interpretation.* New Haven: Yale University Press, 1982.

———. *Structuralism in Literature: An Introduction.* New Haven: Yale University Press, 1974.

Schwarz, Roberto. "*Perto do coração selvagem.*" In *A sereia e o desconfiado,* 53–57. Rio de Janeiro: Editôra Paz e Terra, 1981.

Segal, Lynne. *Straight Sex: Rethinking the Politics of Pleasure.* Berkeley: University of California Press, 1994.

Selden, Raman. *A Reader's Guide to Contemporary Literary Theory.* Lexington: University Press of Kentucky, 1985.

Sellers, Susan, and Milton Keynes, eds. *Writing Differences: Readings from the Seminar of Hélène Cixous.* New York: St. Martin's Press, 1988.

Senna, Marta de. "'A imitação da rosa,' by Clarice Lispector: An Interpretation." *Portuguese Studies* 4 (1988): 159–65.

Severino, Alexandrino. "As duas versões de *Água viva*." *Remate de Males* 9 (1989): 115–18.

Silverman, Kaja. *The Subject of Semiotics*. New York: Oxford University Press, 1983.

Sousa, Ronald. "At the Site of Language: Reading Lispector's G. H." *Chasqui* 18, no. 2 (November 1989): 43–48.

———. "O Lustre." In *Clarice Lispector: A Bio-Bibliography*, edited by Diane E. Marting, 87–89. Westport, Conn.: Greenwood Press, 1993.

———. "Once within a Room." Introduction to *The Passion according to G. H.*, translated by Ronald Sousa, vii–ix. Minneapolis: University of Minnesota Press, 1988.

Sturrock, John. *Structuralism and Since*. New York: Oxford University Press, 1979.

Strand, Mark, ed. *The Best American Poetry: 1991*. David Lehman, series ed. New York: Macmillan, 1991.

Suleiman, Susan Rubin. "(Re)writing the Body: The Politics and Poetics of Female Eroticism." In *The Female Body in Western Culture*, edited by Susan R. Suleiman, 7–29. Cambridge: Harvard University Press, 1986.

———. *Subversive Intent: Gender, Politics, and the Avant-Garde*. Cambridge: Harvard University Press, 1990.

———. "Writing Past the Wall, or The Passion according to H. C." Introduction to *Coming to Writing and Other Essays*, by Hélène Cixous. Cambridge: Harvard University Press, 1991.

Tejada, Cristina Sáenz de. "The Eternal Non-Difference: Clarice Lispector's Concept of Androgyny." *Luso-Brazilian Review* 31, no. 1 (summer 1994): 39–56.

Tompkins, Jane P. "The Reader in History." In *Reader-Response Criticism*, edited by Jane Tompkins, 201–32. Baltimore: Johns Hopkins University Press, 1980.

Johnson, Randal, ed. *Tropical Paths: Essays on Modern Brazilian Literature*. New York: Garland Publishing, 1993.

Varin, Claire. "Clarice Lispector et l'esprit des langues (extrait)." *Trois: Revue d'écriture et d'érudition* 2, no. 3 (1987): 33–37.

———. *Clarice Lispector: Rencontres brásiliennes*. Laval, Quebec: Éditions Trois, 1987.

———. *Langues de feu: Essais sur Clarice Lispector*. Quebec: Trois, 1990.

Vasconcelos, Eliane. "O arquivo de Clarice Lispector." *Letras de Hoje* 28, no. 1 (March 1993): 87–97.

Vieira, Nelson. "A expressão judaica na obra de Clarice Lispector." *Remate de Males* 9 (1989): 207–9.

———. "A linguagem espiritual de Clarice Lispector." *Travessia* 14 (June 1987): 81–93.

———. *Ser Judeu e escritor—três casos brasileiros: Samuel Rawet, Clarice Lispector,*

Moacyr Scliar. Papéis Avulsos, No. 25. Rio de Janeiro: Centro Interdisciplinar de Estudos Contemporâneos, Escola de Comunicação, Universidade Federal de Rio de Janeiro, 1990.

———. "The Stations of the Body: Clarice Lispector's *Abertura* and Renewal." *Studies in Short Fiction* 25, no. 1 (winter 1988): 55–69.

Waldman, Berta. *Clarice Lispector*. São Paulo, Brasiliense, 1983.

Weedon, Chris. *Feminist Practice and Poststructuralist Theory*. Oxford, England: Basil Blackwell, 1987.

Willis, Sharon. "Mis-translation: *Vivre l'orange*." *SubStance: A Review of Theory and Literary Criticism* 52 (1987): 76–83.

Young, Robert, ed. *Untying the Text: A Post-Structuralist Reader*. London: Routledge and Kegan Paul, 1981.

INDEX

"structuration," 45, 83; and "either/
or" thinking, 50; and deconstruction,
55, 200n.5; and binary oppositions, 83,
135; and reinscription, 84; and characterizations, 89; and God, 118, 119; and
signification theory, 150; and "phonocentrism," 152; and psychoanalysis,
156; and undecidability, 200–201n.9
Descartes, René, 28
Desire: and characterizations, 1, 62,
66–67, 72–73, 179, 188, 189; and language, 1, 6, 8, 62, 158, 180, 182–183,
186; and other, 1, 62, 188; and poststructuralism, 1, 67; and writing, 10;
and feminist theory, 22; and language
and being, 62, 180–181, 183; and Lispector, 62, 179; and meaning, 67, 190;
and gender, 69; and identity, 81, 161;
and sociopolitical dimension, 133; and
psychoanalysis, 168, 179, 180
"Différance": and Derrida, 6, 13, 27–28,
39, 40, 49, 106, 131, 144, 189, 190,
205n.21; and meaning, 6, 12; and language, 13, 27; and signifier/signified,
20; and poetry, 38; and binary oppositions, 50; and structure, 50; and
eroticism, 71; and women, 80; and
identity, 81; and characterizations,
97, 104
Discovering the World, 176
Dreams, and psychoanalysis, 157, 177, 179
"Dry Point of Horses," 120, 180

Eagleton, Terry, 4, 135
"Egg and the Chicken, The," 11, 12, 120
Electra complex, and psychoanalysis, 157,
179
Epistemology: and poststructuralism, 1;
and poststructural *textes*, 16; traditional
problems of, 29; and "either/or" thinking, 50, 83; and structurations, 50; and
language, 101, 114, 131, 156, 185; and
androgyny, 112; and characterizations,
115; and "I," 184. *See also* Knowing
Eroticism: and gender, 62, 158; and Lispector, 62; and metamorphoses, 64;
and "différance," 71; and women, 74,

159; and language, 81, 84, 85, 86, 157,
189; and transformative power of, 81–
82, 147; and androgyny, 82, 116; and
language and being, 86, 87, 190; and
characterizations, 90; and being, 111;
and structurations, 173
Existentialism, 2
"Explicação," 133, 169

"Family Ties," 139
Family Ties: and feminist theory, 21; and
poetry, 37; and language, 49; and sexuality, 71, 74, 157; and characterizations, 88–89, 101, 104, 120
Felman, Shoshana, 62, 63, 188
Feminist theory: and Lispector, 2, 21–22,
54–55, 203–204n.11; and poststructuralism, 3, 18, 137; and meaning, 15,
22, 54; and sexuality, 76; and characterizations, 98; and sociopolitical dimension, 137, 141
"Fifth Story, The": and language, 11,
21, 46, 47; and poetry, 35; and literary
form, 47; and meaning, 47; and truth,
47; and decentering, 49, 50; and characterizations, 120
"First Kiss, The": and sexuality, 63, 148;
and eroticism, 64, 81–82, 111, 147;
and identity, 81; and phallogocentrism,
81; and characterizations, 100, 106,
111, 115, 116; and sociopolitical dimension, 147–150
"Flight," 96, 101, 146, 155
"Footsteps": and feminist theory, 22; and
desire, 56; and eroticism, 64; and sexuality, 70, 77; and characterizations,
89–90
"Foreign Legion, The," 120
Foreign Legion, The, 37, 56, 57, 58
"Forgiving God," 28
Formalism, 44
"Form and Content," 47, 57, 60
Foucault, Michel, 3, 4, 5
Freedman, Ralph, 35
Freud, Sigmund, 156, 160, 164, 166–169,
171, 177–180
Froula, Christine, 77, 106–107